MISSISSIPPI

INDEX OF WILLS

1800 - 1900

Compiled By Betty Couch Wiltshire

HERITAGE BOOKS, INC.

Other Books by the Author

Carroll County, Mississippi
Abstracts of Wills, 1834 – 1875, and Divorces 1857 – 1875

Marriages and Deaths from Mississippi Newspapers
Volume 1: 1837 – 1863

Marriages and Deaths from Mississippi Newspapers
Volume 2: 1801 – 1850

Marriages and Deaths from Mississippi Newspapers
Volume 3: 1813 – 1850

Published 1989 By

HERITAGE BOOKS, INC.
1540E Pointer Ridge Place, Bowie, Maryland 20716
(301)-390-7709

ISBN 1-55613-219-0

The Ancestors of Jesus Christ

Abraham begat Isaac; and Isaac begat Jacob; and Jacob begat Judas ... and Judas begat Phares ... and Phares begat Esrom, and Esrom begat Aram; and Aram begat Aminadab; and Aminadab begat Naasson; and Naasson begat Salmon; and Salmon begat Booz ... and Booz begat Obed ... and Obed begat Jesse; and Jesse begat David the king; and David the king begat Solomon ... and Solomon begat Roboam; and Roboam begat Abia; and Abia begat Asa; and Asa begat Josaphat; and Josaphat begat Joram; ... and Joatham begat Achaz; and Achaz begat Ezekias; and Ezekias begat Manasses; and Manasses begat Amon; and Amon begat Josias; and Josias begat Jechonias ...Jechonias begat Salathiel; and Salathiel begat Zorobabel; and Zorobabel begat Abiud; and Abiud begat Eliakim; and Eliakim begat Azor; and Azor begat Sadoc; ... and Eleazar begat Matthan; and Matthan begat Jacob ; and Jacob begat Joseph the husband of Mary of whom was born Jesus, who is called Christ.

Excerpts from St. Matthew 1: 2-16

TABLE OF CONTENTS

INTRODUCTION

In this book I have attempted to index all wills available in Mississippi for the years 1800 (the earliest will I found) through 1900. The date used was the probate date in almost all cases. When no date was actually given, I estimated the date according to the wills on surrounding pages.

Wills were found in probate books, marriage books, inventory books, and other unusual places. Because of this, it is possible that some wills escaped detection. In an effort to be as accurate as possible, when the spelling of a name was not clear, I listed each possible spelling.

Some wills are recorded in more than one county, because besides being probated in the county of the testator, they were often also recorded in the county of an heir. Due to this practice, there are also some wills for testators from other states.

Only a small number of people left wills, and some wills were lost in courthouse fires, etc. More than 10,000 testators are listed in this book. It is my hope that your ancestor's name will be found within these pages.

Betty Couch Wiltshire

MISSISSIPPI INDEX OF WILLS

E. - Estate Book
I. - Inventory Book
M. - Marriage Book
P. - Probate Book

(1) - District 1
(2) - District 2

The following county names have been abbreviated:

Ada - Adams County
Ami - Amite County
Att - Attala County
Ben - Benton County
Car - Carroll County
Chi - Chickasaw County
Cho - Choctaw County
Cla - Claiborne County
Clk - Clarke County
Cly - Clay County
Coa - Coahoma County
Cop - Copiah County
Cov - Covington County
DeS - Desoto County
Fra - Franklin County
Gre - Greene County
Grn - Granada County
Han - Hancock County
Hin - Hinds County
Hol - Holmes County
Isa - Isaquena County
Ita - Itawamba County
Jac - Jackson County
Jas - Jasper County
Jef - Jefferson County

Jon - Jones County
Kem - Kemper County
Laf - Lafayette County
Lau - Lauderdale County
Law - Lawrence County
Lea - Leake County
Lee - Lee County
Lef - Leflore County
Lin - Lincoln County
Low - Lowndes County
Mad - Madison County
Mar - Marion County
Mas - Marshall County
Mon - Monroe County
Mot - Montgomery County
Nes - Neshoba County
New - Newton County
Nox - Noxubee County
Okt - Oktibbeha County
Pan - Panola County
Per - Perry County
Pik - Pike County
Pon - Pontotoc County
Pre - Prentiss County
Qui - Quitman County
Ran - Rankin County

Sco – Scott County
Sha – Sharkey County
Sim – Simpson County
Smi – Smith County
Sun – Sunflower County
Tal – Tallahatchie County
Tat – Tate County
Tis – Tishomingo County
Tip – Tippah County

Tun – Tunica County
Uni – Union County
War – Warren County
Was – Washington County
Web – Webster County
Wil – Wilkinson County
Win – Winston County
Yal – Yalobusha County
Yaz – Yazoo County

NAME	COUNTY	WILL BK & PG	DATE
AARON, Joseph	Wil	3-159	1897
AAY, S. F.	Yaz	B-305	1895
ABBEY, Richard	Yaz	B-270	1891
ABBOT, William M.	Nes	A-44	1856
ABBOTT, Elsy	Wil	2-119	1857
James	War	A-80	1837
John	Mon	I.13-642	1858
Mary	Low	1-96	1862
Mary I.	Low	1-125	1862
Nancy	Wil	2-118	1857
Noah	Jef	P.D-520	1849
William	Ada	4-338	1884
William	Wil	2-10	1847
Willis	Chi(1)	1-75	1886
ABBY, Richard	Tun	2-86	1883
ABERNATHY, Anne F.	Pan(1)	B-344	1881
ABNEY, John B.	New	1-142	1896
Wiley	Nes	A-127	1890
ABRAHAM, Simon	Att	D-48	1898
William F.	Cla	B-175	1843
ABSTON, Joshua Sr.	Mas	P.8-376	1852
ACERMAN, Frederick	War	A-352	1866
ACREE, B. F.	Tat	1-132	1890
ADAMS, Abram Sr.	Nox	B-110	1872
Addie B.	War	B-313	1895
E. G.	Att	B-197	1875
Elias	Cho	A-20	1886
Elisha Bradford	War	A-74	1837
Eliza M.	Mot	1-120	1895
Eliza M.	Yaz	B-252	1890
Ezekiel	Hin	1-273	1851
Francis	Nox	A-93	1846
Grave S.	Lef	A-40	1864
Howell	Car(1)	A-125	1854
Jeremiah	War	B-15	1870
Joannah	Mad	A-41	1838
Joseph	War	A-177	1849
Mary Abigail	Mon	I.6-79	1890
Mary E.	Tal	B-84	1887

1

Mildred F.	DeS	2-417	1895
Nancy	Hin	1-370	1855
Nancy R.	Mad	A-602	1880
Philip	Ada	1-141	1817
R. S.	Kem	A-5	1882
Robert S.	Mon	I.2-27	1873
Thomas B.	Cla	B-246	1854
William	Att	2-473	1865
William Jr.	Ada	2-398	1851
William Sr.	Ada	3-89	1857
Wright H.	Laf	1-254	1875
ADDISON, Andrew L.	Nes	A-29	1853
James W.	Pik	1-97	1896
ADKINS, Allen	Tip	1-22	1867
ADLER, S. P.	Wil	3-153	1896
AGAR, Robert	Ada	1-193	1819
AGNEW, James	Ada	3-64	1856
AGRIEW, Abram	Lee	1-115	1889
AIKEN, Seddon	Was	2-24	1896
William M.	Sha	A-25	1898
AINSWORTH, James	Jas	1-109	1897
AKEN, A. K.	Han	A-267	1894
ALBERT, Sarah	Ada	5-269	1900
ALBERTSON, W. C.	Jon	1-5	1898
ALBRIGHT, J. E. R.	Mas	1-89	1896
ALCORN, James	Coa(2)	1-50	1898
James Lusk	Coa(2)	1-26	1894
ALDERSON, James C.	Mas	P.7-298	1850
Susan	Mon	I.5-589	1890
ALDIGE, Marie Leonie	Han	A-275	1895
ALDRICH, Lyman D.	Ada	4-131	1878
Richard P.	Ben	1-6	1871
ALDRIDGE, F. A.	Yal	B-70	1862
Frank S.	Was	2-122	1900
Lewis	Yal(1)	B-83	1863
Madison L.	Pan(2)	A-156	1900
W. W.	Laf	1-437	1898
ALEXANDER, Adam R.	Mas	P.5-507	1848
Amanda M.	Mon	I.22-295	1871
David	Ada	2-62	1834
George	Pan(1)	A-4	1845
Isaac	Ada	1-141	1817
J. H.	Laf	1-415	1895
Jennie S.	Hin	B-453	1896
John	Hin	B-392	1888
Lilly A.	Tip	1-211	1900
Parker	Mon	I.14-520	1859
Saml. D.	Car	A-82	1849
Uriah	Mas	P.7-636	1851
William H.	Win	1-11	1862
ALFORD, Cade	Tal	A-29	1842

Charles	Low	1-557	1888
Cincinnatus	Ran	1-206	1885
Jackson	Yaz	A-48	1839
James	Tal	A-137	1852
Mahala	Tal	A-168	1855
Nancy S.	Tal	B-78	1885
William P.	Pan(1)	A-112	1852
ALFRED, William	Sun	1-5	1889
ALLAN, Robert M.	Was	1-61	1844
ALLEN, Alfred S.	War	A-246	1858
Ben	War	B-351	1898
Elizabeth	Mad	A-91	1839
H. W.	Mon	I.11-578	1856
Henry	Pan(1)	A-302	1858
Jacob	Mad	A-280	1859
James H.	Pre	1-123	1899
James Madison	Yaz	B-78	1878
John	New	1-48	1876
Joseph	Ita	E.5-281	1860
Louise	Ran	1-311	1899
M. E.	Hol	3-37	1893
Martha	Web	A-105	1895
Martha B.	Coa(1)	1-90	1866
Mary E.	DeS	1-229	1859
Mrs. Nancy A.	Laf	1-426	1896
Olivia Harper	Hin	B-486	1900
Richard	Mad	A-56	1840
Samuel B.	Uni	1-27	1892
Sarah Ann Omega Sandifer	Hol	3-15	1895
Sarah B.	Was	1-515	1893
William	Att	C-72	1889
William	Hin	1-256	1850
William	Lau	1-95	1869
William	Mas	P.2-522	1839
William	War	A-76	1837
ALLISON, John	Low	1-483	1885
ALMEY, Benjamin	Ada	2-110	1835
ALSOP, Jesse	Yaz	A-217	1857
T. V.	Lau	1-229	1887
ALSTON, Alexander S. I.	War	A-110	1834
Bettie	Coa(2)	1-21	1893
Bettie	Coa(2)	1-42	1896
Eleanor E.	Yaz	A-76	1844
James	Mas	P.2-263	1841
Philip	Cla	A-203	1828
Philip M.	Hin	B-192	1866
Phillip S.	Qui	1-5	1892
Ross	War	B-293	1892
William	Pan(1)	B-58	1868

3

ALTOM, Mary F.	Lee	1–188	1897
AMES, Amanda M.	Han	A–27	1867
AMIS, Joseph	War	A–135	1840
ANDERSON, Anna D.	Mad	A–568	1876
Charles	Mad	A–5	1831
D. H.	Ada	2–16	1832
David	DeS	1–191	1858
David W.	Car(1)	A–510	1868
Edward H., Sr.	Nox	A–95	1844
Henry	Mas	P.4–272	1846
J. M.	Laf	1–114	1856
J. M., Sr.	Mad	A–626	1883
Jabez S.	DeS	1–228	1859
James	Hol	1–360	1872
Jemima	Ran	1–62	1863
Joel L.	Car(2)	1–49	1887
John	Cla	B–248	1854
John H.	Mas	P.15–308	1861
John H.	Mon	I.2–471	1876
John W.	DeS	1–440	1868
Killis	Nox	B–284	1883
Louisa Rebecca	Mad	A–414	1865
Margaret	Ada	4–520	1890
Martha A.	Hin	B–229	1867
Martha C.	Ran	1–76	1865
Mary Ann	Hol	1–163	1856
Nancy	Mas	P.15–568	1862
Peter	Mad	A–690	1892
Peter	Mas	P.18–202	1868
Timothy	Mad	A–149	1850
W. H.	Tat	1–184	1893
Warren P.	Hin	B–136	1861
William	Mas	P.15–336	1861
William W.	Yaz	A–142	1851
Y. S.	Mad	2–95	1893
ANDING, Martin	Yaz	A–119&129	1848
Martin	Yaz	B–92	1878
ANDRE, Jack	Ada	1–170	1818
Jacque	Ada	1–199	1820
Jacque	Ada	2–20	1832
ANDREW, Jayne	Ada	1–170	1818
Jayme	Ada	1–199	1820
Jayme	Ada	2–20	1832
ANDREWS, Arthur	Ada	2–244	1841
Brockenborough B.	Tal	A–179	1855
Caroline	Hol	1–481	1885
George	Ada	4–470	1888
George	Jef	P.C–76	1841
Jesse N.	Hin	1–306	1853
John	Mad	2–141	1899
John W.	Mon	I.8–143	1852

Joseph	Yaz	B-1&3	1870
ANTES, David D.	Mon	I.7-40	1897
ANTHONY, Johan Georg	Ada	2-389	1851
APPLEGATE, Susan E.	Car(2)	1-33	1885
APPLETON, James B.	Pan(2)	A-54	1884
APPLEYATE, George S.	Mot	1-92	1887
APPLEWHITE, Rev.			
James	Car(1)	A-536	1871
John	Hol	1-30	1838
APPLING, Joel	DeS	2-296	1888
ARARA, Rosalie	Han	A-55	1869
ARCHER, Harbert	Nox	B-338	1889
James	Cla	A-58	1815
Mariah J.	Nox	C-63	1898
Mary C.	Cla	B-200	1849
Rebecca N.	Nox	B-75	1866
Robert H.	Was	1-445	1885
ARCHUR, William S.	Lef	A-24	1855
ARICH, William L.	Hol	1-4	1834
Asenith W.	Hol	1-32	1840
ARMFIELD, Hance	Ran	1-141	1875
ARMISTEAD, Narcis			
Mimms	Car(2)	1-80	1899
Patrick H.	Pan(1)	A-181	1854
Peter F.	Pan(1)	B-3	1864
Thomas Road	DeS	2-355	1892
William H.	Car(2)	1-14	1878
ARMOR, Davis Willey	Tip	1-46	1870
ARMS, Edward	Pan(1)	A-204	1855
ARMSTEAD, Sarah A.	Cly	1-132	1897
ARMSTRONG, Abraham W.	Pan(1)	A-51	1848
Alexander	Cla	A-301	1834
Andrew Cottrel	Hin	1-404	1857
Drury	Mon	I.21-53	1871
Elias J.	Laf	1-99	1855
Louise E.	Han	A-135	1881
Pamela	Low	1-561	1889
William	Mad	A-1O1	1846
ARNETT, Francis A.	Chi(2)	1-63	1879
ARNOLD, F. L.	Hol	1-466	1884
Feneler	Car(1)	A-52	1834
Ira L.	Lee	1-206	1900
Lucy B.	Mas	1-32	1894
Margaret	Tat	1-109	1887
Stephen B.	Car(1)	A-514	1868
ARRIGHI, Domenica	Ada	4-139	1879
Matilda H.	Ada	4-336	1884
ARRINGTON, Charles	New	1-146	1893
Joseph	Coa(1)	1-189	1887
ASHBY, Andrew	Clk	1-15	1873
ASHFORD, James P.	Ada	2-340	1847

ASHLEY, Charles	Lef	A-70	1882
Elihu Martin	Cop	A-146	1900
J. C.	Att	D-204	1900
J. P.	Hol	3-39	1896
John	Att	2-167	1862
Josiah	Car(1)	A-3	1836
ASKERNIE, Thomas	Cop	A-46	1890
ASKEW, Eli	Mas	P.12-199	1857
John	Pan(1)	A-248	1856
L. M. C.	Hin	B-463	1899
Martha E.	Low	2-36	1891
T. W. L.	Tun	2-117	1890
ASWELL, Kinchen	Wil	2-124	1857
ATCHESON, Elijah F.	Ada	2-354	1848
ATCHISON, Samuel	Car(1)	A-422	1861
ATKINS, Daniel	DeS	1-144	1857
William	War	B-17	1871
William S.	DeS	1-332	1865
ATKINSON, Caledonia	Tat	1-13	1875
Jerome H. B.	Low	1-48	1860
Sarah	Ran	1-308	1899
William H.	Coa(1)	1-92	1866
ATTEBERRY, C. S.	Nox	B-392	1893
ATWOOD, Turpin G.	Att	B-202	1875
AUGUSTUS, Nicholas G.	Nox	A-230	1856
AULTMAN, Cullen	Cov	1-5	1894
AUSLEY, Henry	Laf	1-106	1856
AUST, Absalem M.	Nox	B-49	1863
AUSTIN, Martha E.	Jac	2-19	1898
Nancy	Hin	B-253	1869
William J.	Hin	B-90	1864
AUTER, Abram	War	B-273	1893
AVANT, William R.	Yal(2)	1-14	1881
AVENT, Benjamin	Laf	1-293	1878
AVERA, Alexander	Gre	1-8	1892
John C.	DeS	2-134	1878
Nancy	Gre	1-17	1896
AVERITT, Jesse	Mad	A-514	1870
AXMAN, Martha	Was	1-479	1889
AYCOCK, James			
Jackson	Cly	1-78	1887
AYERS, W. F.	Att	2-410	1864
AYNS, Angus W.	Grn	A-37	1875
AYRES, A. M.	Ben	1-56	1890
BABBITT, Amzi	Chi(2)	1-11	1883
BABERS, J. P.	Wil	2-249	1867
Jane C.	Wil	2-315	1875
BABTINT, William H.	Was	2-31	1896
BACKSTROM, David M.	Nes	A-100	1876
Jonas	Nes	A-3	1840

BACON, Henry	Mad	A–461	1867
Henry W.	Car(2)	1–70	1894
Mary A.	Chi(2)	1–37	1886
Milton E.	Mot	1–80	1886
William	Mad	A–217	1854
William	War	A–100	1839
BADLEY, Elijah	Yal(2)	1–101	1896
BADLY, Thomas	Yal(2)	1–78	1893
BADY, Terrell	Lin	1–62	1900
BAER, Leona	War	B–344	1898
BAGLEY, Josiah M.	Car(1)	A–177	1859
BAGNELL, Samuel	Cla	B–198	1847
BAILEY, David	Mad	A–4	1831
Edward W.	War	A–211	1854
Henry	Uni	1–2	1882
John H.	Hin	1–126	1840
John M.	Laf	1–273	1877
John M.	Laf	1–308	1877
John P.	Yaz	A–203	1855
Jordan	Hol	1–490	1887
Mrs. M. V.	Mad	A–653	1888
Peter A.	Tal	A–35	1843
Richard	Yal(1)	B–59	1861
Richard T., Sr.	Hol	3–84	1899
Richmond E.	Tat	1–231	1899
Samuel	DeS	1–274	1861
Spener	Tal	B–82	1887
Susan	Jef	B–128	1874
William	Mas	P.15–179	1861
William H.	Hin	1–63	1835
William Y.	DeS	1–205	1859
BAILLIE, Alexander	Ada	1–191	1819
BAIN, Alphonse	Jac	1–191	1898
Matthew	Att	A–105	1858
Murdock	Att	C–290	1892
Patterson L.	Was	1–94	1847
BAINS, James	Yaz	A–4	1833
BAIRD, A. C.	Chi(1)	1–72	1886
Felix W.	Hin	1–69	1836
James B.	Wil	1–258	1842
Simon	Chi(1863–1872)–41		1864
BAKER, Adaline H.	Ada	4–220	1882
Archibald	Cop	A–3	1886
Charles	War	A–304	1861
Clifton	Grn	A–108	1894
E. B.	Ada	5–47	1893
Francis	Yal(1)	A–98	1846
German	DeS	2–163	1880
Harriet	DeS	2–489	1899
Henry	War	B–64	1876
Ira	Mon	I.4–552	1883

Isaac D.	Grn	A-49	1882
Jacob	Win	1-118	1890
James M.	Wil	2-188	1863
Jesse R.	Grn	A-79	1886
Jesse R.	Mot	1-84	1886
John C.	Yal(1)	A-117	1848
Joshua	Laf	2-12	1898
Leonard	Coa(1)	1-1	1840
Lewis E.	Ada	3-169	1861
Mary	Ada	2-144	1837
Peter P.	Ada	2-351	1848
Thomas J.	Nes	A-70	1862
BALCH, Hesekiah I.	Jef	A-61	1820
John B.	Pan(1)	B-9	1864
BALDING, J. R.	Lee	1-212	1899
BALDWIN, Archibald P.	Pon	1-257	1839
Harriet	DeS	2-144	1879
Hattie T.	Was	2-16	1895
Hiram	Jef	P.E-23	1851
Lemuel N.	Cla	3-142	1893
Mary Jane	Cla	3-188	1899
Mary A.	Mad	A-603	1875
Owen W.	Mad	A-337	1860
BALEY, Elisha R.	Hin	B-70	1862
BALFOUR, Catherine	Ada	4-10	1871
Emma H.	War	B-174	1884
Joseph Davis	Mad	A-465	1867
William	Mad	A-21	1834
William L.	Mad	A-247	1857
William T.	War	B-75	1877
William T.	War	B-181	1887
BALL, Mary	Tal	A-160	1854
BALLANCE, Eliza	Yaz	A-325	1865
James	Yaz	A-256	1865
BALLARD, Hugh L.	Hin	B-283	1872
Lavina	Nox	B-291	1885
Rice C.	War	A-277	1860
Willis P.	DeS	2-377	1893
BALLENTINE, Mary R.	Pan(1)	B-502	1900
BALLINGER, Jesse	Cla	B-193	1846
BALLOW, Thomas C.	Mad	A-559	1874
BAM, Alphonse	Jac	2-27	1900
BAMBURG, George	Car	A-199	1860
BANDY, Edward	War	A-113	1841
BANES, James	Hol	1-24	1832
BANKHEAD, James	Hol	1-51	1845
James T.	Yal(2)	1-11	1878
BANKS, Dunstan	Low	1-447	1881
George D.	Ada	1-458	1829
George Gerard	Hin	1-343	1854
Lemuel	DeS	1-91	1854

Mary	Ada	1-35	1808
Viney	Chi(2)	1-72	1896
Viney	Lef	A-118	1896
BANKSTON, Augustine			
H.	Hin	1-177	1844
Spencer	Hin	1-287	1852
BANN, Alphonse	Jac	1-191	1898
BANNISTER, Eli	Ada	1-354	1825
BARBEE, Elijah	Coa(1)	1-127	1878
Elizabeth	DeS	2-204	1883
Henry H.	DeS	1-36	1853
W. R.	DeS	2-330	1891
BARBER, Martha A.	Wil	3-186	1900
BARBOUR, John L.	Hol	1-29	1838
Thomas	Laf	1-35	1849
BAREFIELD, Francis	War	A-149	1847
Jesse	War	A-257	1859
Miles	Cla	A-299	1834
Samuel	Was	2-125	1900
BARFIELD, John	Cop	AAA-462	1840
M. A.	Was	1-491	1891
BARINEAU, J. M.	Lef	A-93	1886
BARKER, Andrew			
Segourney	Tal	A-141	1852
Andrew Segourney	Was	1-225	1855
Eldridge	Laf	1-62	1850
Susan	Hin	B-473	1899
BARKLEY, Samuel A.	Tip	1-86	1878
BARKSDALE, Alexander	Yal(1)	A-183	1850
J. A.	Mas	P.17-478	1866
John A.	Jas	1-24	1863
John F.	Laf	1-31	1848
Joseph	Hol	1-194	1858
Josephine	Yaz	B-222	1887
Rebecca	Hol	1-452	1881
William	Low	1-144	1863
William Robert	Grn	A-16	1877
BARLAND, William	Ada	1-132	1816
William	Ada	1-142	1817
BARLOW, Branson	Clk	P.B-89	1839
BARNARD, Elizabeth	Sun	1-6	1881
Joseph L.	Isa	B-5	1853
Thomas	Ada	2-283	1844
William	Ada	2-49	1833
BARNES, A. S.	Lau	1-357	1896
Abram	Cla	A-222	1830
Emily	Yal(1)	A-124	1848
Esther	Cla	A-288	1833
Henry P.	Cop	A-57	1891
Rev. James	Nox	A-130	1849
John	Mar	A1-70	1842

John	Nox	A-83	1846
John A.	Cla	A-263	1833
John M.	War	A-195	1852
Joseph	Cla	A-134	1823
Josiah	Cla	A-35	1811
Lewis Morgan	Nox	A-44	1842
Mary	Cla	B-183	1845
Samuel	Ada	2-196	1839
Shadrack	Tal	B-62	1880
Silas Brown	Mad	A-625	1883
Theophilas	Nox	B-56	1864
Thomas	Cla	A-71	1817
Warren B.	Grn	A-11	1872
BARNET, Nathaniel	Jas	1-62	1871
BARNETT, James R.	War	B-123	1880
Joel	Nox	A-165	1851
Julia M.	War	B-47	1874
Mildred	Nox	A-270	1859
Thomas B.	Mad	A-305	1859
William	Mad	A-428	1866
BARNEY, William H.	Lau	1-299	1892
BARR, H. A.	Laf	2-17	1899
James	Laf	1-46	1850
BARRETT, A. H.	Lef	A-116	1895
George W.	Cla	3-134	1892
John W.	Nes	A-128	1893
Joseph	Nes	A-6	1840
Reuben	Nes	A-51	1858
Squire	Mas	P.15-493	1862
BARRETTE, Henry Elias	Lau	1-102	1872
BARRINGER, Paul B.	Laf	1-286	1878
BARRINGTON, Minnie	Mad	2-80	1897
BARRON, Absalom H.	Isa	A-5	1847
BARROW, William	Wil	1-56	1832
BARROWS, George	Cop	A-48	1891
Sarah Elizabeth	Mad	A-126	1848
BARRY, Andrew P.	Cop	A-75	1892
Araminta	Low	1-487	1885
Charles H.	Low	1-517	1886
Maria F.	Low	2-115	1896
Mary M.	DeS	1-395	1866
R. H.	Low	1-490	1885
Richard	Low	1-266	1869
William S.	Lef	A-74	1883
William S.	Low	1-459	1868
BARTEE, Crotia Ann	Low	1-120	1862
BARTIN, William M.	Wil	1-160	1836
BARTLEY, Agnes	Mad	A-650	1887
BARTON, Armistead	Pan(1)	B-186	1875
BARWICK, W. C.	Cov	1-3	1892
BASKIN, Robert	Hin	1-2	1832

BASKINS, John Sr.	Car(1)	A-124	1854
BASS, Batson	DeS	2-457	1897
Councell	Hin	1-247	1830
Council R.	Was	1-413	1879
George W.	Nox	B-38	1863
Job	Ada	2-162	1836
John	Clk	1-1	1872
John H.	Clk	1-184	1895
May	Cop	A-155	1900
BASSETT, Hanceford	Nes	A-68	1862
William	Cla	A-128	1823
BATCHELOR, Victoria			
A.	Jef	B-128	1874
BATES, John T.	Grn	A-17	1877
Joseph C.	Hol	1-303	1865
BATHOS, John	Ada	1-168	1818
BATTE, John P.	Mas	P.11-79	1855
Lewis	Ran	1-40	1861
William H.	Ran	1-149	1877
BATTLE, Harriet	Ada	4-63	1874
W. H.	Lee	1-60	1881
BATTS, Nathan	Nes	A-23	1849
BAUGH, Martha A.	Ran	1-165	1881
BAUGHMAN, Joel	Mar	A2-11	1887
BAUGHN, L. E.	Hol	3-64	1898
Lorenzo D.	Hol	1-347	1870
BAUM, J. Frederick	War	B-263	1891
BAUMAN, Elizabeth	Ada	3-455	1871
BAUMANN, Maria	Ada	3-348	1868
BAXLER, Mary	Yaz	B-274	1892
BAXTER, Isabella	Cla	A-283	1833
BAY, William R.	War	A-203	1853
BAYARD, Antione Sr.	Han	P.(1853-1860)-77	1849
BAYLESS, Thomas A.	Hol	3-20	1895
BAYLISS, Maria Louisa	Tun	2-145	1897
BAYS, H. F.	Web	A-72	1889
BEACHUM, Daniel			
Shelton	Clk	1-106	1889
BEAFORD, William	Lee	1-34	1877
BEAL, Charles M.	DeS	1-28	1852
BEALE, Thomas B.	Yaz	A-142	1851
BEALL, Daniel W.	Hol	1-436	1880
Otho W.	Hol	1-309	1866
Samuel F.	Tis	1-32	1890
T. T.	War	B-337	1897
BEAM, C. W. Sr.	Pik	1-88	1896
BEAMAN, Edmund	Att	B-149	1874
George G.	Sco	A-460	1884
Levi	Lea	1-68	1873
BEAN, George W.	Mas	P.15-406	1862
BEANE, Melburne	War	B-127	1879

11

BEANJEAN, Marie	Han	A-17	1865
BEARD, A. Z.	Mad	A-422	1866
Aaron	Mar	A2-1	1873
Alexander	Uni	1-8	1883
Mary Ann	Grn	A-45	1879
BEARDEN, Pleasant	Pre	1-33	1876
BEARDSLEE, Joseph			
Heoyt	Jac	1-33	1884
BEASLEY, Daniel	Jef	A-17	1813
Frances	Car(1)	A-4	1836
Middleton	Cop	A-109	1896
Nancey	Nox	A-255	1857
Randolph	Coa(1)	1-22	1850
Willlam	Coa(1)	1-8	1845
BEASON, Permelia	Hol	1-37	1842
BEATY, James G.	Yal	A-44	1839
BEATTY, R. T.	Mad	A-677	1891
BEATY, Thomas	Mas(1838-1839)-115		1838
BEAUCHAMP, B. H.	Hin	1-425	1858
BEAUMONT, Bessy	Wil	3-98	1892
BEAVERS, Allen	Lee	1-6	1869
John	Pan(1)	A-423	1862
BEAVIN, Benjamin D.	Jef	B-53	1861
James E.	Jef	P.E-216	1852
BECK, Elijah M.	Car(1)	A-478	1866
Frank Jr.	Han	B-13	1899
Frank Jr.	Was	2-105	1899
James	Wil	2-37	1848
Orrin	Tip	1-31	1868
Orrin A.	Ben	1-12	1875
W. J. L.	Car(1)	A-458	1863
Wesley	Yaz	B-358	1898
BECKERDITE, J. F.	Coa(2)	1-56	1900
BECKHAM, D. F.	Cop	A-95	1894
Leroy L.	Cly	1-1	1872
BECKWITH, Benjamin F.	Low	2-31	1890
Dempsey	Car(1)	A-454	1863
BEDFORD, Benjamin W.	DeS	2-221	1883
James R.	Hol	1-62	1845
BEEKS, Samuel	Mon	I.12-589	1857
BEIRNE, Andrew Sr.	Nox	A-86	1845
BELENGER, Jacob	War	B-74	1877
BELER, Armsted	Car(1)	A-415	1859
M. L.	Car(1)	A-465	1864
William Y.	Car(1)	A-156	1857
BELEW, Reuben	Pre	1-47	1880
BELK, William	Cly	1-23	1877
BELL, Ben R.	Mas	1-160	1899
Charles Allison	Uni	1-39	1896
Charles Hamilton	Sun	1-53	1900
Dempsey	Yal(1)	B-187	1880

12

Elizabeth H.	Okt	1-3	1881
Harriett	Lee	1-144	1888
Ida F.	Okt	1-44	1899
Isaac H.	Pon	2-388	1844
James B.	Low	1-495	1885
Martha	Lee	1-20	1876
Matthew J.	Att	C-70	1889
Mollie A.	Was	1-456	1886
Robert H.	Hin	1-54	1835
Tabitha	War	A-166	1848
Thomas	Low	1-480	1885
Tykus	Nox	A-183	1853
William B.	Nox	B-229	1879
William I.	Hol	1-27	1837
BELLAMY, John	Yal(1)	B-230	1897
BELLANDE, Rosaline	Jac	1-124	1893
BELLEMI, Dominique	Han	A-143	1883
BELSINGER, Mrs. Sarah	Ada	4-79	1875
BELYEW, Martha	DeS	2-332	1891
BEMBON/BENBOW,			
Gershon	Hin	1-309	1849
BENCH, Washington S.	Jef	P.C-397	1843
BENDER, William G.	War	B-98	1879
BENELLI, Joseph M.	War	B-91	1877
BENJAMAN, Lewis	Ada	1-194	1819
BENJAMIN, John F.	Ada	1-417	1828
BENNETT, Albert G.	Yaz	A-286	1862
Bridget Ellen	Yal(2)	1-131	1900
Christopher L.	Was	1-59	1844
Griffin	Ran	1-33	1861
H. L.	Car(1)	A-457	1863
J. F.	Mot	1-118	1893
Julia B.	Ada	3-312	1867
Mark R.	Ada	2-157	1837
Martha	Chi(2)	1-1	1881
T. J.	Sun	1-3	1889
Will	Mad	A-37	1837
BENOIST, Elizabeth	Ada	2-226	1840
BENSON, Catherine	War	B-262	1892
Edward J.	Jac	1-54	1889
Hardy	Tal	A-162	1855
Hardy	Yal(1)	A-139	1848
Hiram J.	Cop	AAA-459	1861
Lucien Minor	Mas	1-112	1897
U. Jasper	Pan(2)	A-85	1891
BENTLEY, William	Hol	1-294&298	1864
BENTON, Mary E.	Low	2-267	1900
BERESFORD, James H.	War	B-207	1888
BERGIN, Catherine	Jas	1-98	1895
BERK, John M.	Ran	1-64	1864
BERKSON, Simeon	Cop	A-158	1900

13

BERNARD, Joseph	Ada	1–15	1804
BERNHEIMER, Samuel	Cla	3–105	1888
BERRY, E. G.	Lau	1–286	1892
J. B.	Ran	1–205	1885
James William	Grn	A–141	1898
Joel H.	Pre	1–26	1875
Lucinda	Tip	1–93	1880
Mary E. C.	Yal(2)	1–7	1875
Richard T.	Law	1–9	1896
Thomas Y.	Cla	3–157	1895
Uriah	Hol	1–310	1866
W. S.	Cla	B–303	1862
Young	Yaz	A–154	1852
BERRYHILL, Samuel			
Newton	Web	A–66	1887
BERT, Charles E.	Mas	P.15–540	1862
BERTRON, Samuel			
Reading	Cla	3–50	1878
Samuel Reading	Lef	A–67	1880
BEST, Jonathan	Coa(1)	1–13	1848
BETHANY, Thomas N.	Kem	A–3	1881
William W.	Kem	A–8	1882
BETHEA, Mary C.	Cla	3–146	1893
W. D.	Clk	1–122	1891
W. W.	Clk	1–109	1889
BETHELL, William	Ada	2–174	1839
BETTISON, David	Wil	1–11	1823
BETTON, Mary	Jef	A–97	1827
BETTS, A. B.	Tal	B–88	1890
James	Chi(1)	1–55	1886
BEVERLY, Robert	Lef	A–6	1850
BEVIL, George W.	Mas	P.8–411	1852
BIBB, Fird	Car(1)	A–455	1863
John	Car(1)	A–65	1848
Robert	Ran	1–11	1860
Susan W.	Car(1)	A–456	1863
Thomas	Hin	1–325	1853
BEILLER, Thomas			
Calvit	Cla	B–210	1850
BIGFORD, S. W.	Pan(1)	A–398	1860
BIGGER, Johnson N.	Laf	1–30	1847
Samuel	Ada	1–362	1825
BIGGS, Ann	Ada	2–7	1822
Benjamin	Yal(1)	A–128	1848
Margaret	Ada	2–460	1853
BILEM, George	War	B–355	1898
BILES, Willie	Yaz	A–27	1836
BILL, James	Mad	A–177	1852
BILLINGSLEA, Sawyer	War	A–138	1843
BILLINGSLEY, Ann	Win	1–80	1873
Callie	Lee	1–225	1900

14

Sarah H.	Car(1)	A-505	1867
BILLINGSLY, Henry			
Gentry	Grn	A-12	1876
BILLS, John H.	Tun	2-22	1871
John H.	Tun	2-99	1888
BILLUPS, Frances A.	Low	2-17	1890
Ida S.	Low	2-45	1891
Joseph P.	Han	A-175	1887
Joseph P.	Low	1-535	1887
Thomas C.	Low	1-207	1866
Thomas C.	Low	2-211	1898
Wildie Sysles	Low	2-243	1899
BINFORD, John A.	Mot	1-20	1877
BINGAMAN, Adam Lewis	Ada	4-576	1892
BIRCHETT, George K.	War	B-264	1892
BIRD, William G.	Wil	2-231	1865
BIRDSONG, Ann E.	Hin	1-353	1855
George T.	Hin	1-288	1852
L. F.	Cop	A-99	1894
William M.	Hin	1-90	1837
BIRMINGHAM, Mary A.	DeS	2-167	1880
BISCBY, Herbert	Ada	3-209	1863
BISCOE, Bennel	Wil	3-9	1883
BISHOP, Celia Ann	Cop	A-103	1895
Elijah	Sim	A-36	1886
Jane	Pan(1)	B-459	1890
John H.	Mad	A-404	1865
BISLAND, John	Ada	1-221	1819
Mary L. L.	Ada	4-29	1873
Peter	Ada	1-433	1829
William	Ada	2-356	1848
BITTERMAN, Anna Laura	War	B-103	1879
BITTLEMAN, Lucy	Mas	P.2-93	1840
BIXBY, Herbert	Ada	3-209	1863
BIZZELL, Caleb	Nox	C-77	1898
W. H.	Tat	1-221	1897
BLACK, Benjamin	Ada	1-190	1819
David A.	Tip	1-40	1869
James C.	Laf	1-191	1861
R. W.	Laf	1-272	1876
Sarah	Lef	A-53	1876
Sarah	Was	1-409	1876
William	Yal(1)	A-221	1852
BLACKBOURN, A. L.	Tat	1-169	1893
William C.	Mon	I.15-142	1860
BLACKLIDGE, James G.	Jon	1-5	1899
BLACKMAN, Uriah	Pan(1)	A-338	1859
BLACKMON, C. A.	DeS	1-310	1862
Rebecca Ann	Car(1)	A-98	1851
BLACKWELL, Ellemund			
B.	Tip	1-9	1866

Michael Joseph	Mas	P.19–258	1869
BLACKWOOD, E. C.	Pan(2)	A–1	1880
BLAIR, David P.	Low	2–218	1898
Ishmael	Okt	1–29	1885
John	Hin	1–147	1842
John A.	Lee	1–203	1899
BLAIZE, Nicholas	Han	A–168	1886
BLAKE, Benson	War	B–31	1873
Caroline M.	War	A–170	1849
Ruel	Mad	*	1835
* Available only at the Canton Public Library, Canton, Mississippi.			
William	Car(1)	A–60	1846
BLAKELY, Martha M.	Kem	A–44	1891
BLAKEMON, M. H.	War	B–36	1874
BLALOCK, Calvin J.	Mad	A–119	1847
William	Yaz	A–230	1859
BLANCHARD, Horace F.	War	A–95	1838
John	Ada	1–228	1820
Ranson G.	Mon	I.17–101	1862
BLAND, Emeline	Cla	B–268	1856
Isaac	Cla	A–95	1820
BLANKENSHIP, John	Cop	A–87	1893
Sarah A.	Pan(1)	B–405	1885
BLANKINSHIP, Thomas H.	Jef	P.D–584	1849
BLANKS, Arnold	Cla	A–280	1833
Edith	Car(1)	A–502	1867
James	Car(1)	A–417	1861
William	Lau	1–17	1859
BLANNING, George Willington	Lef	A–119	1896
BLANTON, James M.	Mad	A–115	1847
Jefferson	Jef	B–119	1873
Martha R.	Was	2–51	1897
William	Yal(1)	A–62	1842
BLATCHFORD, John M.	Ada	2–159	1837
Richard	Ada	2–137	1836
BLAYLOCK, Levi	Mot	1–62	1883
BLEDSOE, James T.	Cho	A–24	1891
James T.	Mad	A–611	1880
BLEWETT, Thomas G.Sr	Low	1–308	1871
Thomas T.	Low	2–175	1896
BLOCKER, George M.	Nox	A–181	1852
BLOODWORTH, William	Mas	P.15–36	1860
BLOOMENSTEIL, Alexander	War	B–18	1871
BLOOMFIELD, Edw.	Jac	1–186	1898
BLOUNT, Granbury	Car(1)	A–100	1846
Malinda	Cop	AAA–452	1836
William J.	Att	2–52	1862

BLOW, Miles M.	War	A-189	1851
BLUE, Mary	Hol	1-307	1865
BLUM, Jacob C.	War	B-272	1892
BLUMENTHAL, Isaac D.	Mas	1-129	1898
BLUNT, Benjamin E.	Hol	1-64	1845
Beverly	Hin	B-286	1873
Mollie	Tis	1-8	1888
William	Ada	2-40	1833
BLYTHE, Nancy	Nox	B-152	1874
BNFORD, Charles	Att	D-141	1899
BOARDMAN, Robert	War(1827 1832)-156		1829
BOASMAN, James	Hin	1-218	1848
BOATNER, Eliza A.	Laf	1-234	1873
John	Tip	1-11	1866
BOAZ, Elizabeth	Mad	A-657	1889
BOBB. George	War	B-288	1893
BOBBETT, George T.	Pan(1)	A-426	1862
William	Yal(1)	B-46	1860
BOBBITT, Cassandra V.	Yal(1)	B-95	1863
Martha A.	Tip	1-131	1886
BOBO, A. K.	Coa(1)	1-202	1888
Absalom	Cla	A-228	1831
Frances W.	Pan(1)	A-277	1858
James M.	Low	2-27	1890
Missouri	Coa(2)	1-29	1895
Virgil A.	Pan(1)	A-421	1861
BODDIE, John W.	Mad	A-394	1864
BOGAN, R. H.	DeS	2-78	1872
BOGARD, Sarah	Ben	1-59	1885
William	Mas	P.16-18	1863
BOGER, Elizabeth	Ada	4-351	1884
BOHANNON, Robert	Yal(1)	B-213	1888
BOISCLAIR, Peter F.	Tal	A-191	1858
BOLAND, James	Wil	2-226	1865
BOLANDER, Joseph	Cla	3-33	1877
BOLEN, Willaby	Lee	1-62	1881
BOLIAN, Joseph	Pik	1-67	1896
BOLLS, Martha	Hin	B-96	1864
Samuel R.	Hin	B-99	1864
William W.	Hin	B-104	1865
Wilson	War	A-130	1842
BOLTON, James N.	DeS	2-428	1896
Nancy	Mas	P.17-380	1866
Thomas J.	Hin	B-411	1890
BOND, Henry L.	War	B-167	1886
BONDS, Benjamin F.	Chi(1863-1872)-105		1865
John C.	Lee	1-39	1878
Moses	Mas	1-98	1896
BONDURANT, Elizabeth			
P.	Ada	3-95	1857
George P.	Yal(1)	B-182	1879

Mary A.	Ada	5-68	1895
W. E.	Ada	4-39	1874
BONELLI, Barthelomew			
E. S.	War	B-282	1893
Frank	War	B-379	1899
BONNELL. Elias	Ada	1-9	1803
Joseph	Ada	2-231	1840
BONNER, Jane	Cla	B-184	1845
John C.	Cly	1-106	1891
Moses	Jef	A-126	1800
Thomas	War	A-220	1855
William H. '	Jas	1-68	1877
William H.	New	1-86	1877
William T.	DeS	1-444	1867
BONNEY, Jesse S.	Yaz	A-88	1845
BOOKER, Isaac	War	A-123	1841
William	War(1823-1827)-1		1823
BOON, Bryant	DeS	2-171	1881
Daniel	DeS	1-454	1870
Margaret C.	Chi(2)	1-25	1884
Robert L.	DeS	2-469	1897
BOONE, James C.	Mon	I.11-619	1856
William	Laf	1-94	1855
BOOTH, Elizabeth	Ada	3-376	1869
Hester	Cla	B-167	1840
J. F.	Lee	1-180	1897
John	Cla	A-138	1824
Phillip	Hin	B-403	1889
S. S.	War	B-280	1893
Col. William	Car(1)	A-539	1875
William A.	Mad	A-433	1866
BOOTHE, Charles	Cla	A-120	1822
BORDAGE, Edwina	Han	A-184	1889
BOREN, Amanda P.	Pon	1-17	1900
James M.	Pre	1-54	1881
Mahulda A.	Tal	B-12	1868
Thomas	Tal	A-122	1851
William A.	DeS	1-276	1860
BORMAN, Elizabeth	War	B-189	1887
BORN, John	Cla	3-139	1893
BORNARD, Jesse	Jef	A-100	1827
BORROUM, Beverly	Laf	1-19	1846
Peterson	Laf	1-7	1845
BOSLEY, James	Ada	1-286	1823
BOSTIC, F.	Yaz	B-410	1900
BOSTICK, Ann	Tun	2-123	1892
Jonathan	Tun	1-490	1869
BOSWICK, H. K. Sr.	Att	C-4	1887
BOTTERS, Sampson	Hol	1-46	1844
Thomas	Hol	1-172&183	1857
BOTTO, Louis	Ada	5-235	1899

18

BOULAND, Robert	Pon	2-447	1845
BOULDIN, E.	DeS	2-372	1893
BOURNE, N. J.	Ran	1-129	1874
BOVARD, Thomas	Yaz	A-120	1849
BOWDEN, William	Ada	1-380	1826
BOWEN, Catharine D.	Mas	P.15-37	1860
Isabella M.	Mas	1-97	1896
Reese	DeS	1-347	1865
Richard P.	Mas	1-179	1900
BOWER, Adam	Ada	2-31	1833
BOWERS, Carr	Nox	B-85	1861
Clora	DeS	2-448	1896
Franklin	DeS	1-70	1853
Leora Randolph	Grn	A-112	1896
Octavia	Hol	3-56	1898
BOWIE, George A.	Nes	A-45	1856
Luther A.	Nes	A-27	1851
BOWKER, Thomas	Coa(1)	1-95	1866
BOWLEN, John	Att	C-397	1894
BOWLES, David	Yal(1)	A-104	1846
George F.	Ada	5-254	1899
George W.	Sun	1-12	1891
BOWLING, Alexander	Mas	P.8-38	1851
Benjamin F.	Mad	A-506	1870
Martha M.	Tat	1-18	1876
BOWLS, John	War	A-251	1858
BOWMAN, Celeste	Ada	1-47	1809
Elizabeth A.	War	B-196	1888
Henry F.	Tat	1-185	1893
Mary E.	Yaz	B-294	1894
Nancy	Yaz	A-55	1840
Susan Louisa	Yaz	B-233	1889
BOWNING, Dennis	Hin	B-356	1884
BOWREN, Nathaniel	Wil	2-254	1867
BOWRING, Dennis	Hin	B-356	1884
BOX, Jane	Chi(1)	1-100	1890
Joseph	Cla	A-1	1803
William	Low	1-244	1867
William Mitchell	DeS	2-301	1889
BOYCE, Alford	Chi(1)	1-29	1880
Charles M.	Nox	B-234	1880
Harriet E.	Coa(1)	1-204	1888
James	Ada	1-307	1824
N. K.	Coa(1)	1-129	1878
Ker	DeS	2-55	1872
Robert	War	A-55	1836
BOYD, A. A.	Pik	1-158	1900
A. J.	Att	B-276	1879
Alexander	Ada	3-285	1866
Austin	DeS	1-434	1868
Catharine C.	Ada	5-179	1898

Gordon D.	Att	A-290	1859
John R.	Yaz	A-193	1854
Lewis M.	Lau	1-97	1870
Martha Ann	Tat	1-119&124	1889
Richard	Yaz	B-190	1885
Samuel S.	Ada	3-315	1867
Thomas J.	Mas	P.11-255	1856
BOYDSTON, Benjamin	Yal(1)	A-142	1848
BOYED, Thomas	Was	1-101	1848
BOYETT, E. W.	Att	C-147	1890
William W.	Att	B-1	1876
BOYETTE, Thomas W.	Hol	1-149	1854
BOYKIN, John	Hin	1-95	1837
Simon D.	Hin	1-349	1854
Thomas	Yal(1)	A-4	1830
William D.	Nox	B-92	1867
BOYLAN, John H.	Isa	C-155	1892
William	Yaz	A-311	1861
BOYLE, Mary	Hol	1-421	1878
R. L.	Hin	B-384	1888
William	Hol	1-377	1873
BOYLES, Almedia E.	Pan(2)	A-46	1884
John	Hol	1-160	1856
John M.	Pan(2)	A-11	1881
Robert	DeS	2-198	1883
Robert S.	Pan(1)	B-80	1871
William	Pan(1)	A-429	1862
BOZEMAN, Meday	Hin	1-80	1837
BRABSTON, John B.	War	B-269	1892
Thomas	Ada	2-24	1832
BRACEY, William J.	Hin	B-264	1870
BRACK, Benjamin	Low	1-44	1859
Ward	Han P.(1853-1860)-120		1853
BRACKEN, James	Ada	1-343	1822
BRACKETT, Chastain	Nox	B-46	1863
BRADDOCK, Thomas W.	Tip	1-152	1891
BRADFORD, George	Tal	A-18	1836
George S.	Coa(1)	1-34	1852
Lizzie	Tun	2-167	1898
Lyman	Jac	1-69	1890
Lyman N.	Jac	1-134	1895
R. S.	Chi(1)	1-132	1898
BRADLEY, Bradford	Ada	1-391	1827
John L.	Tip	1-84	1877
John R.	Mad	A-170	1852
W. W.	Att	B-309	1880
BRAKENHOF, Charles C.	Wil	2-245	1866
BRAMLETT, A. G.	Laf	1-227	1873
Nancy T.	Nox	A-226	1857
BRAMLETTE, Virginia	Lau	1-82	1868
BRANCH, Eliza H.	Ada	3-191	1862

John	Ada	2–284	1844
Rebecca H.	Ada	5–133	1897
Reuben	DeS	1–199	1859
Sarah	Mad	A–332	1857
BRANDENBURG, Solomon Sr.	Mad	A–100	1845
BRANDER, James S.	War	B–113	1879
BRANDON, Charlotte S.	Ada	4–124	1877
Gerard	Ada	1–294	1823
Louisa A.	Wil	2–291	1874
Mary W.	Mon	I.17–400	1863
Matthew N.	Wil	1–235	1842
William A.	Tat	1–95	1886
BRANIGAN, Peter	Mad	A–482	1868
BRANIN, Harrison S.	Han	A–232	1893
BRANNON, Joseph L.	Yal(1)	B–139	1870
BRANSFORD, John	Tun	2–138	1896
BRASFIELD, J. M.	Mon	I.6–182	1892
BRASHEARS, Eden	Cla	B–162	1839
Martha	Cla	A–51	1814
Turner Bell	Cla	A–276	1833
BRASWELL, James L.	Tun	1–403	1866
James L.	Tun	2–8	1873
BRATTON, John W.	Hol	1–31	1838
BRAUNAGAN, Elizabeth	Mad	A–621	1882
BRAWNER, Henry	War	A–96	1839
BRAXTON, Carter	Cla	3–110	1888
BRAZEALE, Drury W.	Cla	A–293	1833
BRAZIL, Albert	Isa	C–148	1890
BREAZEALE, Elliott F.	Yaz	A–278	1862
Willis	Cla	A–234	1833
BREEDLOVE, John	Kem	A–60	1896
BREENE, Frederic	Ada	1–190	1819
BRELAND, Mary Ann	Gre	1–7	1890
Richard	Gre	1–4	1884
Samuel	Gre	1–6	1890
BRENNAN, Lawrence	Ada	3–367	1869
BRENT, H. P.	Ran	1–299	1894
William	Hin	1–38	1834
BRESHEARS, Marsham F.	Cla	A–230	1831
BREWER, D. C.	Car(1)	B–69	1899
Leroy	Car(1)	A–97	1851
Lewis	Nox	A–213	1855
Rawleigh	Nox	B–199	1875
Samuel	Ada	1–189	1819
William	Nox	A–207	1849
BREWSTER, James	Lau	1–55	1866
BRICKELL, Henry B.	Yaz	A–206	1856
James	Mad	A–63	1841
Susan L. C.	Ada	3–97	1857
BRIDGEFORTH, Caroline	DeS	2–352	1892

James C.	Yaz	B-60	1876
John B.	DeS	1-23	1852
Martha	Hol	1-276	1862
Robert F.	Yaz	A-150	1851
BRIDGERS, Abram B.	Cla	B-204	1849
Benjamin H.	Tal	A-238	1860
Edmond H.	Tun	1-35	1846
Samson	Cla	B-173	1842
William	Cla	B-211	1850
BRIDGES. George W.	Cop	AAA-448	1863
H. D.	Pre	1-9	1873
Hannah	Cla	3-128	1891
John C. C.	Jas	1-35	1861
Richard Roberts	Cop	AAA-442	1846
Seletta	Jas	1-51	1866
William	Jas	1-52	1865
William J.	Att	C-456	1894
BRIEL, William B.	Ada	4-524	1890
BRIGGS, A. A. E.	Mad	A-363	1862
David C.	Hin	1-262	1849
Gray	Yaz	A-23	1836
Matilda H.	Yaz	A-85	1845
Richard	Mas	P.3-448	1844
BRIGHT, M. J.	Lee	1-176	1896
Sarah W. S.	Mon	I.20-368	1871
BRILL, Charles	Mad	2-97	1897
Phillip	Ada	1-436	1829
BRINER, Daniel	Yaz	A-207	1856
BRINKLEY, Eli H.	Ran	1-192	1884
Elijah C.	Tip	1-57	1872
Robert C.	Mad	A-585	1879
Robert C.	Tun	2-48	1878
Squire	Jef	B-187	1893
BRINSON, Gause	Cla	A-140	1825
BRISCOE, Eli C.	Cla	3-48	1878
Elizabeth	Cla	B-190	1846
Emeline	Cla	B-304	1862
George W. T.	Cla	B-241	1853
Jane	Mad	A-368	1862
Notty W.	Mas	P.15-17	1860
Parmenus	Cla	B-212	1850
S. M.	Cla	3-155	1894
Thomas	Cla	A-232	1832
William	Cla	B-282	1858
William P.	Jef	P.E-399	1853
BRISTER, Hockeday	Hol	1-196	1858
John	Yaz	B-116	1880
S. M.	DeS	2-200	1882
Samuel	Att	B-173	1875
Thompson	Yaz	A-162	1853
Z. R.	Hol	1-271	1862

22

BRISTOW, E. H.	Mon	I.7–151	1900
BRITT, Jesse	DeS	1–393	1866
William	Mot	1–115	1893
BRITTENUM, Dempsey E.	Mas	P.5–271	1848
BRITTON, Audley C.	Ada	5–58	1894
Edmond	DeS	2–350	1892
James	Pan(1)	B–301	1879
Ruth	Ada	5–228	1899
Stephen W.	Hin	1–357	1855
BROACH, William P.	Lau	1–255	1889
BROKUS, William	Cla	A–16	1805
BROOKS, Aaron T.	Mas	P.18–607	1869
Allen	Low	1–218	1866
B. H.	Yaz	A–239	1860
Mrs. E. M.	Ada	1–81	1812
Eugene N.	Low	1–510	1886
George	Jef	A–107	1830
James	Cla	B–167	1840
Joe	Yaz	B–238	1889
John R.	Kem	A–82	1899
Joshua	Att	C–533	1871
Mary	Nox	B–161	1874
Mary P.	Ada	3–186	1861
Micajah	Nox	A–153	1851
Oliver C.	War	A–232	1856
Robert	Yal(1)	B–177	1878
Samuel	Ada	1–166	1812
Scythia	Tip	1–108	1882
Susan	Hol	1–493	1888
Terrell	Tip	1–119	1885
Thomas	Yaz	A–164	1853
Thomas B.	Low	1–55	1860
Timothy T.	Chi(1)	1–22	1879
Travis M.	Hol	3–35	1895
Washington	Yal(1)	B–192	1882
William	Ada	1–234	1821
William	Jef	A–95	1827
William J.	Uni	1–55	1884
William R.	Mon	I.14–142	1859
BROOM, Robert P.	Ada	1–363	1826
BROOME, Sarah J.	Hin	B–475	1899
BROWER, William	Ada	1–310	1823
BROWN, Abner	Yaz	A–211	1858
Adolphus	Mad	A–622	1882
Alexander	War	A–310	1862
Anderson R.	Tal	B–25	1870
Andrew	Ada	3–448	1871
Andrew Sr.	Tip	1–153	1890
Bedford	DeS	2–242	1885
Charles L.	Cla	A–305	1834
Charles V.	Wil	2–347	1877

Charlotte	Ada	4-19	1873
Charlotte	Wil	2-377	1880
D. L.	Wil	2-144	1858
Mrs. E. C.	Lee	1-222	1900
Elias	Clk	1-10	1872
Elijah C.	Pan(1)	B-167	1875
Eliza A.	Wil	3-173	1898
Eliza P.	War	B-107	1879
Elizabeth	Cop	AAA-395	1855
Emilene	Yal(1)	B-229	1897
G. T.	Tal	B-100	1892
George	Lee	1-229	1898
George	Yaz	B-289	1893
Hannah	Ada	4-485	1889
Henry	Kem	A-14	1884
Henry	Nox	B-331	1888
Henry W.	Hol	1-427	1879
Isaiah	Car(1)	A-11	1838
J. H.	Coa(2)	1-9	1892
J. L.	Tat	1-148	1890
James	Win	1-49	1867
James C.	DeS	1-421	1865
Jeremiah D.	Coa(1)	1-89	1866
Jesse P.	Mad	A-180	1853
Jesse S.	Yaz	A-19	1836
John	Mas	P.11-123	1855
John	Mas	P.18-441	1868
John	Wil	1-28	1833
John F.	Cla	B-210	1850
John Wilson	Wil	2-120	1857
Joseph G.	Mad	A-601	1880
Joseph Newton	Tis	1-117	1900
Levi T.	Tun	1-489	1869
Lorenzo D.	Wil	1-278	1844
Lucy Ann	Low	1-302	1871
Mary Jane	War	B-334	1897
Matilda	DeS	1-73	1853
Olivia	Yaz	B-50	1876
Osburn	Ada	2-232	1841
Patrick H.	Tal	B-47	1876
Peleg	Pre	1-105	1897
Robert	Mon	I.13-643	1858
Robert C.	Mad	A-407	1865
Robert C.	Mon	I.2-632	1877
Robert Samuel	Wil	2-324	1876
Sarah D.	Wil	2-78	1853
Susan B.	Clk	1-134	1892
Thomas J.	Wil	2-263	1871
William	Nox	B-65	1865
William	War	B-125	1879
William	Yaz	B-46	1875

William H.	Att	2-230	1862
William M.	Coa(1)	1-73	1860
William S.	Hin	B-139	1861
Wyatt M.	Nox	B-247	1881
BROWNE, Margaret	Att	D-134	1899
Miles T.	Yaz	B-34	1873
William	Ada	2-317	1846
BROWNING, A. P.	Laf	1-432	1896
Albert G.	Laf	1-338	1885
Caleb	Laf	1-2	1844
G. B.	Att	D-144	1899
J. A. Sr.	Laf	2-76	1900
J. C.	Laf	1-389	1892
BROWNLEE, Absalom S.	Low	1-93	1862
Fannie C.	Chi	1-130	1896
J. J.	Sun	1-7	1890
John R.	Low	1-105	1862
Joshua S.	DeS	1-43	1853
Lucinda	DeS	1-223	1859
Sarah Ann	DeS	1-46	1853
BROYLES, E. S.	Mon	I.4-532	1883
Ira G.	Mon	I.7-50	1899
BRUCE, John L.	Wil	1-46	1833
BRUNE, William	Ada	3-364	1869
BRUNER, Margaret	Ada	1-411	1825
BRUSER, Henry B.	War	B-100	1879
Lizzie	War	B-366	1899
BRUTON, Joel E.	Coa(1)	1-86	1861
BRYAN, James	Hin	1-12	1833
Lewis H.	Wil	2-194	1863
Mary	Ada	3-81	1857
Mathew	Wil	2-42	1849
P. G.	Mon	I.1-53	1871
Thomas J.	Hin	1-13	1833
BRYANT, A. A.	Yal	B-221	1893
John	Pan(1)	B-441	1888
Nathan	Hin	1-170	1843
Phoebe Ann	War	A-190	1851
Robert H.	Hin	B-289	1872
Sarah F.	Lef	A-50	1876
BRYCE, John	Wil	2-141	1858
BRYSON, Emma L.	War	B-187	1887
James A.	Lee	1-166	1896
James Sr.	Nox	C-30	1897
BUCCUS, John M.	Att	2-81	1862
BUCHANAN, C. J. M.	Chi(1863-1872)-49		1864
Ellen	Wil	3-71	1891
Franklin	Mon	I.7-165	1851
Joseph	Chi(1863-1872)-71		1853
Maximelian H.	Mon	I.13-458	1858
Powhattan H.	Pan(1)	A-368	1859

Sophia W.	Chi(2)	1-59	1893
BUCHANNAN, Benjamin			
B.	DeS	1-418	1867
BUCHEL, Anthony	Han	A-318	1898
BUCK, Benjamin			
Augustus	Jef	P.C-165	1842
Charles L.	War	A-317	1862
D. J.	Nox	C-13	1896
E. H.	Hol	1-374	1872
James T.	Hol	1-482	1886
Maria	Cla	3-24	1875
Mollie D.	Tun	2-29	1874
Richard	Mad	A-155	1850
U. H.	Hol	1-345	1870
William H.	Jef	B-190	1896
Wiiliam K.	Tun	2-29	1874
BUCKELS, Abram	Ada	2-448	1853
Joseph	Lin	1-3	1894
BUCKHOLTS, John G.	Tal	A-1	1835
BUCKHOLTZ, John G.	Hin	1-25	1833
BUCKINGHAM, George H.	Low	1-380	1875
Stephen H.	Mon	I.5-562	1889
Sterling H.	Mon	I.5-562	1889
BUCKLEY, Elijah	Jas	1-2	1855
Even	Jas	1-86	1888
James	Tal	A-96	1848
Joseph Elijah	Jas	1-85	1888
Nancy	Jas	1-30	1863
Richard	Car(1)	A-178	1859
Robert	Yaz	B-85	1878
Timothy	Han	A-164	1886
BUCKNER, Aylette	Ada	4-372	1886
Mary	Mad	A-93	1843
Robert	Was	2-2	1894
Robert H.	Hin	1-195	1846
Sarah F.	Cla	3-132	1892
Sarah F.	Was	1-499	1893
Thomas H.	Was	1-395	1872
William E.	Was	1-493	1893
BUELL, John	War	A-40	1834
BUFORD, Cynthia M.	Laf	1-136	1859
James H.	Hol	1-486	1887
James H.	Mad	A-645	1887
John E.	Laf	1-165	1861
Mary G.	Yal(2)	1-13	1880
Samuel H.	Wil	1-55	1832
BUGG, Frances A.	War	B-296	1894
Martha N.	War	B-17	1870
Nancy	Hin	1-47	1835
BUHLER, Amelia E.	War	B-128	1880
BUIE, Gilbert	Jef	P.D-296	1848

Gilbert M.	Jef	B-132	1873
John	Tal	A-33	1843
Milton	Laf	1-328	1881
Milton	Laf	1-358	1886
Neill	Cop	AAA-389	1861
BULL, Robert	War	A-139	1841
BULLARD, A. B.	Car(1)	A-489	1866
Charles K.	Sco	A-304	1869
David	Kem	A-31	1887
BULLEN, B. M.	Jef	A-82	1824
BULLER, Peter	Yaz	B-267	1891
BULLITT, Alex. C.	Was	1-390	1868
BULLOCK, Edward	Hin	1-416	1857
James	Yaz	A-1	1829
James	Yaz	A-45	1838
Jesse L.	Mar	A2-3	1873
Mary	Cla	A-273	1833
Reuben	Ada	3-378	1869
Stephen	Cla	A-40	1812
BUMPASS, Benjamin K.	Tip	1-140	1887
BUNCH, D.	Yaz	B-332	1897
Henrietta	Sim	A-3	1872
BUNNE, Charles R.	War	B-61	1875
Mary Anne	War	B-333	1896
BUNTIN, Eliza A.	Tal	B-65	1881
BUNTURA, Jose'	Ada	4-104	1875
BURBRIDGE, William R.	War	A-261	1859
Y. T. M.	Pan(2)	A-21	1882
BURCH, John	Hol	1-342	1869
Nancy	Jef	P.C-513	1844
Washington S.	Jef	B-138	1843
BURFORD, A. M.	Tat	1-130	1890
C. M.	Kem	A-56	1894
D. L.	Tat	1-43	1880
BURGES, Christopher	Ada	1-397	1828
BURGESS, Eugene	Lee	1-227	1900
John Sr.	Nox	A-46	1842
William J.	Tal	A-307	1866
BURGET, John	Ada	1-142	1817
BURGETT, Elizabeth G.	DeS	1-456	1870
BURKE, Adolphus			
Thomas	Ran	1-166	1881
Annie J.	Tun	2-132	1892
Michael	DeS	2-389	1894
Michael	Tun	2-127	1892
Mourning M.	Yal(1)	B-169	1877
BURKETT, Gabriel	Per	1-4	1889
BURKHALTER, T. F.	Pan(2)	A-77	1890
BURKILL, B. L.	Mon	I.5-217	1887
BURLEYSON, Elenor	Qui	1-2	1878
Ella G.	Qui	1-2	1887

27

BURLING, Ann Eliza	Ada	1-385	1826
Elizabeth W.	Ada	1-248	1822
BURN, George W.	Low	1-549	1888
BURNELL, Coleman	Hin	1-398	1857
BURNET, Daniel	Cla	A-191	1827
BURNETT, Amos	Cla	B-203	1849
Ann	Tat	1-78	1885
B. C.	Mon	I.17-8	1862
Daniel	Mon	1-223	1845
John H.	Pan(2)	A-90	1892
N. B.	Mon	I.10-266	1854
BURNEY, David	Law	P.B-65	1838
Richard	War	A-15	1831
BURNHAM, Thomas R.	Hin	1-33	1834
BURNS, Agnes C.	Yaz	B-326	1896
Bailus	Yal(1)	A-26	1841
Bailus	Yal(1)	A-48	1841
Caroline	Okt	1-50	1895
Charles	Sim	A-63	1890
Dennis	Yaz	A-103	1848
Henry	Hol	3-63	1898
John	Yal(1)	A-68	1843
BURR, Hudson E.	Lef	A-21	1854
BURRAGE, Rebecca	Win	1-5	1860
BURRELL, Carry	Cly	1-133	1897
Con	Yal(1)	B-236	1898
Nathaniel	Cla	B-160	1839
BURRESS, Ellen V. K.	Wil	1-104	1834
Thomas	Pre	1-100	1895
BURRIS, Samuel	Ami	1-57	1812
BURROW, John	Mas	P.7-555	1851
Peter B.	Nox	A-291	1860
BURRUS, Elizabeth S.	Yaz	B-2	1870
James R.	Yaz	A-302	1865
BURRUSS, John W.	Wil	2-247	1866
Mary E.	Wil	3-37	1885
BURT, William	Low	1-350	1873
BURTON, David	Coa(1)	1-120	1877
John	Ran	1-245	1892
Martha C.	Car(1)	A-93	1850
R. A.	DeS	2-258	1885
BURWELL, Lewis	Lau	1-394	1898
BUSBY, Elizabeth H.	Mon	I.5-59	1885
W. G.	Tat	1-91	1885
BUSE, John	Laf	1-405	1892
BUSH, James	Hin	1-236	1849
John	Hin	1-422	1858
Peter	Car(1)	A-436	1862
BUSICK, David Wesley	Ran	1-203	1885
BUSTAMANTE, M. G.	Att	C-303	1868
BUSTENS, J. T.	Hol	1-335	1869

BUTLER, Charles G.	Laf	1-95	1855
Ellen M.	Cla	3-40	1877
Frank	Ada	2-148	1837
Jane	Ada	2-98	1835
John	Laf	1-107	1856
John E.	Sha	A-27	1898
Martha	Sim	A-18	1878
Mary	Han P.(1853-1860)-67		1853
Mary E.	Pan(1)	A-201	1855
Medora A.	Jef	B-107	1868
Samuel F.	Low	1-131	1862
Zachariah	Fra	A-11	1889
BYARS, Harriet	Mad	A-530	1873
William	Mad	A-491	1869
BYERLEY, Mollie J.	Sha	A-16	1891
BYERS, Alemeth	Pan(1)	B-277	1873
Amzi W.	Pan(1)	B-316	1879
BYNUM, Augustus W.	DeS	2-42	1871
Bettie T.	DeS	2-207	1883
J. M.	Pre	1-127	1899
Joseph	Pre	1-7	1871
Rebecca	DeS	2-364	1893
BYRAM, Ebenezer	DeS	1-128	1856
John H.	DeS	1-297	1861
BYRD, Alexander	Nox	A-222	1855
H. F.	Hol	3-109	1900
Isaiah	Nes	A-1	1838
John	Yaz	A-22	1836
John B.	Hol	1-77	1847
Josiah	Yaz	A-18	1836
BYRNE, Thomas	Coa(1)	1-217	1890
William	Yaz	B-108	1879
BYRUE, Edward	Ada	4-501	1889
CABB, Jacob	Jef	A-62	1820
CABEEN, William	Hin	1-175	1838
CABERN, Jane	Hin	1-105	1838
CABINESS, Anthony R.	Pan(1)	A-413	1861
CABLE, David	Jef	A-11	1808
CADE, W. R.	Car(2)	1-1	1875
CADY, Fannie Leigh	Low	2-8	1889
William	Lau	1-169	1881
William	Low	1-395	1876
CAFFEY, T. Y.	DeS	2-488	1899
W. W.	Mot	1-149	1899
CAFFERY, Mary	Cla	A-143	1825
CAGE, Albert H.	Mad	A-578	1879
Catherine Jane	Wil	2-130	1857
Edward	Car(1)	A-470	1864
Robert H.	Yaz	A-191	1855
Wilson	Yal(1)	A-131	1847

CAHILL, Achrah A.	Ada	3-314	1867
CAHN, Benhomnie	Was	1-438	1884
CAIN, D. B.	Fra	A-7	1886
Eleanor	Hol	1-320	1866
Hardy	Ami	1-142	1814
Hardy	Fra	A-3	1881
James	Wil	1-168	1837
John	Hol	1-141	1854
John G.	Att	B-462	1885
John G.	Att	C-12	1885
CALDER, Amanda	Wil	3-56	1887
Theodosia	Wil	3-26	1883
CALDWELL, Alexander			
S.	Lef	A-34	1859
Andrew H.	Tat	1-234	1899
George	Hin	1-30	1834
Isaac	Hin	1-66	1836
James	Low	2-145	1896
Jesse	Low	1-501	1885
John L.	Hol	1-464	1884
Joseph	Pan(1)	A-14	1847
Juliet G.	Yaz	B-302	1895
Mary R.	Car(1)	B-27	1885
Robert	Ada	1-300	1823
Sarah	Yaz	B-373	1898
CALHOUN, E. W.	Cla	B-172	1842
George	Mad	A-177	1852
John D.	Cla	B-252	1855
John D.	Hol	1-107	1851
Thomas J.	Tal	A-41	1843
Willis B.	Nox	B-132&157	1873
Willis B.	Nox	B-319	1887
CALLAHAN, Fleming	Mas	P.16-191	1864
CALLAWAY, James R.	Laf	1-152	1865
William	Kem	A-9	1883
CALLECOTT, P. H.	Tat	1-200	1894
CALLICOTT, H. M.	Tat	1-233	1899
CALLIHAM, David	Wil	1-66	1833
John Y.	Wil	1-83	1833
CALVER, Russel	Ada	1-301	1823
CALVERT, George	War	B-35	1874
James	Kem	A-41	1891
CALVIN, Nancy	Okt	1-39	1898
CALVIT, Francis	Ada	2-96	1835
James	Cla	A-197	1827
Samuel	Jef	A-89	1826
Thomas	Jef	A-69&71	1821
CAMERON, Granville D.	Pan(1)	B-125	1872
John M.	Nox	A-71	1842
Lucy A.	Lea	1-160	1894
Mary	Mad	A-135	1849

Paul O.	Tun	2–208	1900
Sallie C.	Han	A–310	1897
Sarah Ann	Pan(1)	B–359	1881
CAMMACK, Dorothy	Coa(1)	1–117	1870
CAMP, Cyrus T.	Yaz	A–285	1863
Elizabeth Tennessee	Pan(2)	A–128	1896
Joseph W.	Mad	A–27	1836
CAMPBELL, Andrea D.	Ada	4–344	1885
C.	Tat	1–96	1886
Caroline A.	Pik	1–10	1883
Charles	Han	A–87	1874
Charles C.	Mot	1–72	1885
D. L.	Lea	1–104	1882
Edwin	War	A–107	1840
Henry	Was	1–397	1874
J. G.	Tip	1–3	1866
Jacob	Jef	P.D–466	1848
James	Yaz	A–234	1860
John	Ada	1–30	1807
John	Hin	1–207	1847
John A.	Laf	1–87	1854
John N.	Yaz	A–294	1865
John P.	Yaz	A–175	1854
Judith	Hin	B–42	1861
L. A.	War	B–129	1881
Lorenzo	Hin	1–294	1852
Lucinda	Low	1–150	1863
Lucy	War	B–130	1882
Mary J. E.	Pan(1)	B–448	1889
Richard	Car(1)	A–101	1844
Robert Gray	Was	2–32	1896
Susan	Ada	3–278	1866
William R.	Was	1–170	1852
CAMPE, August	Han	A–262	1894
CAMTHUS, B. G.	Pan(1)	B–479	1892
CANFIELD, James	Yal(2)	1–51	1886
Orlando	Low	1–68	1860
CANNAN, Susan J.	Cly	1–66	1883
CANNAVAN, James B.	War	B–118	1880
CANNON, Albert	Yaz	B–339	1897
Amanda M.	Low	1–469	1884
Eliza Houston	Mas	1–151	1898
Henry H.	Laf	1–150	1864
J. M.	Law	1–1	1884
J. M.	Yaz	B–171	1884
James W.	Ada	4–34	1873
John	Ada	1–351	1825
Thomas E. Jr.	Low	1–177	1865
Virgil M.	Yaz	B–226	1888
William R.	Low	1–6	1858
CAPDEVILLE, John			

Charles	Ada	5-148	1897
CAPSHAW, William W.	Yaz	A-307	1865
CARABINE, Mary	War	B-54	1875
CARAVAXAL, Francisco	Ada	1-198	1818
CARKEET, Richard	Ada	3-234	1865
CARLETON, Rebecca I.	Nox	A-215	1856
CARLILE, John	Jas	1-48	1864
CARLISLE, Alexander	Mon	I.4-412	1882
Henry	Chi(1)	1-120	1895
Henry	Mon	I.6-432	1895
James G.	Att	C-209	1891
CARLOCK, John	DeS	2-49	1872
John F.	Tat	1-191	1894
Lydia	Mas	P.19-120	1869
Moses	Mas	P.4-423	1846
William R.	Mas	P.11-156	1855
CARLOS, M. D.	Laf	1-19	1846
CARLRY, Eliza A.	Tal	A-256	1861
CARLTON, Samuel	Laf	1-4	1845
CARMICHIEL, William	Jas	1-90	1893
CARNES, Ephraim	Cop	AAA-385	1831
John B.	Tun	2-83	1884
Wells G.	Hin	1-102	1838
CARODINE, William G.	Chi(1863-1872)-102		1865
CAROTHERS, James N.	Chi(1)	1-103	1891
Jesse C.	Laf	1-257	1875
CARPENTER, Delila G.	Att	C-247	1868
Edmond L.	Nox	B-374	1891
Horace	Cla	A-323	1836
Ira	Ada	3-222	1865
John	Car(1)	A-147	1857
John	Tip	1-183	1894
N. L.	Ada	5-13	1893
Sarah E.	Ada	4-396	1887
Temple	Cop	AAA-380	1839
CARR, Abraham	Clk	1-29	1877
Charlotte	Hin	1-18	1833
David S.	New	1-43	1884
Elizabeth Ann	New	1-39	1884
Henry	Hin	1-209	1848
John C.	Ada	2-106	1835
John F.	Low	1-482	1885
Salina H.	Low	2-111	1891
Sarah J.	Yal(2)	1-58	1888
CARRADINE, David	Jef	A-22	1818
James	Ada	4-75	1875
Lettetia	Jef	A-80	1824
Mary	Jef	A-19	1813
Parker	Jef	A-67	1819
CARRAGEL, John C.	Yal(1)	B-135	1868
CARRE, Gabriel	Ada	1-79	1812

CARRIEL, John D.	War	A-49&53	1835
CARRINGTON, Alfred	Mas	P.4-390	1846
John D.	Mas	P.15-569	1862
CARROLL, F. A.	DeS	2-411	1894
Giles	Yal(1)	B-114	1866
Jane N.	Ada	5-10	1892
John	Jef	A-30	1818
CARRUTH, John	Ben	1-18	1868
CARSLEY, George W.	Hin	B-147	1862
CARSON, Caroline C.	Ada	1-467	1831
James	Ada	4-476	1889
Jason	Hin	1-156	1831
Joseph	Ada	1-145	1817
Leah Rachel	Hol	1-47	1844
Orville	Mad	A-183	1853
R. B.	Hol	3-32	1895
Sarah A.	Tal	A-173	1857
Thomas P.	Yaz	A-84	1845
William	Tal	A-21	1837
William Henry	Hin	B-466	1899
CARTER, A. G.	Cop	A-144	1900
Asa R.	Jon	1-2	1897
Augustine	Mon	1-262	1851
Charles H.	War	B-301	1894
Damarius	Jas	1-14	1862
E. L.	Smi	1-4	1896
Eliza S.	Tat	1-111	1888
Emily	Mon	I.6-488	1896
Farish	Lee	1-87	1861
Flora B.	Laf	1-122	1857
Freelive	Ada	5-251	1899
James	Laf	1-382	1891
James F.	Lee	1-57	1866
Jesse	Ada	1-147	1816
John	DeS	1-12	1852
John A.	Jas	1-33	1862
John R.	Tat	1-5	1874
Jonathan	Hol	1-128	1853
Josephus	Pan(1)	B-475	1891
Lorenzo	Jon	1-3	1898
Lorenzo	Per	1-14	1898
M. L.	Smi	1-4	1896
Mary B.	War	A-328	1866
Moses Tresmont	Cho	A-34	1893
Nehemiah	Ada	1-107	1814
Nehemiah	Wil	2-403	1882
Richard	Hol	1-34	1841
Richard	Laf	1-123	1858
Rufus	DeS	1-14	1852
Sallie W.	Yaz	B-187	1885
Samuel Y.	Yaz	B-150	1883

Sarah	Cop	AAA-369	1869
William J.	Hol	1-367	1872
William W.	Mas	P.16-217	1865
CARTHCART, William	Ada	1-235	1821
CARTLEDGE, John	Yal(1)	B-167	1877
CARUTHERS, Fannie L.	Pan(1)	B-498	1899
James	Mon	I.14-621	1863
CARVER, Samuel	Web	A-16	1876
CASEY, M. L.	Ben	1-33	1885
William	Ada	3-147	1860
CASON, Canady	Yaz	A-114	1847
Charles	Ada	1-128	1815
Delphine Rebecca	DeS	2-426	1895
Hilly E.	Yaz	A-7	1834
John	Yaz	A-28	1836
John R.	DeS	1-165	1858
Robert	Ada	2-33	1832
William	Yaz	A-81	1845
CASTEEL, Frank S.	Lau	1-254	1889
S. E.	Lau	1-218	1886
CASTELLA, Edward J.	Ada	4-190	1881
CASTEN, Samuel	Jas	1-45	1864
William F.	Hin	1-441	1859
CASTENS, Emily C.	Mad	A-572	1876
Eugene A.	Mad	A-573	1877
CASTLE, T. W.	Web	A-109	1893
CASTLEBERRY, James	Yal(2)	1-45	1885
John	DeS	2-21	1870
CATCHING, Joseph H.	Cop	A-61	1891
Letitia	Cop	AAA-363	1860
CATES, Isaac Thomas	Pon	1-118	1839
CATHELL, Jonathan	Hin	1-79	1837
CATHEY, A.	Tat	1-241	1899
Alexander	DeS	1-290	1861
Elizabeth B.	Tat	1-54	1882
Josiah G.	DeS	2-75	1873
Mathew B.	Mas	P.10-151	1854
William	Mas	P.3-410	1844
Viola	Lau	1-263	1890
CATLETT, John B.	Hin	1-383	1856
R. P.	Hin	1-7	1833
Rachel M.	Hin	1-410	1857
CATO, Joel P.	Lea	1-101	1880
Sarah	Gre	1-12	1894
CATTLETT, Billy	Nox	B-280	1882
CAUTHEN, Ludy	Pan(1)	B-189	1876
Milton	Mad	A-477	1868
Sarah B.	Mad	2-8	1892
CAVANAH, J. A.	Low	1-149	1863
CAVATT, Cicero	Ada	4-5	1871
CAVENAUGH, Eliza W.	Mas	P.18-383	1868

CAVERT, George S.	Lau	1-377	1898
CAVETT, James	Hin	1-283	1852
Walter H.	Nox	B-317	1887
CAVIN, John	Wil	2-190	1863
CAWART, Elizar	Lin	1-47	1898
CAWECY, William	Cla	A-117	1821
CAWTHON, Charles	Car(1)	A-48	1845
CEANE, Catharine	Cla	A-286	1833
CENAS, Hilary Breton	War	A-209	1853
CESSNA, William	Hin	1-197	1847
CHAFFE, Charles	Lef	A-113	1894
Florence Ward	Han	A-213	1892
CHAILLE, Mary	Ada	2-275	1844
William H.	Ada	2-131	1836
CHALMERS, Fanny M.	Mas	P.4-71	1845
James R.	Coa(2)	1-47	1898
Joseph W.	Mas	P.9-221	1853
CHAMBERLAIN, Charles			
T.	Ada	4-7	1871
John	Cla	B-337	1868
Thomas J.	Jef	P.F-16	1854
CHAMBERLIN, A. M.	Kem	A-6	1882
CHAMBERS, Ann	Mad	A-330	1857
Anna	War	A-126	1841
Annie	Sim	A-93	1899
Benjamin	Mad	A-370	1862
Benjamin F.	Lef	A-82	1884
Edward J.	Mon	I.14-487	1859
Julia A.	Lef	A-159	1900
Maria	Ada	3-484	1871
Samuel	Mon	1-230	1845
Wesley	Wil	1-44	1832
CHAMBLESS, Stephen W.	Mas	P.8-96	1852
Susan	DeS	1-324	1862
CHAMBLIN, D. A.	Pan(1)	B-438	1888
CHAMBLISS, Drusilla			
J.	Jef	B-72	1864
Frederic J.	Jef	P.F-488	1856
Rebecca	Cla	A-166	1826
William R.	Cla	A-93	1820
CHAMPENOIS, Isaac	Clk	1-66	1884
Louisa	Clk	1-142	1893
CHAMPION, J. L.	Coa(1)	1-108	1868
CHANCE, John Joseph	Han	A-109	1879
CHANCELLOR, John S.	Chi(2)	1-7	1883
CHANCHE, John Joseph	Ada	2-415	1852
CHANDLER, Bailey	Low	2-194	1897
Early Madison	Laf	2-41	1899
Erastus C.	Chi(1863-1872)-19		1864
George W.	Lau	1-199	1885
J. W.	Cly	1-76	1887

John	Nox	A-184	1853
Maria E.	Low	2-67	1893
Robert W.	Cly	1-39	1879
William Clark	War	B-1	1867
CHANEY, Ann S.	Isa	A-155	1852
Susan H.	Isa	A-130	1851
Thomas Y.	Isa	C-47	1861
CHANTERANT, Antoine	Jac	1-53	1888
CHAPLAIN, Amenaide			
Chotard	Ada	5-113	1896
CHAPMAN, E. E.	New	1-71	1887
Harriet	Ada	5-215	1898
John	Hin	1-217	1848
Mary A.	War	A-299	1861
Rhoda M.	Hin	B-287	1873
Solomon	Laf	1-164	1866
CHAPPELL, Joshua C.	Per	1-8	1889
CHARLES, Arsene	Jac	1-60	1890
Marion	War	B-381	1900
CHASE, Sally	Ada	3-345	1865
CHATHAM, W. P.	Car(1)	B-7	1878
CHEAIRS, Calvin	Coa(2)	1-54	1899
CHEATHAM, Eggleston	Yaz	A-138	1848
M. C.	Yaz	B-33	1873
Sallie Lee	Yaz	B-384	1899
Sarah W.	Mad	A-78	1843
CHEEK, Elizabeth	Car(1)	A-112	1853
Landon O.	Mad	2-139	1900
William A.	Mad	2-85	1897
CHERRY, Daniel	Mas	P.3-396	1844
Robert	Mas	P.7-644	1851
Wiley	Hin	1-397	1857
CHESNEY, J. F.	Ada	4-578	1892
CHESTER, John F.	Ran	1-247	1892
CHEVENDEMANN, Auguste	Cla	A-316	1835
CHEW, Thomas H.	Yaz	A-52	1840
CHICHESTER, George	Hin	1-439	1859
CHICHON, Rose	Han	A-316	1898
CHILD, Emma E.	Hin	B-440	1895
CHILDRESS, Gorn	Mas	P.19-360	1870
Meredith	Laf	1-21	1848
Mitchel	Laf	1-137	1859
Thomas	Ben	1-70	1896
CHILES, Henry	Lau	1-305	1892
CHILTON, Harriet W.	Hin	1-139	1840
John M.	Hin	B-33	1859
CHIM, Thomas	Mad	A-235	1856
CHISHOLM, John	Laf	1-24	1847
John	Pan(1)	A-37	1847
CHISLEY, Ned	Ada	2-39	1833
CHISM, George	Mas	P.7-603	1851

CHOATE, John J.	Yal(1)	A-137	1849
CHOTARD, Fanny	Ada	4-580	1892
CHRISTIAN, John	Laf	1-189	1868
Mariam	Laf	1-271	1876
Thomas	Lau	1-125	1879
CHRISTMAS, Harry H.	Isa	C-128	1871
William	Ada	3-34	1855
CHUNN, Nathan	Cla	B-242	1854
CHURCH, Edward B.	Was	1-97	1847
Mariah L.	War	A-224	1855
CINCLAIR, Jasper	Jcf	A-103	1829
CLAIBORNE, Isabella			
C. H.	Ada	1-144	1816
J. F. H.	Ada	4-363	1886
John F. H.	Han	A-238	1894
Leon	Ada	1-50	1810
CLANCY, Emily F.	Hol	1-467	1884
CLANTON, Mary E. J.	Tat	1-229	1898
Matthew	Pan(1)	B-37	1867
Rebecca W.	Mad	A-680	1891
Robert	Pan(1)	A-238	1856
CLAPP, Emory	Was	1-421	1880
CLARK, Alfred	Cla	3-46	1878
Archibald E.	Tip	1-4	1866
B. A.	Att	D-143	1899
Benjamin	Chi(1863-1872)-196		1870
Cretia	Lef	A-121	1896
Daniel	Ada	1-99	1813
Daniel	Wil	1-209	1839
Edward	War	B-152	1885
Enoch G.	Car(2)	1-5	1876
George W.	Hin	B-408	1890
Gibson	Cla	A-88	1820
J. S.	Hin	B-191	1866
Jacob	Lee	1-109	1889
James A.	Att	C-399	1894
James C.	Att	D-72	1898
James M.	Jac	1-112	1892
John	Coa(2)	1-1	1892
John C.	Ada	3-5	1854
John T.	Cla	B-250	1855
Joseph	Mad	A-325	1856
M. E.	Lau	1-372	1897
Margaret	Ada	4-468	1888
Mary	Ada	2-223	1840
Richard Cottrell	Lee	1-153	1894
Robert	Hin	1-286	1852
Robert	Yaz	B-141	1882
Robert A.	Ran	1-97	1867
Sarah E.	Pon	1-1	1890
Sidney S.	War	B-40	1874

Silas H.	Att	2–389	1864
Thomas G.	Hol	1–389	1876
William	Car(1)	A–33	1841
William	Hin	B–29	1859
William B.	Gre	1–3	1881
William H.	Ran	1–82	1866
Willis	Pik	1–35	1889
CLARKE, Bolling	Mon	I.12–662	1857
Charles B.	Cla	3–75	1882
Edmund S.	Lau	1–154	1881
Elijah	Cla	A–133	1823
J. G.	Cla	A–205	1828
Lewis	Cla	A–206	1828
Margaret M.	Pan(1)	B–105	1871
Mary G.	Cla	3–178	1898
CLAUNCH, Mary Ann	Lee	1–139	1891
CLAY, Mary H.	Nox	C–133	1900
Nancy	Tun	2–168	1898
Royal G.	Mon	I.19–119	1865
CLAYTON, Alex. M.	Ben	1–45	1889
Joseph	DeS	2–165	1880
Ranson	Pon	1–3	1890
Richard B.	Lee	1–17	1871
Rufus K.	Jas	1–50	1862
CLEARMAN, William L.	New	1–100	1890
CLEATON, Acintha	Was	1–449	1885
CLEAVELAND, George	Lee	1–161	1868
J. M.	New	1–135	1895
CLEMENT, George W.	Nox	B–300	1885
Samuel	Ada	2–173	1839
CLEMENTS, Charity	DeS	2–219	1883
James L.	Pan(2)	A–51	1884
John G.	DeS	1–48	1853
Laban	DeS	2–46	1872
CLEMMER, Eli	Ben	1–26	1875
CLENDENEN, Samuel	Hin	B–141	1861
CLEVELAND, Benjamin	Yal(1)	A–166	1850
CLIFTON, Matilda C.	DeS	1–404	1866
T. L.	DeS	2–512	1900
CLINE, Daniel	Ran	1–152	1877
Jacob	Low	2–14	1890
CLINKSCALES, George			
B.	Pan(1)	B–174	1875
CLINTON, Joseph	Lau	1–123	1877
CLOWER, John	Hol	1–391	1876
William	Hol	1–264	1862
COATES, Pollard H.	Hol	1–56	1845
Thomas P.	War	B–298	1894
COATS, William	Car(1)	A–107	1852
COBB, E. S.	Mad	A–643	1886
Jacob	Jef	A–62	1820

Jacob M.	Mad	A–448	1867
William B. Sr.	Kem	A–40	1891
COBBS, William Tellis	Pre	1–62	1870
COBUN, John B.	Cla	B–236	1853
Samuel	Cla	A–42	1813
Samuel	Cla	B–236	1853
COCHRAN, Benjamin F.	Ada	2–384	1850
George	Ada	1–11	1803
George	Jef	A–76	1822
John	Hin	1–168	1843
John A.	Grc	1–18	1896
Jonathan	War(1827–1832)–57		1827
Pattie	Mad	A–639	1886
Robert	Cla	A–308	1834
Samuel C.	Mad	A–600	1880
William M. W.	Ada	3–136	1859
COCKE, Benjamin W.	Tal	A–259	1862
Charles H.	Low	2–139	1896
Chastain	Yal(1)	B–36	1860
John H.	Tat	1–15	1875
John J.	Hol	1–257	1861
Mary J.	Pan(2)	A–117	1894
Philip St. George	Low	1–113	1862
Rebecca Elizabeth	Hin	B–328	1877
S. M.	Tat	1–215	1897
William	Pan(2)	A–2	1881
William R. C.	Low	1–473	1884
COCKRELL, Hillman	Chi(1)	1–38	1882
Samuel S.	Ada	5–94	1895
W. M.	Lef	A–168	1900
COCKS, John G.	Hol	1–378	1874
COE, J. B.	Yal(2)	1–12	1879
COEVAS, Franciosa	Han	A–23	1866
COFFEE, Hiram	Hin	1–66	1836
COFFEY, H. M.	Cla	B–286	1859
J. K.	Hol	3–73	1899
COFFIELD, Amanda E.	Isa	C–132	1879
Elizabeth	Car(1)	A–59	1847
COFFULA, David	Car(1)	A–58	1846
COGAN, Catharine I.	Jef	B–126	1873
COGDALL, Thomas	Mon	I.12–75	1856
COHEA, David A.	Ran	1–118	1871
Perry	Hin	1–213	1848
COHEN, Isaiah	Wil	2–179	1862
Moses	War	B–5	1869
COHRAN, J. B.	Car(1)	A–161	1858
Lee	Laf	2–21	1899
COKER, Thomas	New	1–23	1882
COLBERT, Martha	Lea	1–49	1865
COLBURN, Maria L.	Car(1)	B–20	1883
COLCOUGH, James	Okt	1–54	1900

COLE, A. R.	DeS	1-25	1852
Horatio S.	Lef	A-28	1849
James H.	Lee	1-26	1875
James M.	Pan(2)	A-87	1891
John	Tip	1-14	1866
Josiah	Pan(2)	A-113	1894
Martha	Mon	I.16-79	1860
Samuel	Yaz	A-12	1835
Theodore N.	Nox	C-96	1899
William A.	Mad	A-49	1839
William H.	Pan(1)	B-263	1878
William L.	Lau	1-66	1866
COLEMAN, Absalem	Att	A-145	1859
Annabella	Jef	B-181	1890
Asa	Mad	A-608	1881
Butler	Lea	1-167	1895
Carroll	DeS	1-314	1862
Charles	War(1827-1832)-146		1829
Daniel S.	Jef	B-85	1865
Edwin R.	Mad	A-512	1871
F. B.	Jef	B-142	1875
James	Ada	4-303	1883
James S.	Sun	1-1	1884
Jeremiah	Ada	1-197	1817
John B.	Lau	1-89	1868
John G.	Cla	B-234	1853
John M.	Mad	A-20	1833
John P.	Hol	1-166	1856
John T.	Ran	1-53	1863
Joseph G.	Lau	1-216	1886
Louisa	Jef	P.B-7	1836
Maria E.	Mas	1-47	1893
Nathaniel	Jef	A-120	1833
Pherobah	Jef	B-2	1859
Richard	Tal	A-150	1853
Thomas	Ran	1-75	1865
William H.	Pan(1)	A-116	1852
COLGLAZER, John	Yaz	A-40	1838
COLHAUN, Eliza J.	Ada	5-82	1895
COLLE, Herman	Jac	1-81	1891
COLLIER, Anthonet	Mad	A-252	1857
Hasten	Low	1-139	1863
Ingram Blanks	Mad	2-52	1896
Isaac Sr.	Ada	1-2	1802
John	Ran	1-234	1889
Martin T.	Tal	B-54	1876
COLLINS, Aaron	Low	1-301	1871
Franklin E.	Lin	1-27	1896
George W. Sr.	Pre	1-3	1870
Glaskey	Mad	A-297	1859
J. G. B.	Yaz	B-102	1879

James	Ada	3-175	1861
James	Ada	3-305	1867
James J.	Mad	A-335	1860
James M.	Cly	1-64	1883
James M.	Yaz	A-194	1855
Jane	Ada	1-447	1829
John	Cho	A-8	1882
Joseph	Mad	A-110	1847
Josephine	Mad	A-399	1863
Joshua	Car(1)	A-26	1840
Lydia Melville	Cly	1-96	1890
Melviney	War	B-229	1889
Moses	Tip	1-29	1868
Rich	Mon	I.11-322	1855
Robert	Clk	1-100	1888
Sallie	Mad	A-637	1886
Susan	Lea	1-176	1897
W. S.	Wil	2-81	1854
William	Ada	1-321	1824
William B.	Wil	1-33	1831
William J.	Mot	1-117	1893
COLLY, Annie	Han	A-277	1895
COLQUHOUN, Mary F.	Mad	A-662	1889
COLSON, Joseph	Tip	1-25	1867
COLTEN, John	Hol	1-112	1851
COLTHARP, John A.	Cla	B-333	1871
COMAR, Martin J.	War	B-336	1897
COMBEL, M. A.	Han	A-166	1886
Maria Louise	Han	A-139	1881
Peter	Han	A-93	1875
COMER, John	Wil	1-269	1844
COMFORT, Ellen C.	Mad	A-160	1851
COMMAGERE, Ernest	Wil	3-157	1897
COMPTON, Drury	Car(1)	A-67	1848
Pickens	Was	1-379	1867
Stephen	Jef	P.C-827	1846
W. H.	Lef	A-9	1851
CON, C. Victoria	Mas	P.4-668	1847
Fulker	Mas	P.2-154	1841
CONDY, Ellen	Ada	5-205	1898
CONDREY, John W.	DeS	2-480	1898
Lydia C.	DeS	2-481	1898
CONE, Edward	Mas	P.2-429	1841
CONGER, Amos A.	DeS	1-343	1865
Martha Archer	Cla	B-274	1857
Martin	Hin	1-24	1833
CONIBEL, P. E.	Han	A-160	1885
CONKEY, Zebina	Laf	1-162	1861
Zebina	Laf	1-173	1862
CONKLIN, James W.	War	B-172	1886
CONLY, George	Yal(1)	A-292	1856

CONN, E. B.	Cop	A-135	1899
Richard	Cop	AAA-359	1835
CONNELLY, John K.	DeS	1-161	1858
Patrick	Ada	1-14	1805
Priscilla	Ada	3-99	1857
CONNELY, Redmond	Ada	1-3	1803
CONNER, B. F.	Ada	2-6	1832
Henry L.	Ada	4-109	1877
J. W.	Kem	A-26	1886
James F.	Wil	2-41	1849
Jane E. B.	Ada	5-116	1896
M. L.	War	A-326	1866
Susan E.	Ada	3-117	1858
William C.	Ada	2-262	1843
William G.	Ada	3-217	1865
William H.	Pan(1)	A-322	1858
CONNOR, Andrew	Nox	A-186	1853
William P.	Nox	B-303	1885
CONNORS, Ellen	War	A-318	1862
CONVERSE, J. B.	Isa	C-150	1890
CONWAY, James W.	Hol	3-7	1890
CONWILL, Daniel G.	Mon	I.17-398	1863
CONY, Emeline	Pik	1-14	1884
COODY, Mary	War	A-320	1862
Zephemiah	War	A-18	1831
COOK, Aaron Moore	Low	2-100	1894
Andrew	Ada	5-171	1898
Elijah Sr.	Hin	1-211	1848
Foster	War(1827-1832)-50		1827
Frederic	Han	B-3	1899
Jennie H.	War	B-341	1897
John W.	Mon	1-211	1843
Lily H.	War	B-205	1888
Rufus	Yal(1)	B-226	1896
Ruth	Hin	1-276	1851
W. W.	Cop	A-14	1888
William	Ada	1-30	1808
William	Mas	1-93	1896
William	Nox	B-107	1871
COOKE, Alexander J.	Web	A-139	1899
J. N. Sr.	Okt	1-20	1889
COOKSEY, George M.	Nes	A-96	1870
COOPEN, Thomas J.	Lea	1-112	1883
COOPER, Anthony	Ada	2-242	1841
Carroll	DeS	2-436	1896
David	Ada	1-453	1830
E. J.	Was	1-394	1873
Eaton D.	DeS	1-72	1853
Edward W.	Yaz	A-283	1861
George W.	Yaz	B-224	1887
Hamilton	New	1-131	1894

Harrison	Cla	A-352	1837
Harrison	Cla	B-225	1852
J. A.	Mad	A-408	1865
James A.	Hol	1-158	1856
John A.	Pan(2)	A-100	1893
John J.	Ben	1-39	1886
Joseph	Hin	B-76	1864
Lizzie	Lea	1-149	1890
Maria	Cla	B-310	1862
Matthew	Hol	1-143	1854
Milas M.	Mad	A-525	1872
Preston	Yaz	A-212	1858
Richard	Ran	1-238	1891
Robert	Laf	1-38	1849
Samuel	Ada	2-47	1833
Sarah Lavenia	Hin	1-446	1859
Stephen	Nes	A-111	1880
Timothy T.	Hol	1-322	1867
Tirzah	Mad	A-640	1886
William	Cla	A-127	1822
Wilson	Mad	A-255	1857
COOPREW, George			
Washington	Nox	A-30	1841
COOPWOOD, Eli	Yal(1)	B-224	1895
Prudence W.	DeS	1-428	1868
COOR, Mary J.	Cop	A-24	1888
CORBAN, Gowin Lane	Laf	1-374	1888
CORBILL, Mary	War	B-151	1885
CORBIN, Martha D.	Jef	B-205	1891
CORCORAN, Thomas	Hin	1-350	1854
CORDELL, Lucy	Hin	B-217	1866
Richard	Hin	1-323	1854
COREY, Jeremiah	Ada	1-21	1806
Richard	Ada	1-53	1810
CORLEY, Rhoda	Ran	1-61	1864
CORMMACK, B. L. A.	Coa(2)	1-32	1895
CORN, Catherine	Ada	2-424	1852
CORNBEL, M. A.	Han	A-166	1886
CORNELIUS, Charles	Pon	2-238	1842
F. P.	Laf	1-378	1889
George	Pon	E.(1844-1848)-207	1847
CORNISH, Edward J.	Ada	3-133	1859
Joseph	Ada	2-439	1853
CORTER, Joseph C.	Pre	1-132	1900
CORUTHERS, W. W.	Ran	1-189	1884
CORY, David	Ada	1-270	1822
Jeremiah	Ada	2-396	1851
CORZINE, Reese	Mad	A-46	1839
COSTA, Faustina			
Ignacia	Jac	2-20	1899
COTHER, Benjamin	Mon	I.2-475	1877

COTTEN, James	Cla	B–289	1860
James	Yaz	B–49	1876
Junius Lea	Pik	1–94	1897
Thomas	Ami	1–172	1816
COTTER, Honora	Yaz	B–88	1878
COTTINGHAM, Martha E.	Cop	A–81	1892
COTTON, A. J.	Jas	1–87	1888
J. W. A.	Grn	A–39	1878
James B.	DeS	1–302	1862
Thomas	Cla	A–229	1831
William	Ada	2–269	1843
COTTONGHIM, Jonathant	Hin	1–112	1839
COTTRELL, Lucy	Mas	P.9–339	1853
COUCH, Alexander L.	Mad	A–580	1872
John	Pan(1)	A–21	1840
William N.	Car(1)	A–31	1842
COUGER, Susan R.	Car(1)	A–108	1852
COUGHLAN, Ann	Ada	5–119	1897
COULTER, John	Win	1–75	1874
William J.	DeS	1–457	1870
COUNCIL, Eleana	Coa(1)	1–124	1878
William J.	DeS	2–169	1881
COURTNEY, Jane E.	Was	1–424	1877
John	DeS	1–75	1854
COUSINS, John R.	Chi(1863–1872)–187		1869
COVEY, Bettie	Lee	1–149	1893
COVINGTON, Alexander	War	A–162	1848
J. B.	Win	1–79	1872
John C.	Pik	1–58	1894
Josephus L.	Low	1–66	1860
Levin	Ada	2–287	1844
W.	Tip	1–166	1893
William	Low	1–163	1864
COWAN, A. Z.	DeS	1–399	1866
David	Yal(1)	A–158	1850
David F.	Hin	B–83	1864
Ellen S.	Mot	1–54	1881
Ludwell B.	War	B–266	1892
Mary	DeS	1–164	1858
T. B.	Isa	C–164	1899
T. B.	Was	2–100	1899
Thomas L.	DeS	1–171	1858
William	Pre	1–91	1891
COWAND, Elizabeth	Mad	A–364	1862
COWARD, Floyd	Laf	1–276	1877
William	Laf	1–127	1858
COWART, James G.	Jac	1–15	1882
COWDON, James	Jef	A–112	1831
COWGER, John	Laf	1–347	1885
COWLEY, John C.	Mon	I.11–487	1855
COWSERT, D. M.	Hol	3–2	1894

COX, A. H.	Mad	2–145	1900
Albert G.	Low	1–446	1881
Bray G.	Pan(1)	A–13	1846
Mrs. C. R.	Yaz	B–312	1896
Charles	War	A–327	1866
G. W.	Low	2–260	1900
H. J.	Cly	1–33	1878
Hampton	Yaz	B–209	1886
J. J.	Ben	1–71	1896
John	Cla	A–342	1836
John C.	Ada	1–143	1817
John J.	Cla	A–332	1836
Joseph J.	Mad	A–447	1866
Josiah	Yaz	A–108	1848
Laura Laurinda	Jef	B–154	1883
Lemuel J.	Low	1–107	1862
Martha W.	Jef	B–129	1874
Michael	Tip	1–124	1886
Michael	Tip	1–160	1890
Nancy	Mas	P.8–18	1851
Nancy M.	Pan(1)	A–144	1853
Robert	Jef	B–153	1882
W. L.	Mon	I.7–148	1900
W. M.	Lee	1–208	1898
William B.	Mas	P.18–66	1867
William Emry	Web	A–111&117	1897
William L.	Mon	I.7–164	1899
COYLE, R. M.	Lef	A–107	1892
Stephen A.	Car(2)	1–76	1895
CRABB, A. C.	Mad	A–631	1884
Henry	War(1827–1832)–161		1829
CRADDOCK, Maude	Low	2–280	1900
CRAGIN, Abner	Pan(1)	A–376	1860
CRAIG, Alexander F.	Laf	1–146	1865
David	Laf	1–32	1849
Eliezer	Ada	3–268	1866
Fransis J.	Was	1–439	1884
Henry	Jef	A–43	1820
John H.	DeS	1–17	1852
Mattie A.	Tat	1–47	1881
CRANE, Francis R.	Cla	B–309	1862
James	Cla	B–271	1857
Martha	Cla	3–88	1883
Robert E.	Cla	B–303	1862
Samuel Barnes	Lef	A–42	1860
Waterman	Cla	A–149	1826
CRATON, McNeil	Tal	A–27	1841
CRAVEN, John W.	Tat	1–134	1890
Thomas	Tat	1–201	1895
CRAWFORD, B. A.	Pik	1–167	1899
Conyngham	Hin	1–107	1838

Edward	Hin	1-219	1845
James	Hol	1-170	1857
James D.	Grn	A-117	1896
Margaret	War	B-109	1879
Rosanna	Mad	A-173	1850
Thomas	Nox	A-89	1846
William	Ada	1-146	1817
CRAWLEY, Bird	Tal	A-79	1847
Eliza M.	Pan(1)	B-355	1881
Elizabeth	Gre	1-22	1898
Robert A.	Pan(1)	B-153	1874
W. N.	Pan(1)	B-253	1878
CREGIER, Peter George	Ada	2-405	1851
CREIGHTON, Carolina			
M.	Cla	B-197	1846
Fletcher	Cla	B-341	1872
CRENSHAW, A. B.	Uni	1-26	1891
J. T.	Mot	1-113	1893
Mildred	Yal(1)	A-177	1850
Thomas	Mot	1-38	1879
Thomas C.	Coa(1)	1-57	1858
Thomas C.	Coa(1)	1-82	1860
William	Hol	1-330	1868
William Henry	Chi(1863-1872)-198		1872
CRESWELL, Leander D.	Wil	2-217	1864
Miles	Wil	2-191	1863
CRIDDLE, James	Hin	1-363	1855
CRISMAN, Lucy C.	DeS	2-446	1896
CRISWELL, Jane Hall	Lin	1-42	1897
CRIZER, Jacob	Ada	3-452	1871
Maria P.	Ada	4-494	1889
CROCKETT, E. Susan	Yaz	B-331	1897
Samuel T.	Tat	1-8	1874
CROFFORD, William C.	Tal	A-170	1855
CRONE, Frederick	Ada	4-184	1881
CRONNER, Charles	Cla	3-66	1882
CROOK, Henry	Ran	B.1-151	1842
Jonathan	Tip	1-53	1871
CROOKS, Joseph	Cla	B-331	1871
CROSBY, Christopher	Yal(1)	1-109	1890
John	Mon	1-163	1819
Matilda	Yal(2)	1-66	1890
CROSLEY, Mary	Wil	1-302	1845
CROSS, Oliver	Car(1)	A-11	1838
Tish	Mad	A-684	1892
CROSSITT, Andrew	DeS	2-173	1881
CROSTWAIT, Lucy A.	Tal	B-96	1891
CROUCH, Benjamin T.	DeS	1-378	1866
James	War	A-342	1865
Solomon	Ben	1-1	1871
CROW, Jacob	Att	2-146	1862

Levi	Wil	2-25	1847
William	Laf	1-349	1883
CROWDER, James B.	Car(1)	A-27	1842
CROWE, Annie	Lau	1-172	1881
CROWELL, John	Cly	1-5	1873
CRUMP, George P.	Yaz	B-203	1886
John	Mon	I.22-224	1871
John B.	Cop	AAA-356	1855
Turner W.	Pan(1)	B-8	1864
CRUSOE, Charles R.	Low	1-257	1868
CUEVAS, Ramon	Han	A-58	1869
CULLEGE, Thomas	Hol	1-43	1844
CULLEN, Peter	Yal(2)	1-116	1898
CULLENS, John M.	Yaz	A-106	1848
CULLEY, Mary D.	Mad	2-66	1896
CULLINGSWORTH, John	War	A-145	1845
CULLIPHUR, Henry F.	Mad	2-64	1896
CULLOM, Mortimer	DeS	1-180	1858
Rachael S.	DeS	1-134	1856
CULP, Jane B.	Mon	I.7-31	1851
CULVER, Ella T.	Clk	1-198	1897
Ella T.	Clk	1-204	1899
CUMMINGS, H. F.	DeS	2-226	1884
Julia A.	DeS	2-170	1881
Levi	Mas	1-5	1892
Sarah K.	Ada	2-407	1852
CUNLIFFE, William E.	Hol	1-291	1864
CUNNINGHAM, Ellen	Han	B-43	1900
Francis Ann	Mon	I.6-124	1892
John B.	Hin	1-221	1848
John P.	Was	1-203	1855
William S.	Pan(1)	A-2	1845
CUPP, John	DeS	2-108	1875
CURD, David	Isa	C-153	1892
Elizabeth	Isa	C-157	1893
CURL, Kinchen	Mon	1-243	1847
CURRAN, John	Hin	B-148	1862
CURRAY, Emma G.	Nox	C-115	1899
CURRIE, John	Jas	1-25	1858
Mary	War	A-152	1846
Roderick	Hin	1-5	1833
Sarah	Jef	P.D-8	1847
CURRIER, Francis			
Matilda	Wil	2-338	1877
CURRY, Elanson M.	Grn	A-60	1884
Jacob	Ami	1-118	1814
James	Ada	3-213	1863
John M.	Yal(1)	B-43	1860
William B.	War	A-141	1843
CURTEAIN, Joshua	Ada	5-60	1894
CURTIS, Hannah	Ada	1-62	1807

CURTIS, Mary	Jef	P.B–155	1835
Nancy	Mad	A–197	1853
CURTISS, John	Pan(1)	A–7	1843
CUSACK, Amanda J.	Lau	1–197	1885
James W.	Lau	1–212	1886
Mary T.	Yaz	B–262	1891
CUTCHEN, Sullivan M.	Per	1–27	1900
DABBS, E. H.	Lee	1–50	1880
Mary A.	Lee	1–45	1879
DABNEY, Anderson W.	Nox	A–218	1856
Frederick Y.	Cop	A–142	1900
George F.	Han	B–42	1900
W. T.	Lau	1–386	1899
DACHER, Nancy	War	B–346	1898
DADE, Henry C. Sr.	Nox	A–31	1841
Robert R.	Mon	I.18–372	1864
DAHLGREN, Mary M.	Ada	3–109	1858
DAILEY, Patrick W.	War	A–216	1854
DAINGERFIELD, Mary I.	Jef	P.D–713	1850
DALE, Joshua	Cla	A–175	1826
DALEHITE, James L.	DeS	2–379	1894
DALRYMPLE, Albert D.	Mon	I.7–62	1898
DALTON, Mrs. E. F.	Low	1–528	1887
John L.	Cly	1–59	1883
Laura	Yaz	B–219	1887
DAMERON, Fannie	Mad	2–3	1892
Martha H.	Hin	B–460	1899
W. A.	DeS	1–312	1862
DAMPUR, James M.	Sim	A–50	1888
DANA, Charles B.	Ada	4–20	1873
Elvira R.	Ada	4–377	1886
DANCY, John W.	Mad	A–630	1884
Joseph	War	B–242	1890
Kate M.	DeS	2–442	1896
Kate McCorkle	Mas	1–35	1894
DANDRIDGE, Anne			
McGehee	Pan(1)	B–424	1888
Charles F.	Pan(1)	B–29	1867
Nathaniel W.	Pon E.(1844–1848)–297		1847.
DANGERFIELD, Henry	Ada	1–120	1815
William	Ada	1–204	1820
DANIEL, Ann	Cla	A–218	1830
Erastus	Yaz	B–308	1896
Ezekiel	Lau	1–6	1858
Joseph F.	Mas	P.3–543	1844
Nancy	War	A–3	1830
DANIELL, Smith C.	Cla	A–329	1836
Smith C.	Cla	B–302	1862
DANIELS, James W.	Lau	1–79	1868
DANSON, Henry S.	Was	1–1	1839

DAPONTE, Durant	Jac	1-137	1895
DARBY, Basdel	Yal(1)	A-24&46	1840
DARDEN, Ann	Mad	A-13	1833
Betsey	Jef	P.E-133	1851
J. H.	Jef	B-189	1895
John Henry	Hin	B-470	1899
Washington	Mad	A-2	1830
DARDIN, Rederick	Lau	1-223	1886
DARRILL, John			
Carribee	Lea	1-157	1893
DARSY, Benjamin	Ada	1-27	1807
DASHIELL, Thomas			
Rowan	Low	1-383	1876
DAUGHERTY, Frank	Ada	3-321&326	1867
John B.	Lef	A-26	1855
Sarah	Ran	1-27	1860
DAUGHITY, James	Mad	A-34	1830
DAUPHIN, Maximillian			
Auguste	Han	A-193	1891
DAUTZLER, David A. J.	Nox	B-194	1877
DAVANOY, Nancy	Grn	A-116	1896
DAVENPORT, Dice	Hol	3-38	1896
Ephraim	Cla	B-299	1862
James	Cla	B-170	1842
Joseph	Cla	B-233	1853
Nancy	Hin	B-46	1860
Presley	Cla	B-213	1849
Thomas	Jef	B-177	1893
DAVID, Mrs. E. A.	Yal(2)	1-93	1895
Henry	DeS	1-1	1851
Louis	Ada	4-284	1883
DAVIDSON, Ephrim E.	Laf	1-43	1847
George	Pon	1-246	1840
H. M.	Yal(1)	B-108	1866
John	Lau	1-315	1893
William P.	Nox	B-43	1863
DAVIE, Gabriel	Nox	B-14	1862
DAVIES, John	Nox	A-136	1849
Richard George	Jac	1-8	1878
DAVIS, A. W.	Lau	1-44	1863
A. W.	Tis	1-45	1891
Allen	Ada	3-164	1861
Anne	Ada	4-27	1873
Anne J.	Wil	3-13	1883
Arthur H.	Hin	1-32	1834
Berry S.	Wil	2-20	1847
Mrs. C. U.	Mon	I.7-31	1896
Clement	Hin	B-340	1881
Derry	Hol	1-489	1887
Edward	Att	B-463	1885
Elisha D.	Tip	1-175	1891

Elizabeth	Lee	1–52	1880
Elizabeth	Low	1–185	1865
Elizabeth S.	Ada	4–122	1877
F. A. W.	Ada	4–346	1885
Fielding	Isa	C–18	1859
Gabriel W.	Mad	A–644	1886
Gardner	Ada	2–124	1836
Gea Malin	Ada	4–292	1883
George H.	Qui	1–8	1897
H. M.	Cop	A–117	1897
Isaac N.	Pan(1)	A–409	1860
Mrs. J.	Mon	I.4–410	1883
Joanna	Mas	P.10–74	1854
James R. E.	Mon	1–121	1836
Jane	Tip	1–19	1867
Jane	Wil	2–1	1846
Jesse E.	Chi(1)	1–112	1889
John	Ada	5–150	1897
John	Ami	1–30	1811
John	Jac	1–36	1885
John	Uni	1–64	1900
John C.	Yaz	B–401	1899
Joseph	Ada	1–372	1825
Joseph A.	Mas	P.10–196	1854
Joseph Emory	Cla	3–34	1877
Joseph Emory	Hin	B–318	1875
Joseph Emory	War	B–11	1869
Joseph J.	Car(1)	A–518	1869
Joshua	Ada	1–153	1816
L. H.	Tat	1–166	1893
Levi	Yal(1)	B–99	1864
Levi M.	War	A–243	1857
Louis	Ada	4–583	1892
M. A.	DeS	2–127	1877
M. G.	Lef	A–110	1893
M. M.	Mad	A–492	1869
Margaret	Yaz	A–172	1854
Melinda E.	Hol	3–61	1898
Marmaduke P.	Ada	2–134	1836
Nancy F.	Att	2–339	1867
Nimrod	Low	1–94	1862
Orlando	Mas	1–141	1898
R. H.	Chi(1)	1–26	1880
Redding	Ada	2–410	1852
Reuben	Cla	A–109	1821
Rhoda	Jef	A–65	1820
Robert R.	Hin	B–93	1864
Rosier W.	Clk	1–62	1884
Samuel	Laf	1–83	1851
Sarah	Ada	2–44	1832
Sarah M.	Mas	P.3–70	1843

Siny	Cop	A-69	1892
Squire	Cla	B-279	1858
Susan	Mas	P.10-195	1854
Thomas G.	Mas	P.3-497	1844
Thomas G.	Yaz	A-247	1860
Thomas H.	Mon	I.20-719	1867
Thomas T.	Ada	4-198	1881
W. V.	Att	B-438	1885
Walter	War	A-127	1842
Warler	Laf	1-392	1892
William	Att	A-602	1861
William	Hol	1-477	1885
William	Ran	1-47	1863
Zabon	Cop	AAA-410	1847
Zelpha	New	1-35	1884
DAWSON, Alabama			
Franklin	Mad	A-672	1891
Joseph	Laf	1-58	1851
DAY, Hallie E.	Nox	B-360	1892
DEAN, Aaron	Mas	P.16-202	1864
Jane	Tis	1-83	1896
Joseph	Mas	P.19-621	1871
Seth	Ada	1-152	1816
DEANE, Nathaniel O.	Coa(1)	1-123	1878
DEAR, John	Lea	1-172	1896
John Sr.	Mad	A-353	1861
Sallie A.	Clk	1-74	1884
DEARING, Albin P.	Cly	1-114	1889
James H.	Mon	I.6-350	1895
Martha Anne	Mon	I.6-569	1897
DEARMAN, Solomon	Lau	1-72	1866
DEASE, Edward	Jas	1-28	1860
Lucinde S.	Jas	1-30	1860
DEATON, Emma T.	Pan(2)	A-150	1899
James A.	Was	2-97	1899
M. J.	Pan(2)	A-123	1896
DEBERRY, Delphae	Mad	A-112	1847
DEFRANCE, Elizabeth	Ada	2-298	1845
DELANEY, Patrick	War	A-234	1856
DELANY, N. H.	Jef	B-214	1896
DELEY, William	Laf	1-220	1872
DELOACH, Abbe	Wil	2-163	1860
John M.	Wil	2-366	1880
Ruffin	Wil	1-143	1835
William	Hol	1-25	1832
William	Mas	P.16-273	1865
DELOCK, Madison P.	Isa	A-27	1848
DEMENT, Virginia M.	Was	1-514	1893
W. B.	DeS	2-339	1891
DENDY, O. F.	Chi(1)	1-19	1879
DENISON, Bersheba	Mad	A-167	1851

DENMAN, B. G.	Low	1-76	1860
Thomas	Mad	A-73	1842
DENNING, Joseph	Cop	A-90	1893
DENNIS, Caroline	DeS	2-466	1897
James	DeS	2-215	1883
Sarah	Cla	B-292	1860
Thomas	Win	1-44	1867
DENNY, Mary E.	Jac	2-30	1900
Walter	Jac	1-101	1892
DENSON, Jesse Sr.	Ran	B.1-20	1841
William	Mad	A-106	1846
DENT, Benjamin	Jef	A-78	1821
F. H. C.	Ran	1-209	1885
George R.	Jef	B-98	1867
Mary C.	Nox	B-416	1894
Thomas	Car(1)	A-44	1844
William S.	Jef	A-109	1831
DENTON, Benjamin	Mas	P.4-489	1846
W. A.	Hol	3-66	1898
DETRAY, Harriet S.	Chi(2)	1-53	1891
DEUPREE, Daniel	Nox	B-259	1881
Elijah	Nox	B-243	1880
Thomas M.	Nox	B-17	1862
DEUS, Abraham	Ada	2-74	1834
DEVENNEY, Patrick	War	B-157	1886
DEW, J. T.	Hin	B-35	1860
DEWEES, Oscar L.	Mad	A-317	1859
Theodore	Mad	A-233	1856
DEWOLF, Calvin	Han	B-32	1900
DEWS, Thomas	Ada	1-414	1826
DIAL, J. R.	Lau	1-312	1893
DIBRELL, C. C.	Chi(1)	1-44	1883
DICK, James	Mad	A-137	1849
James	Yaz	A-178	1849
John	Ada	1-10	1803
Robert	Yaz	A-18	1836
DICKENS, James T.	Att	2-398	1864
Nancy	Pan(1)	B-108	1872
T. T.	Pan(1)	B-477	1892
DICKERSON, Pete C.	Coa(1)	1-152	1885
Thomas	Lin	1-58	1900
W. T.	Ben	1-66	1895
DICKENS, Eliza V.	Pan(1)	B-156	1874
DICKINS, John R.	Pan(1)	B-419	1887
William B.	Pan(1)	B-33	1867
DICKSON, David	Ran	1-116	1870
M. J.	Ran	1-212	1885
Parmelia A.	Yal(1)	1-83	1894
Zachariah	Hin	1-340	1854
DIGGS, Lucy B.	Mot	1-161	1900
DILLAHUNTY, Julia B.	Low	2-101	1895

DILLARD, Lewis	Mas	P.4–532	1847
DILLESHAW, Peter	Tal	B–17	1869
DILLIARD, Gaston	Lau	1–171	1881
Joseph S.	Mas	P.3–114	1843
DILLINGHAM, James	Mon	I.16–239	1861
DILTZ, Mary	Yal(1)	B–93	1863
DILWORTH, James			
Caldwell	Yal(1)	A–96	1845
James T.	Mon	I.6–77	1891
Joseph	Ada	1–47	1809
DININGHAM, William H.	Wil	2–122	1857
DINKINS, Eliza	Mon	I.4–404	1883
Joseph Rufus	Mad	A–367	1862
Lucy	Mad	A–146	1850
Rufus K.	Mad	A–40	1838
Simmie Sefronia	Mad	2–136	1899
DINSMORE, John R.	Nox	C–127	1900
DINWIDDIE, Harvey S.	Mad	A–35	1837
DISHONG, Leonidas P.	Mas	P.7–637	1851
DISMUKES, Elisha	Nox	A–204	1855
James W.	Lea	1–20	1858
DIVINE, Elizabeth			
Davis	Mad	A–360	1860
Kinsman	Mad	A–265	1858
DIXON, Adaline V.	Yaz	A–358	1869
Almira Sammorial	Ada	5–18	1893
Amazon A.	Yaz	B–134	1881
Charlotte	Ada	4–522	1890
Edward	Ada	4–102	1876
Freeman	Uni	1–32	1894
George B.	Yaz	A–171	1854
Harriet	Ada	4–472	1889
John	Tat	1–246	1900
Mildred	Jef	P.D–712	1850
R. D. I.	Yaz	A–279	1862
Robert	Pan(1)	B–490	1898
Robert Smith	Ada	5–77	1894
Samuel	Lee	1–13	1871
Willis H.	Mon	1–255	1849
DOAN, James H.	Tis	1–80	1893
DOBBS, John	Hin	1–57	1835
Nancy	Lau	1–29	1862
DOCKERY, Alfred	DeS	2–81	1874
D. Henry	DeS	2–129	1877
DODD, Allen	Att	C–207	1890
George	Att	C–3	1866
J. V.	Att	B–574	1887
J. V.	Att	C–68	1888
John	Tat	1–51	1881
Julius M.	Att	C–335	1893
Richard M.	Hol	1–287	1863

Rodolphus	Hol	1-155	1856
William	Yaz	A-17	1836
DODSON, L. J.	DeS	2-249	1885
Reason	Lea	1-34	1860
W. S.	Jac	1-115	1890
DOERING, Catherine	Ada	5-198	1898
DOGAN, Hamilton	Tal	A-317	1867
DOGGETT, A. B.	DeS	2-289	1887
DOHAN, James	Jef	B-111	1870
DOLLAHITE, R. P.	Tat	1-208	1896
DOMINICK, B/R. N.	Cly	1-108	1891
DONALD, Elizabeth	Att	C-364	1894
DONALDSON, John B.	Pre	1-49	1881
Joseph	Pre	1-88	1891
DONELSON, James K. P.	Hol	1-285	1863
DONNAGHOR, John	Ada	2-128	1836
DONNANT, Denis			
Francois	Ada	1-168	1818
DONNELL, George R.	Tun	2-110	1890
Levi	Low	1-317	1872
DONOHO, Gaines	Jef	P.C-456	1844
DONOHOE, Charles	Ada	3-457	1871
Patrick	War	A-141	1844
DOOLEY, Joseph	Ada	3-57	1856
DOOLY, Catherine	Ada	4-155	1879
DORMAN, Elizabeth	Ada	1-182	1819
DORNEY, Michael	War	A-329	1866
DOROUGH, Catharine	Coa(1)	1-38	1853
Hugh M.	Coa(1)	1-56	1858
DORRELL, John Cornbee	Lea	1-186	1899
DORSEY, R. S.	Yaz	A-94	1846
W.	Yaz	A-93	1846
DOTSON, Eliza	War	B-295	1893
Hattie Finley	War	B-243	1890
Savanna E.	Att	B-225	1876
Savanna E.	Lea	1-91	1876
William	Cla	B-272	1858
DOTY, James B.	Hol	1-40	1842
Minerva	Hol	1-109	1851
DOUGLAS, Willis	Ada	4-297	1883
DOUGLASS, Abram	Nox	B-211	1877
James S.	Cla	A-361	1837
W. H.	Was	1-399	1862
W. H.	Was	1-403	1865
William E.	Yal(2)	1-55	1888
DOUTHAT, Maggie			
Simmons	Hol	3-60	1898
Maggie Simmons	Yaz	B-380	1898
DOW, J. T.	Hin	B-35	1860
DOWD, William F.	Mon	I.3-298	1879
DOWDLE, Andrew	Low	1-462	1883

James M.	Low	1-390	1876
John W.	Low	1-273	1869
John W.	Low	1-286	1870
DOWDY, Willis W. M.	DeS	1-316	1862
DOWLING, Aaron			
Madison	Nox	B-168	1875
Robert S.	Att	B-388	1884
Thomas	Ada	3-35	1855
DOWN, Mary J.	War	B-126	1879
DOWNER, Thomas J.	DeS	2-263	1886
DOWNES, Henry A.	War	A-355	1866
DOWNEY, Gabriel	Tal	B-118	1898
Samuel S.	Hin	1-279	1851
DOWNING, Alexander	Hin	B-187	1866
Catherine	War	B-276	1893
George	Was	1-76	1845
James E.	Chi(1)	1-1	1872
Mary	Mas	P.2-9	1840
DOWNS, A. C.	War	A-242	1857
Edward S.	Yaz	A-160	1853
DOYLE, James	Ran	1-54	1863
Martin	Ada	1-100	1813
Noice	Car(1)	B-6	1877
DRAFUR, Robert W.	Pan(1)	A-418	1861
DRAKE, J. D.	DeS	2-455	1897
J. W.	Nox	C-6	1896
Neely	Nox	B-188	1876
Sophia	Fra	A-14	1896
Willis	Hol	1-35	1841
DRANE, Hiram	DeS	2-317	1889
James	Cho	A-21	1889
DRAPER, H. E.	Tal	B-83	1889
DRATON, J. S. Sr.	Uni	1-61	1900
DRAUGHON, John B.	Wil	2-81	1853
DRAYTON, John	Lef	A-115	1895
John	Lef	A-142	1898
DRENNAN, David	Ami	1-78	1811
DREW, Lucy P.	War	A-248	1858
DREYFOOS, M.	Chi(2)	1-89	1900
DRISCOLL, Patrick	Pan(1)	B-436	1887
DRISH, John R.	Nox	B-96	1867
DRIVER, Eli M.	Tun	1-88	1851
Giles L.	Laf	1-288	1877
DROKE, J. D.	Tat	1-9	1874
DROMGOOLE, James	Jef	A-20	1818
James	Jef	A-63	1820
DRONE, Richard S.	Hin	B-368	1885
DRUHAN, Marie P.	Han	A-187	1890
DRUMMOND, Henley F.	Low	1-200	1866
DRUMMONDS, James	Sim	A-41	1888
Sebron	Sim	A-98	1900

DUBARD, William	Yal(1)	B–117	1866
DUBOSE, Mrs. M. L.	Was	1–485	1889
DUBS, Charles H.	Ada	4–23	1873
Margaret L.	Ada	4–282	1883
DUBUISSON, Delia S.	Ada	2–462	1853
DUDLEY, Mrs. M. A.	Was	1–360	1866
DUELLMAN, Christman	Pan(1)	B–445	1889
DUFF, James M.	Laf	1–15	1845
DUFFIN, Thomas F.	Tun	2–188	1897
DUGAL, Alexander W.	Jef	A–18	1813
DUGAN, Ellen	War	B–378	1899
Thomas J.	Nox	A–105	1848
William M.	Chi(1863–1872)–124		1866
DUGGER, Sarah S.	Mon	I.5–176	1885
DUGGINS, Leander	Tal	B–1	1867
DUGLASS, John	Mas	P.19–594	1871
DUKE, A. B. C.	Tal	B–105	1896
John P.	Laf	1–191	1869
Mary	Yal(1)	B–122	1867
Z. P.	Laf	1–142	1861
DUKEMANIER, Jessee	Cly	1–8	1873
DULANEY, Daniel C.	Chi(1)	1–8	1879
Daniel M.	Hol	1–80	1848
Henry Rozier	Was	1–3	1840
Margaret P.	Mad	A–102	1846
Martha Jane	Cop	A–38	1890
William J.	Mad	A–599	1880
William P.	Mad	A–576	1878
DUNBAR, Ida	Ada	5–168	1898
Isaac	Ada	2–368	1849
James Jr.	Jef	P.C–36	1841
John W.	Jef	P.D–5	1846
Joseph	Jef	P.C–817	1846
Joseph	Jef	B–208	1898
Kate	Ada	5–169	1898
Martha W.	Ada	3–434	1870
Olivia	Jef	B–33	1860
Robert	Ada	1–367	1826
Samuel	Ada	2–22	1832
Sarah W.	Ada	3–155	1860
William	Ada	1–129	1816
William	Ada	2–345	1847
DUNCAN, C. E.	Lau	1–279	1891
Henry L.	Yal(2)	1–5	1875
Henry P.	Ada	4–158	1880
Hinson	Low	2–241	1899
Isaac A.	Laf	1–343	1885
John	Att	B–107	1872
John	Car(1)	A–525	1872
John	Grn	A–3	1872
John	Win	1–62	1872

Robert	Jef	B-68	1862
Stephen	Ada	3-350	1869
DUNIGAN, Samuel	Pan(1)	B-401	1884
DUNKILL, John	Ada	3-162	1861
DUNLAP, A. M.	Yaz	B-221	1887
Alex. M.	Yaz	B-111	1879
G. A.	DeS	2-47	1871
Hugh W.	Hin	1-245	1849
James	Ada	1-422	1823
James	Laf	1-188	1868
DUNLOP, E. H.	Wil	2-147	1859
DUNSLOP, Margaret	Wil	2-69	1851
DUNN, Alfred	Tun	1-34	1846
Isaac	Car(1)	A-463	1864
J. A.	War	B-293	1893
James	Yaz	A-17	1836
Jane E.	Lee	1-41	1878
Jesse G.	Car(1)	A-142	1857
Mary A.	Low	1-408	1878
Mary J.	Lee	1-70	1882
Patrick	Cla	3-120	1882
Patrick	Was	1-420	1882
Sessums	Hin	1-361	1855
T. J.	DeS	2-99	1875
Thomas H.	Nox	A-264	1858
Thomas Hamilton	Cla	B-290	1860
DUNNAVANT, Haley	Mas	P.7-558	1851
DUPREE, James	Hin	1-255	1850
Thomas H.	Hin	B-485	1900
William E.	Nox	A-16	1837
DURANT, John H.	Wil	1-71	1833
DURATY, William	Ada	1-154	1811
DURBIN, Daniel	Cla	A-200	1828
Elisha	Car(1)	B-3	1876
DURDEN, M. C.	Hol	1-500	1888
S. R.	Mot	1-126	1896
DURHAM, Dudley	Hol	1-167	1856
DURLEY, Henry	Tat	1-177	1893
DURRETT, Annis	Yal(1)	A-312	1857
DURRUM, Joseph	Mas	P.4-396	1846
DUSAN, Mary Joseph			
Zoe Deblanc	Han	A-47	1868
DUTCHER, Dennis	War	B-217	1889
DUTY, Ellen B.	Mas	P.18-99	1867
Milton	War	A-93	1838
Thomas	Mas	P.16-105	1864
DUVAL, Alexander D.	Isa	A-260	1853
DUVALL, Algernon S.	Yaz	A-92	1846
John J. H.	Ada	2-241	1841
DYE, Jane	Uni	1-49	1897
DYER, Flora Ann	Was	1-404	1877

DYESS, James M.	Cov	1–17	1900
DYSON, John L.	Hol	1–441	1881
EADS, Joseph D.	Lea	1–182	1899
Louisa Josephine	Laf	1–385	1888
Margaret J.	Lea	1–148	1890
EAGAN, Martin W. Sr.	Cop	A–7	1887
EAKENS, Alfred	Lau	1–272	1890
EARHART, David	Ada	3–138	1860
William	Ada	4–40	1874
EARNHART, Mary L.	Ada	5–286	1900
EARP, George	DeS	1–208	1859
Robert	DeS	1–216	1859
EASLEY, Mary E.	Chi(1)	1–90	1888
T. W.	Yaz	A–223	1858
EASON, Harris H.	DeS	1–230	1859
Nancy H.	Coa(1)	1–47	1856
W. Pitt	Tat	1–89	1883
William Thomas	DeS	1–157	1857
EAST, J. B.	Cla	3–195	1900
Robert	Low	2–63	1892
Sarah J.	Mas	1–32	1894
EASTERLING, Thomas	Ran	B.1–140	1842
EASTLAND, Oliver	Sco	A–467	1899
EASTRIDGE, Tully	Pan(1)	B–15	1865
EATON, J. A.	Per	1–10	1889
J. M.	Tis	1–85	1896
ECHOLS, Joseph	Mas	P.4–669	1847
ECKFORD, James	Nox	B–137	1873
James H.	Low	1–7	1858
Martha L.	Low	2–126	1895
ECKHART, E. A.	Was	1–416	1879
ECKLES, Edward W.	Hin	1–345	1854
EDDE, Elizabeth A.	Mon	I.6–121	1892
Moses P.	Mon	I.4–618	1884
EDDING, Harrison	Cla	3–156	1894
EDENS N. B.	Mon	I.1–638	1874
EDGER, Clement	Grn	A–9	1874
EDINGTON, Phillip	Cly	1–126	1897
EDMONDS, Jefferson L.	Low	1–146	1863
EDMONDSON, Elizabeth			
Rebecca	Lef	A–52	1876
Malinda M.	Clk	1–97	1887
Thomas	Ada	1–51	1809
EDMUNDS, Howell N.	Yal(1)	A–185	1851
EDMUNDSON, Asa	Ran	1–44	1862
Isabella	Pon	E.(1844–1848)–231	1847
EDNEY, Penelope	Laf	1–44	1849
EDWARDS, Anna	Hol	1–331	1869
C. B.	Tis	1–67	1893
Charles	Wil	1–251	1842
Edward D. Sr.	Web	A–2	1874

Edward D. Sr.	Web	A-57	1887
Elizabeth	Han	A-53	1869
Fannie A.	Lee	1-130	1889
Henry	Att	D-249	1900
James H.	Okt	1-1	1885
Jane	Wil	2-3	1846
Jesse	Wil	1-214	1839
John	Cop	AAA-406	1859
John G.	DeS	2-271	1886
John J.	Mad	B-392	1863
Julian F.	Nox	B-386	1893
Melvina	Wil	2-289	1874
Montalbirt	Hin	1-78	1836
Rachal F.	Cly	1-128	1896
Richard	War	A-151	1847
William	Mas	1-159	1899
William Sr.	Pan(1)	A-219	1855
EFFINGER, Edward T.	Ada	2-457	1853
EGG, Catharine	Was	1-461	1887
EGGER, Andrew	Low	1-284	1870
Green B.	Low	1-145	1863
Hugh S.	Low	1-368	1874
John R.	Low	1-85	1861
EGGLESTON, Fanny P.	Hol	1-369	1873
Joseph E.	Yal(1)	B-150	1874
Marianna	Grn	A-136	1898
Mariana Peyton	Hol	3-111	1900
Mary S.	Yaz	B-210	1886
Richard	Yal(1)	A-10	1840
Sarah	Low	2-91	1893
William	Hol	1-56	1845
EHLERS, Henry	Jac	1-63	1890
EICHELBERGER, Henry			
M.	Nox	A-231	1856
EILAND, O. G.	Kem	A-48	1892
EILER, Jacob	Ada	3-371	1869
ELAM, Egbert P.	Mas	P.3-92	1843
Maria L.	Jef	B-1	1857
Thomas A.	Jef	P.B-6	1836
ELBERL, Ed	Was	2-94	1898
ELDER, Jeremiah	Tat	1-2	1873
William G.	Jac	1-132	1894
ELDERGILL, John	Ada	1-28	1807
ELDRIDGE, Mildred T.	Pan(1)	A-386	1860
ELFORD, John	Jef	P.B-588	1840
ELKIN, Thomas B.	Mon	I.5-592	1890
William G.	Mon	I.7-43	1897
ELLARD, Isaac	Att	C-241	1891
Mary Ann	Att	C-78	1889
ELLETT, Archibald	Tal	A-305	1866
Henry T.	Cla	3-98	1887

Henry T.	Mon	1–96	1889
John	Tal	A–302	1865
ELLINGTON. D. A.	Lea	1–106	1882
James B.	Att	B–256	1878
ELLIOT, William			
St. John	Ada	3–15	1855
ELLIOTT, Alexander	Mon	1–3	1873
Anna F.	Ada	4–111	1877
Dan. D.	Ada	1–216	1815
Eliza J.	Yal(2)	1–74	1889
Hampton	Ada	4–15	1872
Nancy	Tip	1–15	1866
Robert	War	A–26	1833
Thomas	Tip	1–16	1866
ELLIS, Abram	Ada	1–155	1816
Blanton B.	Jef	P.E–93	1851
Elisha T.	Pan(2)	A–48	1884
James M.	Tal	B–59	1880
Jesse	Nox	B–99	1869
John	Ada	1–42	1808
John M.	Car(1)	A–43	1844
Littleberry	Hin	1–165	1842
Lott Warren	Cop	AAA–403	1849
Margaret	Wil	2–76	1852
Mary	Ada	1–85	1813
Mary	Cop	AAA–400	1840
Richard	Ada	3–197	1862
Richard Sr.	Ada	2–119	1835
Richmond C.	Cop	AAA–433	1849
Robert B.	Low	1–436	1880
Sarah A.	Tal	B–16	1869
Segesmunda M.	Lau	1–177	1882
Sigismunda M.	Ran	1–176	1882
Thomas	Yaz	B–168	1884
Underhill	Pon E.(1844–1848)–164		1846
William	Hol	1–138	1853
William	Low	1–418	1879
ELLISON, Marie			
Henrietta	Jac	1–19	1882
Moses	Yaz	A–159	1852
Peter	Was	1–457	1886
William Perrine	Jac	1–5	1877
ELLSBERRY, B. L.	Wil	2–165	1860
William	Wil	2–182	1862
Southerd	Wil	1–163	1836
ELLZEY, Elizabeth	Pik	1–161	1900
Maria Ann	Cop	AAA–429	1855
ELMORE, Henry	Pan(1)	A–345	1859
Jane	Lef	A–87	1885
ELSASSER, Catheline	War	B–147	1884
Peter	War	A–257	1859

ELSBERRY, Jacob	Wil	1-218	1840
ELY, Daniel	War	A-137	1843
Mary	Yal(1)	A-297	1857
Thomas	Car(2)	1-29	1883
ELYEE, J. Kingsburry	Wil	2-234	1865
EMANUEL, Jonathan	Low	1-540	1883
EMBREE, Jonathan	Nox	A-119	1848
EMBRY, Parker	Tat	1-1	1873
EMMERSON, Henry	Att	2-420	1864
ENGEL, Philip	Ada	1-171	1817
ENGLE, Mary	Ada	1-274	1822
ENGLESING, Francis			
C.	Cla	3-90	1884
ENGLISH, S. C.	Pan(1)	B-481	1896
ENOCHS, Enoch A.	Ran	1-169	1881
ENWOLDSEN, Enwold	Yaz	B-303	1895
EOERMAN, Margaret B.	Lau	1-104	1873
EPPERSON, Polly	Mas	P.11-443	1856
Sarah	Hin	B-419	1892
William T.	Yaz	B-288	1893
EPPS, Kate	Han	A-200	1891
ERICKSON, Aileen	Yal(2)	1-86	1895
John	Mad	A-595	1879
ERNST, Anna Maria	Mad	A-638	1886
ERVIN, James	Jef	P.D-489	1849
Mary A.	Jef	P.D-224	1847
ERWIN, Archibald	Hin	1-190	1846
James S.	Mas	P.7-606	1851
John A.	Mas	P.8-273	1852
William	Coa(1)	1-35	1852
ESKRIDGE, R. M.	Clk	1-55	1883
Richard	Car(1)	A-406	1860
Thomas L.	Car(1)	A-10	1837
Thomas P.	Cla	A-333	1836
ESTELL, Conwell	Laf	2-47	1899
ESTEMBERG, Elizabeth	Cop	A-86	1892
ESTES, H. B.	Lea	1-187	1899
Samuel Jr.	Yal(1)	A-18	1819
ESTILL, Jane	Car(1)	A-31	1841
ETHERIDGE, Elizabeth	Kem	A-21	1886
Martha Elizabeth	Lef	A-58	1878
ETHRIDGE, Caroline E.	Nox	B-316	1887
Newburn	Cla	B-227	1853
ETTINGER, E. B.	Lef	A-49	1872
EUBANKS, George W.	Low	1-164	1864
EUCKSON, Mana	Jac	1-136	1895
EUDALY, Eliza	Mon	1-152	1899
EUNE, Jethro	Lea	1-107	1881
EUSTIS, Horatio S.	Isa	C-13	1859
EVANS, Annie E.	Nox	B-370	1892
David Sr.	Ran	B.1-294	1847

Emeline	Cly	1–101	1890
Frances	Low	1–321	1872
George	Cla	A–5	1804
H. G.	Ran	1–193	1884
Henry	New	1–67	1876
James H.	Mad	2–91	1897
John	Lin	1–1	1894
John	Mon	I.10–50	1853
John	Pan(1)	A–82	1850
John H.	Yaz	A–335	1866
John P.	Pik	1–8	1883
Lewis	Ada	1–303	1823
Mary	Att	A–92	1858
Mary E.	Win	1–27	1863
Moses	War	A–45	1834
Nancy Ann	Low	1–250	1867
Richard	Mad	A–142	1849
Robert C.	Ada	3–158	1860
S. E.	Mas	1–161	1899
Samuel W.	Laf	1–133	1860
Susan A.	Hol	1–206	1859
Thomas	Att	A–114	1858
Thomas	Cla	A–46	1813
W. C.	Cla	A–119	1822
William	Hin	1–260	1850
William G.	Mon	I.5–52	1885
William W.	Jef	P.C–829	1846
EVERETT, James	Yaz	B–21	1872
James A.	Car(1)	A–83	1848
EVERHART, Michael	Isa	C–144	1887
EVRETT, James	Cop	AAA–427	1834
EWIN, Lucy D.	Yaz	B–91	1878
EWING, James	Hin	B–174	1863
Jesse H.	Mad	A–264	1857
John T.	Mad	A–642	1886
Margaret A.	Mad	2–28	1894
Mitton P.	Mad	A–35	1837
Stephen S.	Mon	I.20–730	1871
FADER, Margaret	Att	D–205	1900
FAHRENBACK, John	Hin	B–51	1860
FAIR, Ellen	Ada	3–173	1861
FAIRCHILD, Brit	Was	2–61	1897
Loftin B.	Lau	1–105	1873
Robera	Hin	B–418	1893
S. B.	Lau	1–109	1874
FAIRCHILDS, Susannah	Hin	1–184	1846
FAIRES, Lee T.	Chi(2)	1–94	1900
FAIRFIELD, S. S.	Grn	A–97	1893
FAIRLEY, Charlotte	Jac	1–71	1890
Peter	Jef	P.E–236	1852

FAIRLY, Mary	Jef	B-57	1861
FALKNER, Alfred	Mas	P.15-586	1862
Jonathan	Mas	P.15-581	1862
Nathan	Web	A-31	1880
Patsey	Mas	P.19-360	1870
W. C.	Tip	1-156	1889
FALL, Eliza A.	Was	1-501	1893
FALLS, Theophelus	Hol	1-116	1852
FANT, A. E.	Cly	1-68	1884
Benjamin S.	Mas	P.16-223	1865
J. C.	Nox	B-343	1889
James T.	Mas	1-45	1895
William B.	Mas	P.2-419	1841
FARBRE, Joseph	Ada	2-123	1836
FARE, Martha V.	Ran	1-109	1869
FARLEY, Charles Henry	Pan(1)	A-424	1862
Mary Jane	Pan(1)	B-81	1871
R. J.	DeS	1-374	1866
Robert M.	Pan(1)	A-164	1854
FARMER, Henry S.	Car(1)	A-533	1873
FARR, B. R.	Hol	3-28	1895
Delilah	Han	P.(1853-1860)-595	1857
Ephraim L.	Mas	1-5	1890
J. Wilson	Hin	B-260	1869
Susan J.	Hol	1-205	1859
W. B.	Isa	C-84	1866
FARRAR, Alice V.	Ada	4-9	1871
Stephen C.	Hin	B-236	1868
FARRELL, Bridget	Yaz	B-259	1891
FARROW, William	Mas	P.9-215	1853
FASE, Martha V.	Ran	1-109	1869
FASER, Jacob	Nox	B-379	1892
FASLIP, Redman	Mad	A-125	1848
FAULK, Orran	Cla	A-121	1822
FAULKNER, Allen	Chi(1)	1-81	1887
John	Ada	2-120	1831
FAUST, Sarah C. W.	Yaz	A-262	1863
FAVRO, Mary	Han	A-64	1871
FAWLKES, Joseph	Mon	1-158	1840
FAX, Hally	Cly	1-125	1897
FEAMSTER, Samuel T.	Mad	A-95	1845
FEARS, John	Sco	A-346	1869
FEATHERSTON, Edward	Mon	I.13-346	1858
FEEMSTER, C. H.	Low	1-410	1878
Isabella D.	Low	2-124	1895
James K.	Low	1-46	1859
Jeptha M.	Low	1-525	1886
Margaret E.	Low	1-412	1878
Silas J.	Low	1-246	1867
FEISER, Ferdinand	War	B-368	1899
FEITIG, Jacob	Jac	1-119	1893

63

FELLOW, L/S. J.	Mas	P.15–351	1861
FELLOWS, L. R.	Mad	A–687	1892
FELTON, Patrick	Kem	A–51	1892
FELTS, Lafayette	Car(1)	B–58	1889
FELTUS, Abram M.	Wil	2–166&174	1861
FENNELL, Bettie W.	DeS	2–322	1890
John	DeS	2–136	1878
FENNER, Elizabeth	Wil	2–193	1863
Richard	Hin	1–128	1828
FERGUSON, Alexander			
C.	Ada	3–304	1867
Anne R.	War	B–111	1879
Francis	Coa(1)	1–65	1858
Hannah	Coa(1)	1–87	1862
Hattie M.	Cla	3–70	1881
James A.	Att	C–489	1870
Jane	Ada	3–137	1860
Jesse B.	War	B–320	1896
John	Jef	A–65	1820
Joseph	Ada	3–83	1857
Kate M.	Ada	5–75	1895
Martha M.	War	A–49	1835
Mary B.	Yal(1)	B–174	1878
Moses J.	Cop	A–119	1897
P. M.	Yaz	A–141	1851
Paulina	Jef	P.D–475	1849
Pinckney L.	Ada	5–281	1900
Sarah	War (1823–1827)–160		1825
Thaddeus T. C. S.	Sha	A–8	1879
Thomas	War	A–91	1838
Thomas Jefferson	War (1823–1827)–153		1825
William	Ada	3–46	1855
FERNANDEZ, Walter H.	Laf	1–195	1870
FERRALL, Eliza O.	Ada	4–163	1880
John A.	Ada	4–26	1873
George W.	Mon	I.12–591	1857
Warren	Yal(1)	B–33	1860
FERRIS, Tennie	Nox	C–10	1896
William S.	Nox	C–48	1898
FIELD, Andrew	Pan(1)	B–73	1870
Joseph	Han	A–13	1865
Levi B.	Ada	4–359	1884
Osborne K.	Ada	4–399	1887
Thomas G.	Low	1–233	1867
Virginia H.	Ada	5–231	1899
FIELDS, Henry	Tal	B–107	1896
FIGG, Alfred H.	Pan(1)	B–100	1871
FINANE, Mary Ann	War	B–360	1899
FINCH, James B.	Yal(1)	B–38	1860
FINGES, Abram	Tip	1–117	1884
FINLEY, James	Ran	1–25	1860

James Lockhart	Lee	1-169	1896
Martha A.	Wil	3-176	1898
William	Mad	A-241	1856
FISHER, Elijah	Hin	1-119	1839
Mary E.	Cla	3-131	1892
Samuel	Ran	B.1-498	1849
Southey	Lau	1-4	1858
FISK, Abijah	Ada	2-371	1845
Alvarez	War	A-212	1853
FITTS, Ulysses	Mad	A-58	1840
FITZ, Gideon	Lef	A-39	1857
FITZGERALD, George	Ada	1-37	1808
James	Ada	1-165	1816
Martha	DeS	1-254	1860
Thomas	DeS	1-108	1855
William H.	Mon	I.7-218	1900
Willie	DeS	1-64	1853
FITZHUGH, J. W.	Ran	1-225	1889
Nelson	Ada	3-337	1868
Robert W.	Ada	4-289	1883
Thomas	Ran	1-21	1860
FITZPATRICK, Ann			
Lightfoot	Hin	1-142	1841
FIZER, John B.	Pan(1)	B-90	1872
John C.	Tun	2-72	1880
FLACK, Rufus K.	Mad	A-321	1860
FLEITAS, J. Manuel	Han	A-80	1873
FLEMING, Dinah	Ada	2-360	1848
Mary	Mad	2-133	1899
Moses	Nox	B-213	1878
William	Mad	2-103	1898
FLEMMING, James	Mas	1-8	1891
Jefferson	DeS	2-227	1883
John	Ada	1-184	1819
Margaret	War	A-142	1844
FLESHAS, Joseph	Jac	1-23	1883
FLETCHER, James L.	Pan(1)	A-131	1897
James L.	Qui	1-10	1898
James L.	Tal	B-116	1898
John	Ada	3-193	1862
Lenard R.	Hin	1-449	1859
Richard	Ada	1-276	1823
FLEWELLEN, Mattie			
Fredonna	DeS	2-460	1897
FLINN, Mary	Clk	1-40	1878
Mary L.	DeS	2-54	1872
W. H.	Mas	1-96	1896
FLINT, William	Mon	I.17-368	1863
FLOOD, Alfred	Ada	5-237	1899
Oliver V. E.	Ada	5-261	1900
FLORA, B. E.	Kem	A-58	1895

FLORIN, Henry	Hin	B-278	1872
Margaret	Hin	B-279	1872
FLOURNEY, Mary E.	Lau	1-259	1889
Victor M.	Was	1-418	1878
FLOURNOY, Matthews	Was	1-80	1846
Elisha	Cla	A-111	1821
Elisha	War	A-75	1837
FLOWER, Nancy	Cla	A-130	1823
FLOWERREE, Dan W.	War	B-93	1878
FLOWERS, Armstrong E.	Jef	B-21	1859
Eliza	Mot	1-68	1884
Henry	DeS	1-292	1861
James	Cla	B-288	1859
W. W.	Cla	3-78	1882
William	Mot	1-46	1881
William O.	Pik	1-50	1892
FLOYD, John	Pan(1)	A-267	1857
FLUKER, David	Hin	1-76	1836
FLY, Joshua	Yal(2)	1-8	1875
FLYNN, Elizabeth	Ada	2-341	1847
FLYNT, Martha	Nox	B-420	1894
Martin	DeS	2-140	1878
FOERSTER, John	Han	B-9	1899
FOGG, Andrew J.	DeS	1-97	1855
Eliza J.	DeS	2-92	1874
George W.	DeS	2-180	1881
William W.	DeS	1-136	1857
FOGO, S. W.	Was	2-42	1897
FOLEY, Burrel	Ada	4-175	1880
Catherine	War	B-73	1877
FOLKES, John M.	Jef	B-124	1873
FOLKS, John M.	Jef	B-131	1870
FOLTZ, Theodore	Wil	2-224	1864
FONDA, A. C.	Tal	B-104	1895
FONDREN, Herrod	Cho	A-9	1882
T. R.	Laf	1-326	1883
Thomas	Laf	1-116	1854
FOOTE, George	DeS	1-188	1858
George H.	Nox	A-214	1856
George P.	Pan(1)	A-426	1862
Gilson	Nox	A-158	1851
H. W.	Nox	C-138	1900
Helen M.	Ran	B.1-189	1844
Hezekiah William	Nox	C-83	1899
William	Nox	A-1	1833
William H.	Tip	1-109	1882
FORBES, Christopher			
B.	Lee	1-10	1870
H. J.	Lee	1-43	1879
John	Lee	1-36	1878
William T.	Lee	1-190	1895

FORCE, Albert B.	War	A-176	1849
FORD, Christopher	Ada	2-379	1850
Elizabeth	Ada	3-328	1867
Fielding T.	Ada	4-81	1875
John F.	Tip	1-82	1877
Joseph	Ada	1-20	1804
Joseph	Ada	1-218	1820
Lavinia	Ada	2-426	1853
Manly	Isa	C-45	1861
Mary A.	Cop	A-149	1900
Mary C.	Ada	4-178	1881
Robert	Ada	1-411	1828
Samuel H.	Pan(1)	B-128	1872
Sizzie D.	Hol	1-434	1880
Thomas	Ada	2-170	1838
Thomas J.	Ada	2-310	1845
Washington	Ada	4-418	1887
FORDHAM, James	Ada	1-98	1813
FORE, Appie Louisa	Ran	1-73	1865
FOREMAN, Sarah	Jef	P.D-477	1849
FORMAN, Joseph	Ada	1-157	1816
FORMSWSKI, Albert	War	B-213	1889
FORNIQUET, Louis I.	Pik	1-105	1898
Maria A.	Pik	1-16	1884
FORREST, Aaron H.	Lef	A-43	1864
John D.	Mot	1-16	1876
FORT, Dorothy F.	Low	1-461	1883
Jacob H.	Hin	1-28	1834
James D.	Yaz	A-308	1865
James W.	Tat	1-23	1877
Martha W.	Low	1-400	1877
Mary R.	Mad	A-436	1866
William Anthony	Mad	A-87	1844
FORTENBERRY, Hugh	Mar	A2-15	1894
FORTNER, Allen	Chi(1)	1-81	1887
Arthur	Hin	1-51	1835
Gilbert J.	Kem	A-36	1889
Patsey	Jac	1-16	1882
FORTSON, John T.	Mon	I.14-312	1859
FOSC, Mary	Ada	5-243	1899
FOSCUE, Lewis	Cla	A-318	1836
FOSH, William	Win	1-52	1868
FOSTER, A. H.	Win	1-176	1897
Agnes O.	Tal	A-207	1859
Albert Gallatin	Wil	1-265	1843
Augustus R.	Wil	1-148	1835
B. P.	Was	2-139	1900
Edward	Win	1-121	1891
Ephraim	Ada	1-318	1824
Gibson	Cla	A-355	1837
Guilford D. D.	Wil	1-152	1836

Hardy A.	Hol	1-301	1865
Isiah	Cla	B-222	1852
James	Ada	2-29	1833
James	Ada	5-202	1898
James	Ada	2-115	1835
James	Cop	AAA-419	1850
John G.	Ada	2-331	1847
John Tillman	Isa	C-97	1868
Joseph Allen	Cop	A-133	1899
Lerona	Low	2-61	1892
M. J. V.	Yaz	B-364	1898
Mattie Matilda	Okt	1-45	1898
Moses	Cop	AAA-412	1860
Rachel	Ada	2-393	1851
Samuel	Ada	3-292	1866
Sarah	Ada	2-149	1837
Thomas	Ada	1-431	1829
William	Ada	2-66	1833
William	Cla	A-38	1812
FOTHERINGHAM, William	War	A-307	1862
FOUNTAIN, William	Jef	B-210	1899
FOURMAN, George R.	Mas	P.12-252	1857
FOWLER, Ally E.	Pon	1-15	1900
Daniel	Ada	3-246	1865
Jacob	Ada	1-361	1825
John R.	Hol	3-108	1900
Joseph W.	Coa(1)	1-4	1844
L. G. B.	Tat	1-142	1890
Samuel	War	A-159	1847
FOX, Ellen L. C.	War	B-348	1898
Jacob	Web	A-56	1885
James A.	War	B-121	1880
James R.	Yal(1)	B-40	1860
Julia T.	Yal(1)	A-190	1851
Lucy A.	Jas	1-95	1890
Mary A.	Pan(1)	A-151	1853
Sophia A.	War	B-33	1873
Thomas B.	Pan(1)	A-141	1853
Thomas B.	Pan(1)	A-198	1855
FOXWORTH, Stephen M.	Mar	A1-133	1844
FOY, Edwin H.	Was	2-124	1900
Margaret B.	Jac	1-122	1893
FRAKER, Jacob	Cly	1-131	1896
FRANCIOLI, Joseph	Hin	B-212	1861
FRANCIS, John M.	Was	2-86	1897
FRANEY, Thomas	War	B-339	1897
FRANK, Christian	War	A-47	1835
Elizabeth J.	Pik	1-149	1900
Margaret B.	War	B-328	1896
FRANKLIN, Hardin P.	Mas	P.8-44	1851
Rebecca	Ada	1-298	1823

Stepany	Lea	1-94	1879
FRANSIOLE, Charles	War	B-142	1883
FRASIER, George W.	Ada	4-562	1891
William P.	Lea	1-96	1879
FRASSLE, Mary	Ada	5-246	1899
FRAZEE, Eliza	Chi(2)	1-35	1886
George	Low	1-313	1872
FRAZER, Elizabeth	Cla	A-64	1816
John A.	DeS	1-132	1856
FRAZIER, George E.	Wil	1-220	1840
Jane G.	Car(1)	A-116	1847
Mary	Wil	2-138	1858
Mastin	Uni	1-1	1882
William	Was	1-85	1846
FREELAND, Frisby	Cla	A-81	1818
Frisby A.	War	A-244	1857
Thomas Sr.	Cla	B-253	1856
FREEMAN, George	Jef	A-79	1823
George W.	Tat	1-89	1885
Henry	Ada	3-170	1861
Joseph A.	DeS	1-416	1867
Sallie G.	Okt	1-52	1899
Thomas	Ada	1-237	1820
Z. T.	Uni	1-44	1896
Zana	Tat	1-102	1887
FRELICK, James	Law	P.Min.B-152	1841
FRENCH, George	DeS	1-433	1868
Mary J.	Mon	I.7-65	1899
Uriah	War	B-158	1886
William	Nox	C-28	1897
FRETWELL, John	Ada	1-312	1824
FRIDAY, Emanuel	Att	A-136	1858
FRIEDLANDER, Samuel	Yaz	B-314	1896
FRIERSON, C. C.	Tal	B-112	1897
S. R.	Okt	1-24	1880
Sarah M.	Low	1-32	1859
FRILEY, Martin M.	Yaz	B-19	1871
FRISBY, Abraham	Jef	P.B-74	1834
FRITZMAN, Elizabeth	Cla	B-189	1846
FROMHERZ, Catherine	Yaz	B-18	1871
FROST, E. D.	Pik	1-32	1887
Isack N.	Yal(2)	1-80	1893
FRUEX, John William	Pik	1-27	1887
FRUIPO, Cesar	War	A-224	1855
FRYAR, Ellen E.	War	B-39	1874
Henry	Tip	1-215	1900
John	Tip	1-114	1884
John	War	A-42	1834
M. M.	Ben	1-17	1877
FULGHAM, Henry	Cop	AAA-375	1840
Patience	Cop	AAA-438	1845

FULKERSON, W. B.	Cla	3-160	1895
FULLER, Caswell	Mon	I.1-5	1872
Elizabeth	Ada	3-242	1865
Jasper L.	Laf	1-83	1853
Jonathan Sr.	Laf	1-90	1854
William P.	Mon	I.11-116	1855
FULLILOVE, David D.	Han	A-170	1887
Thomas J.	Car(2)	1-45	1888
FULTON, David Mackey	Mad	A-582	1879
Duncan	Lea	1-51	1868
Henry	Ada	1-98	1813
John	Coa(1)	1-1	1841
FUNCHESS, Samuel	Hin	1-135	1840
FURGERSON, Charles	Nox	A-43	1842
FURNEY, George	Ada	2-14	1832
FUSSELL, William Sr.	Ran	B.1-14	1836
FUTCH, Jacob B.	Ami	1-67	1812
GABRIEL, Henry	Han	A-234	1893
GADBERRY, William P.	Yaz	A-5	1833
GADDIS, Benjamin F.	Lau	1-14	1859
GADDY, James A.	DeS	1-351	1865
William	Mas	P.11-212	1856
GAGE, Matthew	Hol	1-238	1860
GAILLARD, Isaac	Ada	1-67	1811
GAINES, C. A.	Tat	1-162	1893
John P.	Nox	B-366	1891
GAIRDNER, James	Cla	B-299	1861
GALAWAY, Margaret	War	A-67	1836
GALE, Josiah	Hin	B-57	1861
William A.	Yaz	A-269	1862
GALINGER, Joseph	Yaz	B-147	1882
GALLAGHER, S. F.	Ada	1-360	1826
GALLEHER, Amzi	Low	1-271	1869
GALLOWAY, Alfred	Mad	A-314	1860
Mary	Ada	4-150	1879
GALTNEY, Abraham	Ada	1-283	1823
GALVIN, Patrick	Low	2-261	1900
GAMBLE, James G.	Mad	A-168	1852
GAMBRELL, Maria			
Adaline	Hol	1-215	1859
GANNON, Rosanna	War	B-182	1886
Sallie A.	Mon	I.6-454	1895
William	War	B-182	1886
GANONG, William L.	Coa(1)	1-103	1867
GANT, Louis Sr.	Sun	1-32	1899
GANTT, Frances Emma	Att	B-215	1876
GARARD, Walter J. E.	Jac	1-165	1897
GARAWAY, Jesse	Cop	AAA-372	1845
GARCIA, Manuel	Ada	1-164	1817
Maria	Han	A-307	1897

GARDEBLED, Hipolite	Han	A-156	1884
GARDINER, John H.	Low	1-102	1862
GARDNER, Ashel B.	Yaz	A-15	1835
John H.	Low	1-133	1862
Laura E.	Kem	A-28	1887
Marmaduke	Clk	P.B-30	1839
Robert B.	Tis	1-58	1893
Shadrack	Mas	P.2-492	1841
William	Ada	2-180	1839
GARIBALDE, Mannel	Han	A-230	1893
GARLAND, Ben	Hin	B-265	1869
Pembroke	Hin	1-400	1857
Samuel	Hin	B-161	1862
GARNER, Daniel H.	Kem	A-54	1893
Elizabeth S.	Mas	1-106	1897
Lou	Yal(1)	B-239	1899
Samuel H.	Grn	A-69	1873
Vina	Tal	B-101	1895
GARONNE, Mariah	War	B-340	1897
GARRAWAY, S. T.	Per	1-13	1891
GARRETT, Benjamin	Mad	A-527	1872
Dorcas	Lee	1-85	1884
Frances	Mot	1-9	1873
Henry	Tip	1-147	1889
Mary E.	Mas	1-2	1892
Phillip H.	Mas	P.17-294	1866
GARRIGUES, A. G.	Win	1-131	1893
GARRIOTT, Wilson L.	DeS	1-69	1853
GARRISON, Dorrell	Yaz	B-213	1887
GARROTT, James	DeS	1-425	1867
Robert C.	Tat	1-197	1895
GARTLEY, Lewis	Mad	A-17	1834
Susanna	Mad	A-156	1850
GARTMAN, Susan	Lin	1-17	1895
GARTRELL, William C.	DeS	1-200	1859
GARVIN, Benjamin	Cla	B-269	1856
Charles	Nox	A-74	1824
Harriet J.	War	B-309	1895
William	DeS	2-1	1870
GARY, Allen	Mot	1-28	1878
Charles F.	Nox	B-55	1865
John	Car(1)	A-69	1843
Lucretia	Clk	1-94	1887
Martha	Jac	2-28	1900
Thomas	Ada	3-243	1865
William B.	Pon	E.(1844-1848)-1 1844	
William G.	Hol	1-10	1834
GASKINGS, Charles W.	War	B-162	1886
GASKINS, Starkey	Ada	2-271	1843
GAST, Charles F.	Low	1-422	1879
GASTEN, Elizabeth	Low	2-156	1896

GASTON, J. N.	Low	2-191	1897
Lafayette	Low	1-452	1881
Maria A.	Clk	1-145	1893
Sophia A.	Low	2-257	1900
GASTRELL, Henry M.	Ada	4-497	1889
GATES, Charles S.	Chi(1)	1-46	1883
William	Cop	AAA-353	1870
William W.	Car(1)	A-135	1856
GATEWOOD, Grafton	Car(1)	A-126	1855
Roland	DeS	1-103	1855
Thomas	Mas	P.19-71	1869
GATHINGS, Mary L.	Cly	1-137	1900
Mary L.	Mon	I.7-141	1900
GATLIN, Andrew Lucas	Tip	1-192	1895
William P.	Pik	1-179	1900
GATTIS, Margaret	Yal(1)	A-267	1855
GAULDEN, Elizabeth	Wil	2-50	1850
GAULDING, William	Uni	1-62	1900
GAULT, Elizabeth	Mad	A-44	1821
GAVIN, A. A.	Clk	1-207	1899
G. W.	Nox	B-325	1887
John E.	Nox	B-275	1882
John E.	Nox	C-131	1900
GAYDEN, Reuben	Car(1)	A-110	1853
GEE, Lucas	Wil	2-53	1850
Nancy	Mot	1-18	1877
Robert C.	Low	1-19	1858
Thomas M.	DeS	1-397	1866
William H.	Laf	1-106	1858
GEIGER, John	Ada	2-343	1847
GEISENBERGER, Walf	Ada	5-248	1899
GEMMELL, Peter	Ada	2-153	1837
GENELLA, Flora	War	B-150	1885
Lawrence	War	B-8	1869
Lucinda	War	B-302	1894
Serephina	War	B-134	1882
GENTRY, Lorenzo D.	Mas	P.4-420	1846
W. C.	Yal(1)	B-125	1867
GEORGE, J. Z.	Car(1)	B-52	1897
Joel A.	Hol	1-26	1837
John	Grn	A-70	1886
William Sr.	Yaz	A-75	1844
GERALD, Louisa E.	Car(1)	A-46	1843
GERDINE, W. L. C.	Cly	1-27	1878
GEREN, Abraham	Car(1)	A-190	1859
S. C.	Car(1)	A-81	1850
GERMANY, Charles C.	Wil	3-103	1892
GERREN, A. Adelaide	Car(1)	A-122	1854
GERRMANY, John	Wil	1-149	1836
GETER, Argless	Wil	2-125	1857
GEVINS, Samuel W.	Pon	2-550	1845

GHOLSON, Margaret A.	Mon	I.5-386	1888
S. C. Jr.	Mas	1-26	1893
GIBB, Andrew	Yaz	A-334	1867
GIBBES, Henry D.	Hin	B-312	1875
GIBBON, John	Hin	1-172	1844
GIBBONS, John C.	Mas	P.9-263	1853
GIBBS, Louisa Johnson	Yaz	B-109	1879
Martha A.	War	B-278	1892
Spencer	Tip	1-103	1882
Wilmott R.	Hin	B-405	1890
GIBNEY, Michael	War	A 169	1849
GIBSON, Amarilla C.	Low	2-234	1899
Anderson Lee	Mon	1-241	1846
Ann	Cla	A-216	1830
C. W.	Yaz	B-379	1898
Catharine N.	Jef	B-169	1890
David	Jef	B-7	1859
David J.	Cop	A-26	1888
Frances E.	War	A-363	1867
Gadi	Cla	B-212	1850
Gilford W.	Low	1-335	1873
James	Cla	A-136	1822
James S.	Clk	1-6	1872
John B.	War	B-219	1890
Lewis C. Sr.	Sim	A.44	1888
Maria	Ada	5-73	1895
Mary	War	A-260	1859
R. H.	Tip	1-77	1877
Randal	War	A-60	1836
Sam	Ada	2-28	1830
Samuel	Cla	A-79	1818
Sarah	Jef	B-43	1861
Sarah	War	B-227	1889
Sarah S. D.	Cop	A-150	1900
Tobias	Cla	A-11	1805
William L.	Hin	1-202	1847
William L.	Hin	1-390	1847
GIFFORD, Timothy	Ada	1-342	1825
GILBERT, Christian	Ada	1-140	1816
Dicy	Jef	B-29	1859
Evan S.	New	1-27	1883
J. C.	Kem	A-46	1892
James W.	Ada	1-180	1818
Mary	Ada	1-382	1826
Matthias	Ada	2-446	1853
Nancy	Ada	1-395	1827
Thomas	Ada	1-309	1823
Thomas	Ada	3-159	1860
Webster	Cop	AAA-348	1860
William	Ada	1-452	1829
GILCHRIST, Archibald	Coa(1)	1-39	1853

Halcomb	Coa(1)	1-9	1846
John	Coa(1)	1-41	1853
GILDART, Francis	Ada	1-117	1814
GILE, Jacob	Ada	1-76	1812
GILES, Matilda Nevett	Ada	3-342	1868
Wm. Mason	Ada	2-366	1849
GILESPIE, George	Wil	2-359	1880
J. A.	Tat	1-189	1894
GILL, Emiline	Tat	1-225	1898
J. M.	Lea	1-82	1876
James	Cly	1-115	1894
Lydia Ann	Hol	1-479	1885
GILLAND, John D.	War	B-320	1896
GILLESPIE, A. M.	Tat	1-57	1882
Allen C.	Mad	A-128	1848
Andrew J.	Mon	I.3-295	1878
C. D.	Hin	B-433	1894
Catharine A.	Hol	1-332	1869
Catherine A.	Nox	B-4	1861
Charlotte C.	Grn	A-29	1878
D. P.	DeS	1-367	1866
James	Mad	A-72	1842
James A.	Ada	4-153	1879
James M.	Cla	3-140	1892
John F.	Ada	3-42	1855
Lucullus	Nox	B-37	1863
William E.	Mad	A-290	1859
William P. Sr.	Chi(1)	1-110	1892
GILLEYLEN, John Sr.	Mon	I.6-527	1896
Margaret C.	Mon	I.6-527	1896
William H.	Mon	I.8-285	1852
GILLIAM, Littleberry	Chi (1863-1872)-48		1864
Mary	War (1827-1832)-10		1827
Patrick T.	Chi(2)	1-43	1887
GILLISPIE, Lemuel	Cla	A-353	1837
GILMER, Ann A.	Mad	A-326	1860
John	Low	1-52	1860
Mary Peachy	Cop	AAA-344	1840
Nicholas I.	Low	1-195	1866
Samuel B.	Nes	A-92	1869
Susan C.	Low	1-363	1874
Thomas A.	Mon	I.19-742	1866
GILMORE, Mary Jane	Tat	1-56	1882
GINN, Moses	Wil	2-101	1855
GIPSON, Estelle	Ran	1-309	1899
William	Laf	1-422	1896
GIRARD, Marie			
Virginie	Han	A-207	1892
GIRAULT, John	Ada	1-101	1813
R. D.	Tal	A-296	1862
GIREAUDEAU, Felicite	Ada	3-188	1862

Gabriel	Ada	1-396	1827
Nancy	Ada	2-256	1842
GISH, Lewis K.	Was	1-217	1855
GITTER, Catharine	DeS	2-14	1870
GIVANS, J. D.	Lau	1-326	1893
GIVENS, John	Mas	P.3-188	1843
William	Mon	1-168	1841
GLADDEN, Edward	Fra	A-2	1881
GLASBURN, Godfrey	Ada	1-158	1817
GLASCOCK, Alexander	Lau	1-63	1865
GLASENER, George W.	Clk	1-47	1883
GLASGOW, John	Mas	P.2-102	1840
GLASS, Anthony	War	A-44	1834
J. Clark	War	B-135	1882
Joel	Wil	1-156	1836
L.	Yal(2)	1-54	1888
GLASSCOCK, Peter	Hin	B-342	1882
GLEN, Samuel	Ada	1-48	1809
GLENN, John C.	Uni	1-3	1882
William D.	Mad	A-485	1868
GLOVER, Edwin A.	Lau	1-115	1876
James	Ben	1-19	1878
James	Mas	P.19-458	1870
Mary	Low	1-108	1862
GOAD, Peter	Hin	1-268	1851
GOBEAU, John Baptist	Ada	1-233	1821
GODBER, Thomas K.	Low	1-169	1864
GODFREY, Allen L.	Tat	1-14	1875
Richard	Yal(1)	A-208	1852
GODWIN, Samuel	Cla	A-271	1833
GOFF, D. J.	Pan(2)	A-71	1889
John K.	Cop	AAA-339	1833
GOGGIN, Thomas	Chi (1863-1872)-32		1864
GOING, Samuel	Cla	A-281	1833
GOLD, Sarah Ann	Hin	1-183	1845
GOLDEN, Anthony	Hol	1-329	1868
S. A.	Laf	1-115	1856
GOMILLION, Matilda	Grn	A-46	1871
GOOD, Thomas	Hin	1-420	1857
GOODLOE, Ann J.	Mad	A-522	1866
David S.	Mad	A-359	1859
David S.	Mad	A-540	1873
Martha A.	Mad	2-122	1899
GOODMAN, H. H.	War	B-314	1895
Walter	Mas	P.17-287	1866
GOODNIGHT, Abraham	Pan(2)	A-147	1899
GOODOE, David S.	Mad	A-306	1859
GOODRICH, Chauncery	War	A-84	1838
John Wells	Yal(1)	B-127	1867
GOODSON, William	Hin	1-44	1834
GOODWIN, Asa S.	Mas	P.16-19	1863

Charity A.	Low	1-505	1886
Crafford	Pan(1)	A-93	1850
Crawford Greenberry	Laf	1-200	1870
John	Mon	I.10-449	1854
John H.	War	A-262	1860
Josiah K.	Laf	1-307	1878
Mrs. M. P.	Yal(2)	1-110	1897
Sarah	War	A-299	1861
William W.	Nox	B-145	1873
GOOLSBY, A. J.	Laf	1-428	1896
Margaret	Low	1-77	1860
Pleasant	Low	1-231	1866
GOORE, Eleazar	Mon	1-156,	1840
GOOSEY, Elizabeth	Yaz	A-330	1866
H. C.	Yaz	B-422	1900
GOOSHORN, John	Cla	B-244	1854
GORDON, Adam	Cla	A-339	1836
Bazil	Ada	2-348	1847
Charles B.	Cla	3-62	1880
E. M. Sr.	Kem	A-34	1888
George N.	Hol	1-136	1853
Henry	Yaz	A-16	1835
Martha	Yal(2)	1-67	1890
Mary A.	Wil	1-249	1841
Mary A.	Yal(1)	B-185	1880
Missouri H.	Pan(1)	B-507	1900
Robert	Hol	3-77	1888
Sarah E.	Tat	1-34	1877
William	Laf	1-267	1875
GORE, Davis	Ada	1-77	1812
Mrs. F. M.	Yal(2)	1-72	1892
Mary	Mon	I.14-388	1859
GORLZER, A.	Jac	1-56	1889
GORMAN, Elijah	Nox	A-124	1849
George	Mas	P.18-506	1869
Laura	Ben	1-64	1894
Mary	Ben	1-49	1889
Oliver	Hin	1-206	1847
Patrick	Car(2)	1-24	1880
Starling	Was	1-124	1848
GOSA, William	Cly	1-104	1891
GOSSOM, Willie Webb	Tal	B-123	1899
GOUGE, William M.	Ran	1-86	1866
William M.	Yaz	A-359	1869
GOULD, John A.	War	B-95	1878
GOWER, J. H.	Car(1)	A-476	1865
John H.	Nox	B-68	1865
Mark R.	Yaz	A-151	1851
GOYLER, Maggie J.	Mas	1-140	1898
GOZA, Jos. B.	Cop	A-74	1892
Joshua	Chi(1)	1-118	1894

GRACE, Green B.	Lau	1–210	1886
John B.	Hol	1–244	1860
Mary A. T.	Uni	1–30	1892
GRACY, John	Pan(2)	A–24	1882
GRAFTON, Allan	Jef	A–131	1809
Andrew	Ada	2–249	1842
Elizabeth S.	Cla	B–265	1856
George W.	Mad	A–651	1887
Jennet	Ada	2–212	1840
John	Ada	1–229	1820
Susan	Mad	A–675	1891
GRAHAM, A. L.	War	B–359	1899
Andrew	Car(1)	A–19	1841
Barnett	Pan(1)	B–42	1866
C. P.	Laf	2–7	1898
Columbus	Tat	1–249	1900
Demarus	Sco	A–471	1893
E. G.	Tat	1–112	1888
George W.	Mas	P.11–415	1856
J. C.	Tat	1–146	1891
Joseph	Ada	1–29	1807
Nancy	Ada	3–450	1871
Narcissus D.	Jas	1–92	1892
Robert	Laf	1–364	1885
Samuel L.	Was	1–503	1893
Susannah	Hin	1–251	1850
W. L.	Tip	1–206	1899
William	DeS	1–197	1859
William	Nox	B–282	1883
William M.	Hin	B–439	1895
GRANBERRY, Jesse D.	Hin	B–267	1870
Loammi	Clk	P.B–177	1842
Mary Jefferson	Cop	A–162	1900
Seth	Cop	AAA–328	1853
Seth F.	Hin	1–322	1853
GRANDERSON, Lillie			
Ann Eliza	Ada	4–503	1889
GRANT, Alexander G.	Mad	A–355	1861
Aunas	Isa	C–151	1890
George W.	Cop	AAA–334	1855
GRASS, Charles L.	Mad	2–108	1898
GRAVES, A. B.	Yaz	A–170	1854
B.	Mas	1–91	1896
Eli	Cop	A–118	1897
Elizabeth	Mad	A–153	1850
Grandison A.	Grn	A–9	1874
Jacob	Ben	1–16	1876
James	Jef	P.D–556	1849
James E.	Ben	1–38	1886
John	Hin	1–72	1836
Stephen	Hol	1–176	1857

Thomas Sr.	Hol	3-12	1893
GRAY, Alexander	Car(1)	A-498	1867
Coleman C.	Chi(1)	1-106	1891
John F.	Lea	1-54	1861
John M.	Isa	B-55	1854
Joseph	Hin	B-353	1884
Joseph P.	Jas	1-1	1856
Louisa	Low	1-481	1884
Sam	Tal	B-115	1897
Thomas	DeS	2-39	1871
W. B.	Sim	A-86	1898
William	DeS	1-151	1857
William H.	Low	1-101	1862
William M.	Lea	1-41	1864
GRAYSON, Sarah	Yaz	A-80	1845
GREAR, Booker	Yaz	B-392	1899
GREAVES, Charles	Ada	2-387	1851
GREEN, Abner	Ada	1-149	1816
Abraham	Hin	1-162	1823
Abraham	Mas	P.2-138	1823
Abram	Cla	A-168	1826
Amanda R.	Cop	A-33	1889
Andrew S.	Laf	1-406	1892
Daniel	Cla	B-240	1853
E. D.	Car(1)	A-435	1861
Elizabeth	Ada	2-358	1848
Elizabeth	Jef	A-114	1833
Everard	Jef	A-14	1813
Filmer Wills	Jef	P.C-660	1845
George M.	Clk	1-64	1884
George W.	Car(1)	A-7	1837
Harrison H.	Sun	1-34	1899
Hester Zelia	War	B-192	1888
J. Jasper	Lin	1-57	1899
James	Ada	2-8	1832
John H.	Nox	B-130	1873
John W.	Ada	4-511	1890
Joseph K.	Jef	A-3	1815
Lewis	Low	2-88	1894
Lucy	Low	2-122	1895
Mrs. M. A.	Gre	1-23	1899
Mary H.	Ada	1-335	1825
Moses	Pan(1)	A-173	1854
Pheleneaus	Lin	1-60	1900
Rebecca	War	A-221	1855
Richard E.	Yaz	A-8	1834
Samuel C.	Jef	P.B-176	1836
Samuel C.	Jef	P.C-499	1844
Thomas	Jef	A-12	1813
Thomas H.	Ada	1-49	1809
Thomas H.	Ada	1-52	1810

Thomas K.	Ada	5-122	1897
Thomas K.	Mad	A-184	1853
Thomas M.	Jef	A-4	1814
William	Was	1-423	1880
William M.	Jef	A-104	1829
Zanetta	Low	1-497	1885
GREENBERRY, Norvel R.	Mad	A-151	1850
GREENFIELD, Jesse	Ada	1-292	1823
GREENHOOD, Morris	Clk	1-126	1891
GREENLEAF, Daniel	Hin	1-115	1839
Eliza R.	War	A-57	1836
GREENLEE, Joseph			
Hough	Mad	A-71	1842
Nancy	Att	2-496	1865
GREENWALL, Jacob	Cla	B-166	1840
GREENWOOD, A. G.	Mon	1-141	1840
D. C.	Mon	I.4-338	1882
Samuel	Lea	1-31	1860
GREER, Adam G.	Nox	C-135	1900
Aquilla	Mas	P.3-407	1844
D. W.	DeS	1-373	1866
Edmond	Car(1)	A-105	1852
Henry	Nes	A-32	1854
GREEVES, John Greer	Cla	B-188	1845
GREFFING, Hiram	Lau	1-77	1867
GREGG, E. C.	Pan(1)	B-39	1867
John	Mon	I.5-239	1887
Mary Francis	Mon	I.7-13	1897
GREGORY, Austin	Tat	1-205	1895
James	Ada	3-283	1866
Margaret E.	Yal(2)	1-90	1895
Sarah W.	Win	1-96	1881
GRESHAM, James F.	Pre	1-85	1890
T. L. C.	Uni	1-59	1900
GRICE, Bella	Grn	A-126	1897
H. A.	New	1-122	1891
GRIFFIN, Anderson	Kem	A-91	1900
Benjamin Franklin	DeS	2-309	1889
Charity	DeS	2-86	1874
Clarisa	Was	2-103	1899
Fannie	Was	1-393	1870
J. T.	Chi(1)	1-95	1889
Jackson A.	Mas	P.2-468	1841
James C.	DeS	1-226	1859
Jeremiah	Mad	A-118	1847
L. L.	Ran	1-158	1879
Maria L.	Ada	4-361	1886
Richard W.	Chi (1863-1872)-75		1864
Thomas	War (1827-1832)-11		1827
Thomas M.	Hin	B-330	1878
William De	War	A-290	1860

William S.	Nox	B-22	1862
GRIFFING, Amelia A.	Lau	1-332	1889
John J.	Jef	B-162	1885
William	Jef	B-4	1859
William S.	Cla	B-305	1862
GRIFFIS, Jesse	Grn	A-87	1889
M. L.	Tat	1-67	1883
GRIFFITH, Elias B.	Ada	1-385	1825
J. C.	Win	1-126	1891
John T.	Ada	2-443	1853
John T.	Ada	3-249	1866
Joseph W.	Ada	3-248	1866
Mary	Ran	1-138	1875
GRIGGS, Anderson C.	Nox	A-134	1849
GRIM, Bella	Grn	A-126	1897
GRIMES, William	War	B-32	1873
William	War	B-367	1899
GRIMSTEAD, Martha	Hol	1-145	1855
GRIMSTED, Wiley Y.	Hol	1-139	1853
GRISHAM, G. W.	Lee	1-217	1900
GRISSELL, George	War	A-33	1834
GRISSOM, Edwin	Tip	1-197	1896
GRISWALD, Benjamin	Hin	B-349	1884
Maria	Hin	B-361	1884
GROCE, George L.	Tal	A-126	1851
GROENINGER, George	Cla	A-126	1822
GROOM, Valentine C.	Wil	2-77	1853
GROVE, Henson	Mas	P.2-580	1842
GROVES, Bridges	Ada	4-181	1881
GRUBBS, George W.	Yaz	A-271	1863
Lewis T.	Cla	B-158	1838
T. H.	Uni	1-12	1884
Z. M. P.	Coa(1)	1-19	1848
GUERRY, John	Yaz	A-232	1859
GUESS, Zebediah B.	Att	B-271	1878
GUICE, Edwin J.	Fra	A-16	1899
Ephraim	Yaz	A-187	1854
Lucilla	Ada	4-526	1891
Stephen L.	Ada	4-161	1880
GUIDICE, Clement	War	B-50	1874
GUILLON, Julian M.	Ada	3-206	1863
GUILLOTTE, Laura			
McCaleb	Cla	3-64	1880
GUINARD, Charles			
Frederick	Ada	2-64	1834
GUINES, W. J.	Ada	5-222	1899
GUINN, Morris E.	Yaz	A-39	1838
GULLETT, Anderson	Mon	I.6-107	1891
Louisiana J.	Lau	1-276	1890
GUNN, D. B.	Ran	1-221	1887
James	Pon E.(1844-1848)-169		1847

John	DeS	1-402	1866
Susan P.	Ran	1-224	1888
William P.	Car(1)	A-191	1859
GURLEY, Jesse	Mas	P.3-366	1844
Sarah E.	Mad	A-569	1876
GURLIE, Henrietta	Jac	1-190	1898
Nancy Clara	Jac	1-28	1884
GURNEY, Marsh J.	Ada	3-116	1858
GUSCIO, Annie	War	B-374	1899
GUSTIN, Lemuel P.	Ada	2-48	1833
Richard	Ada	1-118	1814
GUSTINE, Samuel	Ada	2-312	1846
GUY, Leander R.	Mas	P.3-342	1844
Lurana	Lee	1-72	1882
Martha	Pik	1-138	1900
William T. D.	Hol	1-202	1859
GUYTON, A. W.	Att	B-406	1884
GWIN, C. V.	Hol	3-62	1890
Elizabeth	Tun	2-80	1883
J. N. B.	Mas	1-54	1896
William	Lin	1-8	1893
William	Lin	1-44	1898
HACKETT, Alice	War	B-143	1883
HACKLEMAN, James	Low	1-181	1865
HADLEY, Hampton	Nes	A-76	1865
HAGAN, Hiram	Isa	A-21	1848
Sarah A.	Yaz	B-295&299	1894
HAGANY, Benjamin	Laf	1-18	1846
HAGEMAN, Laura D.	Yaz	A-130	1847
HAGINS, Malacheo	Jef	A-95	1826
HAILE, Lucy	New	1-31	1884
HAINING, Louisa	War	B-109	1879
HAIRE, Milton Smith	Hin	B-482	1900
HAIRSTON, Elizabeth			
P.	Low	1-15	1858
Georgia E.	Car(2)	1-42	1888
Hardin	Low	1-122	1862
John H.	Low	1-137	1863
Marshall	Yal(2)	1-22	1882
N. E.	Low	1-538	1888
Peter C.	Low	1-572	1889
Peter W.	Low	1-513	1886
Robert	Mas	P.2-411	1841
Robert Percy	Low	2-80	1894
HALBERT, Henophen	Low	1-158	1864
Joel J.	Low	1-382	1875
HALE, Mary	Hin	1-376	1856
Shadrach	Yal(2)	1-43	1885
Thomas	Han	A-36	1867
HALEY, Burruss	Mad	A-83	1843

David	Mad	A-95	1845
Maria Louisa	Mad	A-116	1847
HALFORD, Washington			
B.	Lea	1-11	1857
HALL, A. H.	Cov	1-10	1895
Ann Jane	War	A-156	1846
Alexander	Mad	A-5	1831
Alexander G.	Mas	P.8-376	1852
Armelia	Mas	P.7-389	1850
Bethany	Hin	1-428	1858
C. Evans	Wil	1-158	1836
Caleb	Ada	3-17	1855
Catharine H.	Yaz	B-158	1883
D. G.	Uni	1-65	1900
David	Ada	4-413	1886
Eliza M.	Pan(1)	B-274	1879
Elizabeth C.	Cla	B-317	1862
Green H.	Hin	B-429	1894
Hiram	Tat	1-106	1888
J. P.	Mas	1-113	1897
James G.	Pan(1)	B-452	1890
John	Kem	A-11	1883
John	Low	1-342	1873
John	Mad	A-685	1892
John	Mad	2-6	1892
John	War	A-106	1840
John A.	Mas	1-158	1899
John R.	Mas	P.16-6	1863
Laurena M.	Yaz	A-293	1865
Margaret	Ada	1-392	1826
Mary E.	Mas	1-152	1899
Moses	War	A-186	1850
Nancy	Tal	B-76	1884
Norton J.	War	B-173	1886
O. C.	Grn	A-147	1900
P. M.	Cla	B-321	1867
Porter	Pan(1)	A-441	1864
R. J.	Lea	1-86	1877
Susan	War	B-377	1899
Thomas C. H.	Tip	1-1	1866
W. M.	Lea	1-114	1884
William	Wil	1-272	1844
William McK.	Mas	1-105	1897
William W.	Grn	A-27	1878
HALLIBURTON, Bursheba	DeS	1-67	1853
HALLIDAY, James T.	Hin	B-299	1874
Margaret J.	Mot	1-135	1897
HALLIGAN, Edward	Tun	2-90	1886
HALSEY, Jehaida	Coa(1)	1-101	1866
William F.	Ada	2-452	1853
HALSTEAD, Benjamin	Hol	1-498	1888

HALY, D. W.	Mad	A-258	1857
HAM, J. A.	Tat	1-227	1899
John	Nes	A-134	1898
Ruth	DeS	2-141	1879
HAMAN, Standford	Hin	B-423	1893
HAMBLEN, Edwin	Mad	A-543	1873
HAMBLET, William W.	Yal(1)	B-165	1876
HAMEL, S. A.	Yaz	B-268	1891
HAMER, C. F.	Yaz	A-259	1865
Joseph L.	Ben	1-81	1900
Sallie C.	Ben	1-78	1897
Thomas	Ben	1-11	1871
W. T.	Ben	1-75	1896
HAMICK, Isaac	Jef	B-148	1880
HAMILTON, Anna E.	Lef	A-76	1883
Darius	Cla	A-172	1826
David A.	Mas	P.13-460	1858
John	Hol	1-8	1835
John O.	Coa(1)	1-179	1885
John T.	Mas	P.15-266	1861
Oscar	Ran	1-42	1862
Richard	Ada	1-54	1810
Richard P.	Hin	1-97	1837
Samuel	Cho	A-13	1883
Sarah	Hol	1-242	1860
Sarah Jane	Lea	1-125	1886
Syrus	Cla	A-206	1828
Vaden	Car(1)	A-81	1847
William	Chi(1)	1-21	1880
William	Tip	1-113	1882
William S.	Yal(1)	A-192	1851
HAMLEY, John	Nox	C-17	1896
HAMLIN, Frank R.	Cly	1-134	1897
John F.	Tun	2-194	1900
HAMM, J. S.	Lau	1-392	1898
HAMMET, William H.	Was	1-313	1861
HAMMETT, Absalom	Wil	1-151	1836
Mary	Hin	1-442	1859
Mary H.	Coa(1)	1-132	1879
HAMMOND, Martha E.	Tat	1-187	1894
HAMPTON, Annie F.	Was	1-440	1876
George A.	Laf	2-59	1900
James M.	Mon	I.7-202	1851
John	Ada	1-195	1818
Margaret	Wil	1-231	1840
Nathaniel E.	Mas	P.15-246	1861
Wade Jr.	Was	1-415	1879
William	Hol	1-65	1845
William M.	Mon	I.2-34	1873
HAMRICK, Willis	Clk	1-89	1886
HANCOCK, George M.	Yaz	A-170	1854

J. Cal.	Tat	1–182	1893
John A.	DeS	1–442	1868
Joshua	Mas	P.15–254	1861
Richard C.	DeS	1–140	1857
W. L.	Mas	1–21	1893
HAND, Albert P.	Clk	1–162	1895
Mary	Low	1–387	1876
Ransom	Lau	1–32	1863
HANDY, Horace	Mad	2–111	1898
HANENSTEIN, William	Nox	B–398	1894
HANES, F. M.	Mad	A–142	1849
Mary L.	War	B–225	1889
HANGHEY, James	Kem	A–61	1896
HANKINS, Benjamin	Jef	A–75	1821
Edward S.	Hol	1–69	1846
Elias C.	War	A–301	1861
Margaret G.	Grn	A–35	1879
HANLIN, Mary A.	War	B–247	1891
HANN, Jackson M.	Was	1–128	1850
HANNA, Andrew	Att	2–273	1865
James	Cla	A–160	1826
Jane S.	Win	1–84	1873
Mattie	Att	B–409	1884
Mijumium B.	Hol	1–199	1859
R. Y.	Win	1–111	1888
William A.	Mad	2–36	1894
HANNESY, John	War	B–354	1898
HANRAHAN, Michael	Pik	1–70	1895
HANWAY, John	Was	2–58	1897
HARALSON, Vincent	Mas	P.4–414	1846
HARBIN, John	Car(1)	B–11	1880
Newton	Car(1)	A–466	1864
HARBOR, John	Ran	1–65	1864
HARDAWAY, John P.	Mas	P.15–211	1861
Thomas R.	War	A–199 .	1853
Thomas Stith	Ben	1–4	1870
HARDEN, William	Hol	1–60	1845
HARDEE, Margret	Clk	1–60	1884
HARDIE, David	Hin	1–98	1835
Robert	Pan(1)	B–16	1863
HARDIN, David	Mas	P.3–479	1844
Littleton Yarbrough	Yal(1)	A–260	1855
Mark	Nox	A–52	1843
HARDING, E. W.	Jef	B–167	1887
Elizabeth M.	Cla	3–127	1891
F. S.	Laf	1–275	1877
HARDWICK, Amanda A.	Yal(1)	B–61	1861
Amelia	Hin	1–174	1844
L. Adeline	Yaz	B–286	1893
HARDY, A. H.	Mad	A–624	1883
John H.	Win	1–68	1873

Mumford	Low	2-34	1891
HARGEN, Elizabeth V.	Mad	A-623	1883
HARGIS, James	Tat	1-64	1883
HARGON, Evaline E.	Mad	A-678	1891
John	Mad	A-463	1867
William O.	Mad	A-663	1889
HARGROVE, Isiah	Ada	4-557	1891
Seaborn	Mas	P.15-312	1861
William H.	Low	1-372	1875
HARKEY, David	Ita E.(1871-1876)-7		1872
HARKIN, Patrick	Lea	1-17	1858
HARKLEROAD, Hiram S.	DeS	2-268	1886
HARKREADER, A. G.	Lee	1-157	1895
HARLOW, Alfred	Cla	B-171	1842
Margaret M.	Yaz	B-343	1897
HARMAN, Benjamin	Ada	2-138	1836
HARMES, Sophia	Pik	1-91	1897
HARMON, Charles	DeS	1-163	1858
Eli	Mad	2-1	1892
James	Cla	A-83	1818
Samuel	Laf	1-16	1844
Sarah	Laf	1-132	1859
William	Cla	B-157	1838
HARNER, Lydia A.	Mas	P.4-283	1846
HARPER, Billy	Hin	B-263	1869
Frances G.	Lau	1-92	1869
George W.	Hin	B-427	1894
Harriet	Ada	5-25	1893
Hucynela	Lin	1-29	1896
James E.	Lin	1-29	1896
Louisa	Jef	B-90	1866
Mary A.	Cla	3-30	1877
Mary S.	Tal	A-242	1860
Richard W.	Mad	A-99	1845
Robert W.	Cla	B-322	1867
Samuel	Mas	P.2-398	1840
Susan L.	Mas	1-4	1891
W. Y.	Clk	1-4	1872
William	Ada	4-173	1880
Yandy	Jef	B-157	1883
HARPOLE, Julia A.	Web	A-63	1887
HARRA, Rosalie	Han	A-55	1869
HARRELL, Isaac	Hin	1-4	1832
John J.	Mas	P.19-176	1869
Lavina D.	Pre	1-82	1890
HARRES, James	Mot	1-7	1873
HARRINGTON, Abel M.	Yaz	A-146	1851
Annie E.	Low	2-56	1891
Bartholomew	Coa(1)	1-126	1878
James B.	Fra	A-15	1898
James F.	Chi(1)	1-53	1885

Margaret W.	Chi(1)	1–24	1880
Patrick	Mas	1–119	1897
HARRIS, Albert B.	Hol	1–282	1863
Arthur	Mas	P.17–609	1867
Barton	Hin	1–131	1840
Benjamin W.	Yal(1)	B–214	1877
Carey A.	Tun	1–32	1842
Charles	Ada	4–17	1872
Charles	War	A–15	1831
Charles R.	Chi (1863–1872)–199		1872
Charles T.	Pan(1)	A–69	1849
Claborn	Mas	P.9–453	1854
Claiborne	Cla	A–124	1822
Clara	War	A–53	1835
Daniel T.	Pan(1)	B–138	1873
Daphney	Cla	3–65	1880
David N.	DeS	1–168	1858
Drury B.	War	A–200	1853
Elizabeth R.	Yaz	B–118	1880
Emily	Tal	B–120	1899
Evaline	Tat	1–138	1890
Fleming W.	Ada	3–195	1862
George W.	Lee	1–210	1900
H. T.	DeS	1–391	1866
Hardy	DeS	1–468	1870
Harriet	Car(2)	1–58	1891
Hartwell	War	A–41	1834
Henry A.	Tal	B–120	1899
Henry C.	Ada	4–25	1873
J. M.	Tun	1–488	1868
James	Mot	1–7	1873
James D.	Hin	1–18	1833
James F.	Wil	2–262	1869
James M.	Lee	1–104	1887
James M.	War	B–346	1898
James R.	Isa	C–35	1860
James W.	Low	1–551	1887
Jesse Winston	Lef	A–44	1864
John A.	Yal(1)	A–144	1849
John E.	War	A–264	1860
John Porter	Nox	B–363	1891
John W.	Pan(1)	A–17	1847
Lewis B.	Cop	A–49	1891
M. M.	Low	2–254	1900
Malissie	Att	D–112	1896
Martha W.	Mon	I.7–42	1897
Mary A. E.	War	B–380	1900
Mary B.	Mon	I.16–168	1861
Mary H.	Tun	2–91	1887
Mary M.	War	B–179	1886
Mary W.	Low	1–34	1859

Matthew T.	Att	C-146	1889
Mordica	Ran	1-322	1900
Nancy	Chi(1)	1-37	1881
Nancy	Pan(1)	A-270	1857
Nancy E.	Web	A-37	1887
Patience	Sha	A-10	1882
Reuben	Mad	A-14	1832
Robert A.	Lea	1-39	1864
Robert E.	Cop	AAA-322	1850
Robert P	Lea	1-43	1864
Robert P.	War	B-65	1876
Samuel	Was	1-472	1888
Samuel M.	War	A-230	1856
Sherrod	Mas	P.18-610	1869
Stephen	Mas	P.10-247	1854
Stephen J.	Mas	P.15-288	1861
Thomas	Pan(1)	B-379	1883
Thomas W.	Low	1-232	1866
W. F.	Sun	1-26	1898
W. S.	Low	2-169	1897
William H.	Car(1)	A-79	1850
William R.	Lee	1-110	1888
HARRISON, Benjamin C.	Grn	A-149	1900
Elizabeth	Jef	P.B-477	1839
Emily	Yal(1)	A-123	1848
Epheus G.	Ada	3-194	1862
Henry	War	B-308	1895
Isham	Low	1-167	1864
James A.	Yaz	A-261	1865
James T.	Low	1-417	1879
Jeremiah Sr.	Law	P.B-60	1838
John C.	Pan(1)	B-159	1874
Levi G.	Ada	3-113	1858
Mary S.	Ada	4-233	1882
Nannie J.	Hin	B-378	1882
Nathan	Wil	3-178	1899
Nathaniel	Jef	B-122	1873
Newton S.	Att	B-359	1882
Peyton	War	B-211	1888
Philip B.	Jef	P.F-80	1854
R. G.	Yal(1)	B-220	1892
Regina	Low	2-29	1890
Richard	Jef	A-1	1800
Richard C.	Low	1-526	1887
T. R.	Jef	B-185	1885
William A.	Nox	A-139	1849
William H.	Hin	1-169	1843
William H.	Nes	A-107	1879
HARPER, Martha M.	Yal(1)	A-6	1832
HARRY, John F.	Jas	1-75	1880
HARSHE, Joanna P.	Was	2-95	1898

HART, Delila	Yaz	A-236	1860
Edward C.	Mad	A-420	1866
James E.	Ada	1-287	1823
Stephen	Mad	A-679	1891
Thomas	Ada	3-323	1867
William H.	Hin	1-104	1838
HARTMAN, Belle L.	Was	2-15	1895
Margaret	War	B-125	1879
HARTSFIELD, William S.	Pan(1)	B-237	1878
HARTWICK, Frederick	War	B-97	1878
HARVARD, Thomas	Wil	2-258	1868
HARVESON, Albert G.	Car(1)	A-480	1866
HARVEY, Alexander S.	Pan(1)	B-20	1866
Augustine W.	Att	B-436	1885
E. A.	Okt	1-8	1885
George	Tis	1-20	1889
Henry P.	Cly	1-122	1893
Henry P.	Low	2-64	1892
Mary P.	Low	1-378	1875
Rebecca	Hin	1-346	1854
Rebecca	Low	2-195	1898
Richard	Tal	B-87	1889
Sallie B.	Tal	B-114	1897
Thomas	Car(1)	A-155	1857
Thomas	Coa(1)	1-137	1880
Thomas C.	Hin	1-295	1852
W. R.	Hin	B-85	1864
Wade	Att	A-488	1860
HARVISON, Matilda	Gre	1-1	1878
HARVY, Anderson	Mot	1-53	1881
Henry P.	Nox	B-383	1892
HARWELL, Henry	Laf	1-229	1873
Nathaniel	Laf	1-108	1856
HARWOOD, Agnes E.	Isa	C-130	1876
HASHER, Granville H.	Ben	1-82	1900
HASKET, David	Jef	P.D-226	1845
HASKINS, Elvira P.	DeS	1-271	1861
Henry	Ran	1-167	1881
HASLETT, J. A. H.	Car(1)	A-534	1872
HASTINGS, James F.	Pan(1)	A-121	1852
O. A.	Cla	3-168	1896
R. M.	Cla	3-61	1879
HATCH, Alice	Nox	A-285	1860
Edmund	Nox	A-168	1851
W. W.	Low	1-435	1880
HATCHER, Lucinda	Cla	B-164	1840
HATCHETT, Morris	Mas	P.5-416	1848
HATFIELD, Elizabeth	Wil	1-193	1838
HAUFMAN, Barney	Yaz	B-228	1888
HAUGHTON, Caroline F.	Mon	I.5-235	1887

James H.	Mon	I.22–235	1871
Mary Silvia	Chi	(1863–1872)–137	1866
HAVER, Michael	War	B–276	1892
HAWELL, B. P.	Laf	1–388	1892
HAWK, Ann	Yaz	B–420	1900
HAWKINS, C. A.	Tun	1–441	1868
Cherry	Tal	B–86	1889
Edward S.	Hol	1–233	1860
Fannie C.	Tat	1–176	1893
Frank Jr.	Mot	1–133	1896
Hinson	Tat	1–244	1900
J. M.	DeS	2–197	1882
James M.	Yal(1)	A–174	1850
Joseph W.	DeS	2–73	1873
Mary F.	Low	1–397	1877
P. H.	Tat	1–195	1894
Richard	War	A–33	1834
Thomas	Mas	P.13–576	1858
Thomas Jefferson	Car(1)	A–20	1840
HAWL, John W.	Yal(1)	A–57	1861
HAWLEY, Q. N.	Fra	A–1	1880
HAY, Anthony	Sim	A–77&81	1897
HAYCRAFT, William A.	Was	1–450	1886
HAYDEN, James	Low	1–140	1863
Parthenia	Low	1–61	1860
HAYES, N. W.	Mad	A–556	1873
V. A.	Web	A–18	1876
HAYGWOOD, Lewis	Law	P.B–41	1837
HAYMAN, Henry	Yaz	A–152	1851
HAYNE, Robert Y.	Ada	2–195	1839
HAYNES, Bythell	Wil	1–48	1833
Charles G.	Tip	1–73	1875
Henry	Clk	P.B–167	1842
Nancy	Wil	2–4	1846
Thomas F.	Wil	3–150	1895
HAYNIE, John	Ada	1–7	1803
HAYS, Jas.	Hol	1–495	1888
James	Wil	2–103	1855
John G.	Web	A–52	1887
Nathaniel W. S.	Jef	B–93	1866
Polly	Sim	A–4	1880
Robert	Sim	A–72	1894
Sarah M.	Cla	B–216	1851
Thomas M.	Wil	2–180	1862
William C.	Yaz	A–95	1846
Jake	DeS	2–340	1891
HAZLIP, John	Ada	3–135	1859
Rebecca	Wil	2–73	1852
William	Wil	1–291	1845
HEAD, John L.	Web	A–121	1898
Sarah P.	Yaz	A–196	1855

HEALEY, James	War	A–120	1841
HEARD, C. C.	Hin	B–347	1883
Francis S.	Hin	B–223	1866
G. A.	Hin	B–397	1887
J. M.	Cly	1–130	1896
Jesse	Mad	A–188	1853
Jesse	Mad	A–222	1854
Jesse F.	Yaz	B–48	1875
Joshua O.	Clk	1–91	1885
Joshua T.	Ran	1–199	1885
Martha M.	Clk	1–84	1885
Moses	Mad	A–457	1867
Sallie W.	Tat	1–193	1894
Samuel Smith	Hin	B–398	1887
Sarah A.	Hin	B–329	1877
Stephen	Hin	1–153	1815
Thomas W.	Hin	B–173	1863
HEARON, A. S.	Mot	1–164	1900
Milton	Mot	1–93	1886
HEATH, Adolphe M.	Yaz	B–212	1886
Jesse	Car(1)	A–158	1857
Lawrence G.	Mas	P.8–266	1852
Mary M.	Yaz	B–180	1884
Saw G.	War	A–157	1847
HEBRON, John	War	A–311	1862
HEDRICK, Peter	Cla	B–211	1850
HEENE, Lawrence	Ada	4–355	1885
HEFLIN, Wiley J.	Nes	A–90	1869
HEFNER, Leander	Hol	1–42	1844
HEGEMAN, Joseph W.	War	A–64	1836
HEIDLEBURG, Samuel			
C. Sr.	Jas	1–101	1895
Thomas C.	Jas	1–67	1877
W. W.	Clk	1–33	1877
Washington Irving	Jas	1–117	1900
HEIGHWAY, James H.	Cop	A–12	1888
HEIMMS, Jesse	Hin	1–180	1835
HEINE, Henry Sigmund	Ada	4–423	1887
HEINRICK, Annie	Ben	1–25	1879
HEITZMANN, Charles	Pik	1–152	1900
HEIWAY, Frank E.	Cop	A–156	1900
HELMISKES, Abraham	Jef	A–19	1813
HEMINGWAY, David			
Myres	Mad	2–98	1897
Wilson	Car(1)	A–182	1859
HEMPHILL, James	Win	1–59	1871
James L.	Sim	A–31	1885
James S.	Car(1)	B–29	1888
Marcus	Hin	B–166	1863
Mary E.	Car(1)	B–39	1890
HENDERSON, A. B.	DeS	2–449	1897

Alexander C.	Ada	3-254	1866
Elisha Williams	Pan(1)	B-408	1885
Elizabeth	Mad	A-141	1849
Isaac H.	Ada	4-2	1871
John	Ada	2-236	1841
John	Mas	P.3-561	1844
John	War	A-81	1837
John Lynn	Mon	I.12-253	1856
Julietta	Lau	1-113	1876
Lawson F	Mad	A-272	1858
O. W.	Yaz	A 240	1860
Sarah Lucinda	Wil	3-145	1895
Thomas	Ada	3-251	1866
Wallace A. J.	Mad	A-161	1851
Walter C.	Mad	A-144	1850
William	Cla	A-284	1833
William G.	Nox	A-7	1836
HENDREN, Sephrona P.	War	B-149	1884
HENDRICK, Fannie B.	Ada	5-176	1898
Jeremiah E.	DeS	1-353	1866
HENDRICKS, D. W.	Yaz	A-292	1864
Henry C. L.	Win	1-21	1863
John M.	Yaz	A-198	1855
Nancy	Yaz	B-251	1890
Redin	Mad	A-670	1890
William W.	Yaz	A-258	1861
HENDRIX, Mrs. C. A.	Yaz	B-335	1897
HENINGTON, Henry J.	Cop	A-37	1889
John	Cop	AAA-318	1843
HENKLE, Mary			
Josephine	Yaz	B-329	1897
HENLES, Howard	Yal(2)	1-1	1878
HENLEY, Elizabeth A.	Wil	1-130	1835
HENLY, George P. A.	Cla	3-160	1896
HENNEGAN, Catherine	War	B-235	1890
HENNESSEE, Richard	Ada	2-385	1850
HENRY, Ada	Jac	1-77	1891
Elizabeth P.	Mad	A-594	1880
Emily A.	Car(1)	B-23	1884
Fram W.	DeS	2-452	1897
James	Att	2-186	1862
James	Low	1-162	1864
John	Cla	B-199	1849
John H.	Mon	1-122	1838
John W.	Car(1)	A-414	1860
Lavinia Helen	Lef	A-130	1898
Margaret	Mad	A-237	1856
Mary L.	Hin	B-457	1898
Mary Louisa	Hin	B-490	1900
Robert W.	Hin	1-199	1847
Sarah A.	Car(1)	B-24	1884

William K.	Ada	2-450	1853
HENSON, W. D.	Tip	1-106	1882
HENWOOD, Anna M.	Mon	I.6-115	1892
HERBERT, James H.	Hol	1-137	1853
Thomas S.	Wil	1-284	1845
HERD, Emma Windham	Jas	1-69	1878
HERLEY, Jeremiah	Hol	1-71	1847
HERMAN, Julia R.	Nox	B-359	1891
Julia R.	Win	1-123	1891
HERNANDEZ, Besantee	Ada	1-112	1814
HERNDON, Osborn D.	Mon	1-143	1840
Thomas I.	War	A-51	1835
William	Hol	1-396	1876
HERNTHAL, Julius	War	B-20	1872
HERRIN, James	Yal(1)	A-213	1852
HERRING, George	War (1823-1827)-206		1826
Icabod	Car(2)	1-12	1878
Jacob B.	Jef	B-150	1878
James	Pan(2)	A-44	1884
L. W.	Car(1)	A-453	1863
Mary S.	Uni	1-17	1889
Violet	Ada	4-196	1881
HERRINGTON, Hezekiah	Hol	1-132	1853
Isaac	Jas	1-70	1878
John	Nes	A-98	1875
John	Nes	A-125	1888
HERRON, Andrew	Laf	1-9	1842
Andrew	Yal(1)	A-146	1849
D. L.	Yal(1)	B-72	1862
F. P.	Yal(1)	B-179	1878
G. N.	Tal	A-264	1862
John N.	Yal(1)	B-90	1863
Lurenia Susanah	Pan(1)	B-399	1884
Marion F. N.	Tal	B-30	1873
HESLEP, Almoth B.	Cla	3-55	1879
HESTER, Elijah	Mad	A-652	1888
Francis	Mad	A-652	1887
Mary Jane	Mot	1-155	1899
HETHERINGTON, Pinkney	Wil	2-206	1864
HEWES, Thomas	Ada	1-387	1827
HEWETT, Josephus	Ada	4-136	1878
HEWLETT, Sarah	Pan(1)	B-11	1864
Thomas	Pan(1)	A-325	1858
HIBBLER, Eldred M.	Coa(1)	1-79	1860
James L.	Nox	B-237	1880
Mary Ann	Nox	C-40	1898
William H.	Nox	B-29	1862
HIBLER, E. B.	Pan(1)	A-439	1864
HICKEY, George W.	Hin	B-159	1862
Joseph	Laf	1-153	1865
Thomas	Ada	2-395	1851

HICKMAN, Joseph W.	Mad	A-194	1853
Paris	Nes	A-2	1838
Peter	Cla	B-164	1840
W. Brinkley	Cop	AAA-314	1852
HICKS, Eliza R.	Hin	B-376	1886
J. G.	War	B-271	1892
John C.	Wil	1-115	1834
John M.	Low	1-127	1862
Joseph T.	War	A-131	1842
HIDE, John G.	Nox	A-274	1859
HIESLAND, H. C.	DeS	1-424	1867
HIGDON, Isaac	Ada	4-118	1876
Mary	Ada	1-25	1805
R. D.	Tis	1-13	1888
Vina	Ada	5-101	1896
HIGGINBOTHAM, Tabitha W.	DeS	1-270	1861
HIGGINBOTHAN, Robert P.	Yaz	A-136	1849
HIGGINS, Bennett J.	Yal(1)	A-28	1840
Mrs. C. M.	Ada	5-270	1900
Ebenezer	Yaz	B-325	1897
Kate	Low	1-439	1880
Mark M.	Nox	B-172	1875
Randall G.	Isa	C-146	1890
William	Laf	1-12	1846
William E.	Yaz	B-385	1899
HIGGS, Elisha	Hin	1-9	1814
HIGHGATE, Mrs. J. M.	Grn	A-125	1897
HIGHLENDER, William R.	War	A-194	1852
HIGHTOWER, James	Pan(1)	A-435	1863
Jane F.	Pan(1)	B-242	1878
John	Pan(1)	B-376	1882
Joshua	Chi	(1863-1872)-26	1864
Stephen	Pan(1)	A-392	1860
Sue F.	War	B-241	1890
HILBORNE, Vaughn	Hin	1-41	1834
HILBURN, F. A.	Tun	2-12	1873
HILDEBRAND, Daniel	DeS	1-146	1857
HILL, Abel W.	Tip	1-115	1884
Abram	Car(1)	A-106	1852
Abram M.	Car(1)	A-113	1853
Brook	Mad	A-21	1835
Caleb	Jef	A-18	1813
Charles	Hin	1-113	1839
Charles	Was	1-447	1885
Duncan	Mas	P.3-481	1844
Geahard	Ada	1-401	1826
Harry R. W.	Isa	B-22	1853
Isaac	Cla	B-328	1868

J. L. S.	Chi(2)	1-92	1900
James	Wil	2-272	1873
James	Wil	3-125	1894
Jane K.	Wil	3-122	1894
John	Ada	4-4	1871
John	Jef	A-99	1827
Joseph H.	Mot	1-1	1872
Josiah P.	DeS	1-149	1857
Julia Ann	Pre	1-84	1890
Lucy	Cla	A-233	1832
Mary	Pon	1-5	1890
Mary E.	Mad	A-609	1881
Mary Jane	Kem	A-73	1899
Nancy	War	A-313	1862
Polly	Chi(1)	1-137	1899
Rebecca G.	Cop	AAA-308	1860
Robert A.	Laf	2-48	1900
Samuel	Mot	1-123	1896
Samuel L.	Mas	P.13-481	1858
Solon	Wil	1-116	1835
Thomas	Jef	A-92	1826
Wiley W.	Nes	A-65	1861
William	Ada	A-454	1829
William	Mad	A-347	1861
William	Mon	I.12-75	1856
William E.	War	A-314	1862
William M.	Kem	A-24	1886
William R.	Mad	A-441	1866
HILLHOUSE, Jesse L.	Web	A-29	1879
HILLIARD, Isaac	Yal(1)	A-250	1854
HILLSON, George			
Washington	War	A-160	1847
HILTON, Truman	Car(1)	A-137	1856
HIMES, John C.	Han	A-106	1877
HINDS, Henrietta	Ada	3-346	1868
Mary F.	Mad	2-32	1894
HINES, C. E.	Nox	B-333	1888
Dolly	Was	2-4	1894
Harrison H.	Hol	1-96	1850
James L.	Mad	A-234	1856
Martha	Cly	1-16	1876
Mary F.	Att	B-351	1881
Richard D.	Yaz	A-33	1837
Thomas	Hol	1-61	1845
Walter B.	Pik	1-124	1899
HINKLE, Mary	Nox	A-219	1853
HINSON, Brooks	Car(2)	1-51	1889
Elizabeth	Clk	1-105	1888
HINTON, George W.	Nox	A-201	1855
George W.	Nox	B-404	1894
HIROCH, Jacob	Was	1-431	1883

HIRSCH, David	Yal(2)	1-94	1895
HITCH, J. Oscar W.	War	A-324	1862
Mary Elizabeth	War	A-235	1856
HITT, David	New	1-15	1882
HOBART, M. B.	Yaz	A-153	1852
HOBBS, Emily B.	Hol	3-71	1899
Robert Gibbs	Cla	B-220	1850
HOBBY, John W.	Low	1-26	1858
HOBERT, Zebulin	Cla	A-86	1819
HOBGOOD, Charles H.	Lau	1-390	1899
HOBSON, Albert	Ran	1 321	1900
J. E.	Chi(1)	1-109	1887
R. G.	Chi(1)	1-98	1890
Sarah A.	Ran	1-306	1896
HOCKSTRASSER, Jacob	Jef	B-105	1868
HODGE, Allen L.	Laf	1-192	1869
Perkins A.	Yaz	A-45	1839
Robert Sr.	Mad	A-62	1841
Susan	Mad	A-272	1858
HODGES, Alex	Qui	1-3	1888
Benjamin	Lef	A-30	1857
Charles A.	Low	1-256	1868
Ezekiel	Pon	1-30	1837
G. W.	Pon	1-11	1899
HODGES, James	Pon	1-301	1840
James Wyatt	Lin	1-11	1894
Samuel Nicholas	Hol	1-131	1853
Sybba	Lee	1-24	1877
Terry	Win	1-1	1860
HODNETT, William	Yal(1)	A-189	1851
HOFFMAN, Anthony	Han	A-121	1880
Louisa	Mad	A-574	1878
Martha	War	B-170	1886
R. H.	Mad	2-25	1893
HOGAN, Daniel	Cho	A-30	1893
Mary C.	Mon	I.20-724	1871
William	War	A-172	1846
HOGG, Hallen M.	Hin	1-274	1851
HOGGATH, Wilford	Ada	1-138	1816
HOGGATT, Anthony	Ada	2-467	1854
Grissilla	Ada	2-248	1842
James W.	Yaz	A-321	1865
John	Ada	2-113	1835
Nathaniel	Ada	1-104	1814
Nathaniel	Ada	3-437	1870
Nathaniel Sr.	Ada	2-463	1853
Philip	Ada	3-19	1855
Sally	Ada	2-253	1842
Wilford	Ada	2-228	1841
William	Ada	1-214	1820
HOGUE, Mary H.	Laf	1-40	1849

HOLBROOK, Andrew			
Jackson	Okt	1-14	1888
HOLCOMB, Thomas A. E.	Jac	1-174	1897
HOLCOMBE, John	Tip	1-163	1890
N. G.	Tip	1-165	1890
William H.	Tip	1-26	1867
HOLDEN, Mary	Ada	5-52	1894
HOLDER, James A.	Tat	1-113	1889
John W.	Jas	1-60	1872
HOLDERNESS, Elizabeth	Low	1-128	1862
HOLIMAN, John	Mot	1-101	1891
HOLLAND, Elizabeth	Nes	A-58	1859
Fannie V.	Mad	2-10	1892
Herman	War	B-302	1894
HOLLEDAY, Andrew J.	Law	P.B-201	1842
HOLLENSWORTH, William	Hin	1-303	1852
HOLLEY, Benjamin	Tun	2-88	1884
Elizabeth	Laf	1-217	1871
HOLLIDAY, Isaac N.	Mad	2-16	1893
John	Mon	I.4-108	1881
Thomas	Mon	I.20-138	1871
HOLLIMAN, Robert	Wil	2-13	1847
HOLLINGSWORTH, Isham	New	1-4	1879
J. M.	Jac	1-99	1892
Jacob	Mad	A-192	1853
Sarah	Yaz	B-383	1899
HOLLIS, Maheal	Yal(1)	B-215	1885
HOLLOMAN, Needham	Low	1-70	1860
Rebecca A.	Yaz	B-40	1874
Thomas R.	Yaz	B-304	1895
HOLLOWAY, Caroline			
Frances	Law	1-8	1896
Chesley	Car(1)	A-186	1859
Letha Caroline	Mad	A-176	1852
Simon M.	Lee	1-106	1888
Thomas	DeS	1-250	1860
W. C.	DeS	1-365	1866
HOLLOWELL, Jonathan	Mas	P.16-21	1863
Seaney Ann	Mas	P.18-288	1868
HOLLY, Christopher	Cla	B-252	1855
Gracy	Tip	1-138	1887
Harriet	Hin	B-363	1881
HOLMAN, Elijah	Car(1)	A-138	1856
John	Car(1)	A-129	1855
Sarah M.	Mas	1-173	1900
HOLMES, Ahab	Wil	1-140	1835
Benjamin R.	Yaz	B-126	1881
Bryant	Pre	1-11	1873
Caroline Roberts	Yaz	B-122	1880
David	Ada	2-34	1832
Finley	DeS	2-228	1884

G. W.	Cho	A-51	1897
John	Ada	2-434	1853
John	Ada	3-239	1865
John L.	Mas	P.18-137	1867
K. H.	Jef	P.B-264	1838
Sarah	Ada	1-27	1807
HOLT, Robert S.	Yaz	A-342	1867
HOMES, Charles	Yaz	B-282	1892
James	Ran	1-95	1866
HOMMEDIEU, Sylvester			
Y. L.	Ilin	1-138	1840
HOOD, Mary Ann	Smi	1-3	1894
HOOE, Nathaniel			
Harris	Nox	A-63	1844
HOOEMEYER, Sarah A.	Was	2-68	1895
HOOK, Francis H.	Wil	2-229	1865
HOOKE, Moses Josiah	Wil	2-83	1854
HOOKER, Calvin M.	Grn	A-53	1884
Nathan B.	Hol	1-229	1859
Zadock	Cop	AAA-301	1861
HOOPER, Benecy G.	Lea	1-158	1893
Icyphena M.	Yal(1)	B-66	1862
Johnson M.	Lea	1-45	1864
Mrs. V. P.	Lau	1-329	1893
HOOTSELL, John T.	Ada	2-413	1852
William	Ada	1-289	1823
HOOVER, C.	Pik	1-18	1886
Charles	Hol	1-358	1871
Thomas B.	Mad	A-225	1855
HOPKINS, Elizabeth	War	B-216	1889
John	Jef	A-105	1829
Louisa B.	Low	2-277	1900
Nathan	Nox	A-242	1856
Octave	Wil	3-41	1886
Wade Sr.	Nox	B-122	1872
William A.	War	B-67	1874
William Henry	War	B-67	1876
HOPPER, David	War	B-210	1888
John D.	Cop	A-137	1899
Susannah	Tip	1-47	1870
William M.	Tip	1-199	1897
HOPSON, G. B.	Coa(1)	1-14	1847
John	DeS	2-51	1871
Susanna	Hol	1-236	1860
HORD, Lewis	War	A-68	1836
HOREW, W. W.	Lee	1-68	1881
HORN, David S.	War	A-105	1840
Henry T.	Tal	B-94	1891
Jacob L/S	Mas	P.9-47	1853
Mary R.	Mas	1-126	1898
Mary R.	Was	2-63	1898

Preston A.	Mad	A-667	1890
Theoden	Pan(1)	B-1	1864
HORNBURGER, Elijah	Mon	I.16-155	1861
HORNE, Benjamin Green	Lea	1-56	1865
HORRELL, E. W.	Kem	A-1	1880
HORRISON, T. R.	Jef	B-184	1885
HORTON, Maria T.	Att	B-446	1885
Robertson Sr.	Grn	A-20	1878
Thomas Fitzpatrick	Yaz	B-52	1876
HORY, Isaac H.	War	A-171	1849
HOSEA, Branson D.	Ada	3-79	1856
Ephraim	Yaz	A-6	1833
HOSEY, Isaac Sr.	Jas	1-88	1890
HOSMER, Charles H.	Pik	1-114	1898
Lydia	Ada	1-188	1819
HOSSLEY, Mary Elizabeth	War	B-99	1879
HOUCK, James S.	Tun	2-64	1879
HOUGH, Joseph	Was	1-183	1853
HOUGHSON, Benjamin	Low	2-236	1899
HOULDITCH, Jane	Uni	1-13	1887
HOUSE, Delilah	Hol	1-311	1866
Elizabeth B.	Hol	1-337	1869
Howard B.	Car(1)	A-30	1842
James T.	Car(1)	A-45	1844
Theophilas	Low	1-138	1863
Wiley J.	Nes	A-102	1877
HOUSTON, A. A.	Laf	1-421	1896
Ambrose Pinkney	Pan(2)	A-109	1894
David H.	Laf	1-11	1845
E. C.	Mas	P.19-416	1870
James A.	Tal	B-36	1874
Lillie R.	Mas	1-169	1900
Lucinda C.	Tis	1-88	1896
Margaret E.	Lee	1-126	1887
Robert H.	Tal	A-205	1859
HOUZE, Isham R.	Mas	P.12-465	1857
Samuel	Hin	1-100	1837
HOWARD, Agnes P.	Grn	A-38	1879
George B.	Laf	1-128	1859
George W.	Ran	1-4	1858
Groves	Nox	A-22	1839
Joshua	Ada	1-256	1820
Louis T.	Car(1)	A-471	1865
M. L.	Low	2-178	1896
Robert	Hol	1-212	1859
Titus	Car(1)	A-140	1856
HOWE, Jabez C.	Pan(1)	B-284	1879
HOWELL, Adam R.	Hol	1-407	1877
Geo. Ann	Mad	A-631	1884
George W.	War	A-226	1855

Henry B.	Mas	1–10	1884
Henry B.	Tun	2–95	1888
James M.	Yal(1)	B–228	1895
Jane	Mas	P.16–108	1864
Lewis	Mon	1–149	1840
Nancy K.	Laf	1–430	1896
S. G.	Pan(1)	B–396	1884
HOWES, Lavinia S.	DeS	2–111	1876
HOWZE, W. D.	DeS	2–324	1890
W. J.	Clk	1–196	1897
HOY, P. B.	Mad	A–503	1870
HUBBARD, Ann L.	Wil	1–282	1844
John	Tal	B–111	1897
P. B.	Sim	A–23	1883
Vind	Clk	1–215	1899
HUBBELL, Robert A.	War	A–23	1832
HUBBLE, F. L.	Yal(1)	B–106	1865
HUBER, Edward W.	Cla	3–194	1899
HUBERT, Elizabeth	Yal(1)	B–188	1881
HUDDLESTON, A. W.	DeS	2–184	1882
William	Low	1–430	1880
HUDENREICH, Alexander	Pik	1–61	1895
HUDGINS, Abijah	Pan(1)	A–89	1850
W. H.	Low	1–300	1871
HUDLESTON, Elizabeth B.	Sco	A–464	1884
HUDNALL, Elizabeth F.	Ran	1–297	1894
Joseph	Ran	1–156	1879
HUDSON, Caleb B.	Hol	1–14	1834
Comfort T.	Mas	P.4–508	1847
E. G.	DeS	1–247	1860
James	Cly	1–74	1886
Joe	Yaz	B–400	1899
John	Nox	A–260	1857
Lawson Henderson	Lin	1–55	1899
M. H.	Laf	1–416	1895
McM.	Kem	A–17	1884
Mary J.	Car(1)	A–522	1869
Mrs. N. E.	Yaz	B–413	1900
R. J.	Nox	C–66	1898
Richard	Ada	2–245	1841
Robert S.	Yaz	B–235	1889
Sarah	DeS	2–360	1893
Thomas J.	Ben	1–31	1884
Ward	Mon	I.16–323	1863
HUDSPETH, Airs	Laf	1–8	1845
Jennie E.	Yaz	B–340	1897
Thomas J.	Yaz	B–333	1897
HUFFMAN, William	Att	2–1	1861
HUFMAN, Jno.	Car(1)	A–479	1866
HUGGINS, Matthew F.	Was	2–38	1896

HUGHES, Beverly	War (1827–1832)–1		1827
Edward W.	Grn	A–41	1873
Felix	Jef	A–81	1824
Felix	War	A–314	1862
Henry Sr.	Cop	AAA–295	1851
J. H.	Tat	1–155	1892
John	Hol	1–142	1855
Major	Nox	B–290	1884
Margaret	Jef	P.E–523	1853
Michael W.	War	B–387	1900
Nancy McKibben	Win	1–171	1896
Thomas J.	Win	1–2	1860
W. J.	Yal(2)	1–63	1890
William I.	Nox	A–24	1840
Willis L.	Nox	C–103	1899
HUGHEY, Samuel A.	DeS	1–449	1869
Sarah J.	DeS	2–18	1870
HUGULEY, Anna	Yaz	B–156	1883
HUIE, Robert	Tat	1–36	1876
HULL, Dabney H.	Coa(1)	1–219	1890
Daniel	Ada	1–159	1817
Elizabeth	Mas	P.4–22	1845
Elizabeth H.	Laf	1–303	1879
Isaac	Coa(1)	1–207	1888
Pinkard C.	Cla	3–43	1878
William	Ben	1–51	1889
HUMPHREY, John T.	Pre	1–15	1873
HUMPHREYS, D. George	Cla	3–187	1899
David George	Cla	B–346	1874
Jesse	Laf	1–381	1890
John	Coa(1)	1–28	1850
John C.	Cla	3–28	1876
John T.	Pre	1–21	1874
Mrs. M. F.	Laf	1–384	1891
Robert H.	Tun	1–310	1862
Ruth D.	Cla	B–267	1857
HUMPHRIES, Abram S.	Low	1–324	1873
Allen	Laf	1–413	1895
Eliza Tucker	Low	1–357	1873
W. W.	Low	1–413	1878
HUNDLEY, Thomas	Hin	1–362	1855
HUNDLY, John W.	Ada	1–469	1829
HUNT, Abijah	Ada	1–65	1811
Abijah	Jef	P.D–794	1851
Andrew	Ada	1–417	1828
Andrew	Jef	B–31	1859
Anna	Jef	B–183	1894
Daniel	Tip	1–94	1880
David	Jef	B–46	1861
David	Jef	B–95	1866
David	Sha	A–6	1879

Elijah	Pan(1)	A-56	1840
Eliza T.	Laf	1-240	1873
George	Jef	B-83	1864
Henry	Ada	1-116	1814
James	Mon	I.18-299	1865
James M.	War	B-205	1888
Jane	Mon	1-161	1841
Jeremiah	Ada	1-261	1821
John	Tip	1-17	1867
John H.	Mas	P.2-443	1841
Jonathan	Mas	P.12-441	1857
Margaret W.	War	B-154	1886
Martha Evelina	Tip	1-190	1894
Nathaniel	Ada	2-56	1834
William	Was	1-358	1866
William R.	Tun	2-135	1895
HUNTER, A. B.	New	1-175	1899
Bashaba	Hin	1-166	1843
Elizabeth A.	Yaz	B-201	1886
Mrs. Ghasky	Nox	A-116	1848
Isaac M.	Lau	1-1	1858
John	Ada	3-207	1863
John A.	Yaz	B-201	1886
Joseph L.	Nox	B-174	1876
Mary Ann G.	Hol	1-263	1861
Milford	Car(1)	B-5	1877
Samuel	Ada	2-1	1832
Silvanus G.	Web	A-146	1900
Thomas O.	Pan(1)	A-391	1860
W. O.	Pan(1)	B-433	1888
HUNTINGTON, Eliza W.	Ada	5-63	1894
HURD, Mary	Tal	A-45	1843
Samuel	Tal	A-65	1846
HURLBUTT, Levi	Lau	1-174	1881
HURST, Ann Eliza	Yaz	A-248	1863
Thomas	Hol	1-17	1835
HURT, Albert J.	Pan(2)	A-79	1890
Cread Lewelling	Pan(1)	A-93	1893
HUSBANDS, Elizabeth	Sim	A-33	1886
Sarah E.	Chi(1)	1-17	1879
HUSSEY, Mary E. H.	Lee	1-21	1875
HUSTON, Andrew J.	War	B-307	1895
Eli	Ada	2-107	1835
Felix	Ada	3-92	1857
Hannah	Ada	3-366	1869
James	Ada	1-166	1818
HUTCHENSEN, William	Lau	1-192	1882
HUTCHERSON, Richard	Mon	I.15-26	1859
HUTCHINGS, Thomas	Win	1-86&90	1877
HUTCHINS, Ann	Ada	1-71	1811
Eliza	Ada	4-1	1871

J. J.	Lea	1-156	1893
James	Cla	B-232	1853
John	Ada	2-466	1853
R. E.	Was	1-480	1889
R. M.	Hin	B-422	1892
Samuel	Ada	1-91	1812
Thomas J.	Cla	3-171	1896
HUTCHISON, Robert	Win	1-42	1866
HUTCHISON, W. B.	Lee	1-79	1883
HYATT, C. J.	Tis	1-89	1897
Christopher Columbus	Lef	A-145	1899
Leonard L.	Yaz	A-289	1865
HYDE, Jesse	Jas	1-66	1876
John G.	Nox	A-274	1859
HYLAND, Eve	War	A-17	1831
HYNES, John	War	A-296	1861
M. T.	War	A-355	1866
HYNSON, Ringgold	Cla	B-263	1856
HYSLAPS, Samuel	Wil	3-38	1886
ILER, Abram	Wil	1-120	1835
INCISA, Ella	Was	1-412	1880
INGATE, Clarence			
Louis Adrian	Chi(2)	1-97	1900
INGERSOLL, William K.	War	B-200	1888
INGLE, Albenis	Han	A-295	1896
INGRAM, Jeremiah Sr.	Mas	P.12-75	1856
Jeremiah Sr.	Mas	P.13-12	1857
John	Nox	B-141	1873
John I.	DeS	2-348	1892
John U.	Yal(1)	B-12	1858
Joshia O.	Cla	B-336	1871
Thomas	Mas	P.19-19	1869
INMAN, Mrs. L. A.	Wil	3-95	1892
William E.	Tal	B-4	1867
IRADALE, Thomas A.	DeS	1-388	1866
IRBY, Caroline	Tat	1-202	1895
Charles	Yaz	A-155	1852
Francis M.	Nox	A-191	1854
Freeman B.	Pan(1)	B-223	1877
James Jackson	Sha	A-4	1878
John	Ada	2-132	1836
John H.	Low	1-242	1867
Maria L.	Pan(2)	A-60	1886
IRELAND, Martha	Ada	4-208	1882
IRION, McKinney	Low	1-134	1862
McKinney Sr.	Low	1-239	1866
IRISH, Ann E.	Cla	B-163	1840
George	Cla	A-327	1836
Henry T.	Was	1-88	1846
IRVINE, J. W.	Ada	5-160	1897

John S.	War	A-122	1841
Mary	Ada	3-55	1856
Mary	Jef	A-68	1820
Walter Sr.	Ada	2-181	1839
IRVING, John	Att	C-528	1871
John	Isa	C-139	1885
IRWIN, David	Yaz	A-56	1841
H. F.	Yaz	B-170	1884
Hugh	Jef	A-123	1805
Mary	Jef	A-68	1820
ISAM, A. J.	Lai	1-282	1877
ISOM, John	Mas	P.9-272	1853
IVES, John	Wil	2-154	1860
IVEY, Caroline V.	Ada	2-118	1835
Edward	Lee	1-215	1900
Laura Helen	Ada	2-245	1842
Samuel	Ada	2-93	1834
IVEYS, Mary E.	Hol	3-96	1900
IVY, Henry	Laf	1-190	1869
J. W.	Mas	1-29	1894
IZSON, Martha O.	Pan(1)	A-61	1848
JACKSON, A. S.	Yal(1)	B-222	1893
Albert W.	Tat	1-163	1893
Alexander Morgan	Nox	B-27	1862
Alford	Tip	1-180	1892
C. B.	Tat	1-11	1875
Cavil O.	War	A-223	1855
Chelly B.	Yaz	B-257	1891
David H.	Hin	1-314	1853
Delia J.	DeS	2-79	1873
Isabella	Tat	1-99	1887
Isaac	Hol	1-11	1835
Jathro M.	Mon	I.13-415	1857
James	Ada	1-313	1824
Jefferson	Mar	A2-17	1898
John L.	Tat	1-98	1887
John N.	Mas	P.4-509	1847
Joseph	Hol	1-447	1880
Maria J.	Ada	5-5	1892
Martha A. E.	War	A-246	1858
Mary	Hin	1-266	1851
Mary E.	Ada	4-448	1887
Mary E.	Lin	1-59	1900
Rhoda	Tip	1-48	1870
Robert R.	Pan(1)	A-422	1861
Samuel A.	Att	C-366	1894
William	DeS	1-410	1866
William L.	Ada	5-99	1896
JACOBS, Walter	Hin	1-20	1833
Walter	Yaz	A-2	1832

JAMAQUN, H. L.	Nox	B–306	1886
JAMES, Daniel L.	Hol	1–499	1888
Isaac	Nes	A–109	1880
John	Jas	1–53	1865
London	Mad	A–665	1890
Nancy	Wil	2–304	1875
Patrick	Gre	1–13&15	1894
Peter	Hol	3–97	1900
Peter	Yaz	B–412	1900
S. L.	Yaz	B–415	1900
Samuel L.	Hol	3–101	1900
Samuel L.	Yaz	B–231	1889
Thomas J.	Cop	A–9	1887
JAMESON, Albert	Mon	I.5–192	1886
JAMISON, George	Nox	B–218	1878
R.	Tat	1–212	1896
Stephen W.	Att	2–428	1864
William E.	Pan(1)	B–200	1875
JANIN, Benjamin	Ada	2–191	1839
JANUARY, Philip B.	Jef	B–216	1899
JARMAN, Larkin Thomas	DeS	1–344	1865
JARRATT, Nathaniel R.	Mas	P.15–407	1862
JEFFERIES, Lucy R.	Cla	3–91	1884
William	Mas	P.8–339	1852
JEFFERSON, Peterfield	Hin	1–296	1852
JEFFRESS, Albert G.	Clk	1–165	1893
R. T.	Tat	1–245	1900
JEFFRIES, Charles H.	Nox	B–377	1891
Curtis M.	Coa(1)	1–22	1852
Francis A.	Nox	B–345	1890
Susan J.	DeS	2–381	1894
William R.	Laf	1–186	1863
JEFFRESS, Richard J.			
Jr.	DeS	1–452	1869
JELKS, Discon	Hin	1–15	1833
JELL, Thomas H.	War	B–30	1873
JEMISON, Susan	Low	1–370	1874
JENCKS, John	Wil	1–167	1837
JENKINS, Benjamin	Lau	1–374	1897
Elias	War	B–163	1886
James	DeS	2–251	1885
James T.	Kem	A–18	1885
John B.	Mad	A–505	1870
John C.	Ada	3–23	1855
M. C.	Kem	A–36	1889
Robert Bowman	Hol	3–75	1899
Robert C.	Hol	1–398	1876
Walter	Mas	P.17–50	1866
Walter S.	Mas	P.11–131	1855
William	Nox	B–103	1871
William M.	War	A–368	1867

JENNI, Benjamin	Ada	2-191	1839
JENNINGS, Arteman	Low	1-262	1869
Franklin H.	Att	B-387	1884
J. T.	Yaz	B-229	1888
James	Mon	1-231	1846
John	Cla	A-282	1833
Peggy	Hin	B-395	1889
Pheby	DeS	1-21	1852
Robert	Pan(1)	A-299	1858
Washington	Grn	A-65	1884
JETER, George W.	Cla	B-193	1846
H. M.	Tat	1-61	1883
JEWELL, Alexander M.	Was	2-5	1894
John D.	Was	2-43	1897
Robert George Washington	Pik	1-46	1892
JIGGITTS, David E.	Mad	A-654	1888
Lewis M.	Mad	A-424&430	1869
Lewis M. Jr.	Mad	A-494	1869
JINKINS, Elias	Mon	I.2-342	1876
JOBE, W. S.	Low	2-189	1897
JOHNS, Mary A. R.	Wil	2-354	1879
Sarah	Yaz	B-124	1880
Thomas	Wil	3-67	1889
JOHNSEY, John	Mon	I.6-176	1892
JOHNSON, Mrs. A. F.	Chi(2)	1-57	1893
Abraham	Coa(1)	1-70	1859
Albert G.	Hin	1-387	1856
Alfred M.	Yaz	A-228	1859
Amon	Mad	A-487	1868
Andrew J.	Yaz	B-259	1891
Ann	Mot	1-158	1899
Apsey K.	Hin	B-257	1867
Benjamin	Lea	1-65	1871
Benjamin W.	Yaz	A-325	1865
Mrs. C. C.	Hol	1-195	1859
Catherine	Ada	3-217	1865
David H.	Pre	1-41	1879
Edward P.	Was	1-372	1867
Eleanora	Yaz	B-23	1872
Eliza P.	Hol	1-249	1860
Emily D.	Mad	2-134	1899
F. W.	Win	1-182	1899
Francis	Ada	1-57	1810
G. M.	Laf	2-61	1900
H. P.	Att	B-433	1884
Harriet	War	B-331	1897
Harry H.	Pon	2-29	1841
Henry	Was	1-346	1865
Hughey	Hol	1-161	1856
Isaac	Wil	1-31	1833

Isreal P.	Mon	I.8–141	1852
J. H.	Clk	1–87	1885
James	DeS	1–340	1865
James H.	Hol	1–247	1860
James O.	Web	A–76	1889
James W.	Was	1–367	1866
Jessee	War	A–228	1856
John	Nox	A–23	1840
John	Yaz	A–207	1856
John C.	Att	D–175	1899
John C.	Cla	B–217	1851
Joseph	Wil	2–27	1848
Judeth N.	Hol	1–455	1882
Julia H.	Was	1–476	1889
Lourain	Yaz	B–98	1879
M. C.	Fra	A–10	1887
M. D.	Tat	1–30	1877
M. D.	Tun	2–119	1891
M. Laura	Pan(1)	B–103	1871
Martha	Was	2–108	1899
Mary Jane	Tis	1–97	1898
Milly	Wil	2–345	1877
Moses J.	Mas	P.12–415	1857
Nancy	Yal(1)	B–235	1897
Rebecca M.	Nox	A–287	1860
Richard M.	Yaz	B–104	1879
S. L.	Tat	1–242	1899
Samuel C.	Low	2–60	1892
Thomas	Ran	B.1–180	1844
Thomas J.	Yal(1)	A–255	1854
Thomas Jefferson	Mot	1–90	1887
Thornton N.	Yaz	A–306	1865
W. B.	Win	1–148	1894
W. D.	Hol	1–444	1881
W. T.	Yal(2)	1–88	1895
Warren H.	Nox	B–1	1861
William C.	Laf	1–93	1855
William C.	War	B–70	1877
William E.	War	B–193	1888
William P.	Tip	1–36	1868
William R.	Yaz	A–139	1849
JOHNSTON, Ann	Nox	A–234	1857
David	Ada	1–63	1806
Ellen	Yaz	B–367	1898
Francis	Yaz	B–115	1880
G. W.	War	A–318	1862
Gideon	Hin	1–302	1852
Isacks	DeS	2–487	1899
Isacks	Tun	2–171	1899
James	Han	A–70	1872
Jennie	Low	2–270	1900

John	Att	A–569	1861
Mary	DeS	1–299	1862
Mary	Yal(1)	B–30	1859
Ruth S.	Laf	1–375	1887
Samuel	DeS	2–280	1887
Samuel	Yaz	B–31	1873
Stephen D.	DeS	1–338	1865
T. J.	Yaz	A–273	1863
Vernon H.	Hin	B–153	1862
Walter R.	Mad	A–1	1829
William	Car(1)	A–1	1834
William	DeS	2–137	1878
William J.	DeS	2–491	1899
JOHNSTONE, Margaret			
L.	Mad	A–598	1880
JOINER, Allena R.	Lef	A–109	1893
Joshua	Nox	B–106	1871
JOLLY, Ida	Chi(2)	1–70	1890
John Henry	Hol	1–41	1843
JONES, A. B.	Okt	1–49	1885
A. J.	Yal(2)	1–122	1899
Albertine	Grn	A–131	1898
Alfred M.	Hol	1–110	1851
Ann R.	Mon	1–237	1846
Augusta	Car(1)	B–59	1898
B. W.	Web	A–107	1895
Ben	Lef	A–80	1883
Benjamin F.	Jef	B–39	1860
Cabe M.	Mon	I.6–476	1895
Catherine	War	B–120	1880
Charles	Car(1)	A–493	1867
Clinton	Hol	1–208	1859
David	Pan(1)	A–66	1849
Dora	Mas	1–117	1897
Dorothy C.	Hol	1–76	1847
Dudley	Nes	A–75	1865
Elijah	Ran	B.1–331	1847
Elijah C.	New	1–110	1891
Eliza C.	Lee	1–113	1888
Elizabeth	Ada	4–487	1889
Elizabeth	Nox	B–335	1888
Elizabeth J.	Cly	1–116	1893
Ellen F.	Ben	1–30	1879
Enoch S.	Gre	1–9	1884
Gaden	Nox	A–81	1846
George	Cla	A–285	1833
Harriet M.	Cop	A–84	1892
Henry Spratley	Laf	2–6	1898
Hill	Mad	A–105	1846
J. B.	Cop	A–132	1899
J. C. H.	Nox	C–147	1900

J. L.	Pan(1)	B-332	1880
James	Pre	1-31	1876
James	Mas	P.15-75	1861
James Sr.	Low	1-288	1870
Jane	Cla	3-177	1897
Jane T.	Mas	P.5-396	1848
Jeremiah	Cop	AAA-291	1832
Joel W.	Nox	B-190	1876
John	Att	B-464	1886
John	Cla	A-269	1833
John	Jef	A-73	1821
John	Wil	1-7	1830
John	Yaz	A-43	1838
John C.	Ada	1-341	1825
John H.	Mas	P.18-474	1868
John J.	Hin	B-149	1862
John W.	Hin	1-64	1835
Jonathan	Jef	A-20	1814
Jordan	Ran	1-122	1873
Joseph	Hin	1-269	1851
Joseph E.	Cla	B-222	1852
Judith B.	Mad	A-315	1857
Levi N.	Yaz	A-83	1845
Lewis	Laf	1-96	1855
Malinda	Ada	5-65	1894
Martha B.	Low	1-352	1873
Montfort	Mad	A-570	1876
Montfort Sr.	Att	D-67	1898
Montfort Sr.	Mad	2-143	1900
Moses	Nes	A-53	1858
Nancy	Ran	1-172	1882
Nancy	Was	1-513	1893
Ned	Coa(2)	1-13	1892
Pauline Jane	Pan(1)	B-78	1870
R. D.	Mas	1-107	1897
Ralph Stovall	Hin	B-447	1898
Reubin T.	Grn	A-61	1884
Robert	Ada	1-19	1805
Rufus	Mas	P.12-339	1857
S. B.	Hol	1-445	1881
Sallie	Mas	1-116	1897
Samuel B.	Lef	A-146	1899
Seaborn	Car(1)	A-148	1857
Susan L.	Grn	A-19	1877
Susanah	Cla	A-84	1819
Susanah	Pre	1-73	1888
Tamsey	War	B-45	1874
Terrel	Pan(1)	B-306	1879
Thomas	Yaz	A-244	1860
W. L.	Was	1-494	1892
W. T.	DeS	1-33	1852

Wachael	Pan(1)	A-47	1848
William	DeS	2-320	1889
William	Mas	P.12-311	1857
William	Mot	1-127	1896
William A. Sr.	Pan(1)	B-163	1875
William E.	Clk	1-116	1890
William M.	Mon	I.7-642	1852
William S.	Lee	1-96	1886
William Smith	Hin	B-111	1861
William T	Wil	2-74	1852
William Watts	Yaz	A-73	1844
Willie	Mad	A-666	1890
Willis W.	Pan(1)	A-154	1853
JOOR, Emily	Wil	2-214	1864
John	Wil	1-154	1836
JOPLING, Jesse	Hin	1-85	1837
Thomas	Hin	1-83	1837
JORDAN, Charles C.	Ran	1-103	1868
Eliza F.	Lea	1-165	1895
Frederic W.	Clk	1-49	1881
James E.	Mas	P.12-384	1857
Judith E.	Low	1-558	1888
Margaret L.	Lea	1-73	1874
Susan	Jef	P.C-131	1842
William M.	Clk	1-217	1896
JOSEPH, Edward	Wil	2-411	1882
JOSLIN, John	Laf	1-36	1850
William	DeS	1-380	1866
JOYCE, Eskaline M.	Hol	3-80	1899
John Franklin	Han	B-31	1900
Luella C.	Car(2)	1-53	1889
William	Car(2)	1-73	1894
JOYES, Clarence	Was	1-426	1881
JOYNER, A. C.	Laf	1-185	1866
Benjamin H.	Pan(1)	A-19	1847
Elizabeth E.	Laf	1-149	1864
Elizabeth E.	Laf	1-179	1863
Maria L.	DeS	2-342	1891
Turner	Was	1-212	1855
William	Tun	2-108	1889
JUDGE, Hill	Jas	1-82	1884
JULIENNE, Claiborne	War	B-120	1880
JUNGHERR, Theodore	Hin	B-199	1866
JUNKIN, Sarah A.	Ada	5-218	1898
JURTH, Emit	Coa(1)	1-208	1883
JUST, Annie Catherine	War	B-297	1894
KAIGLE, Esaias	Wil	1-1	1825
KAIGLER, Elizabeth H.	Wil	1-222	1840
Henry	Car(2)	1-32	1885
Vandy V.	Wil	2-295	1875

KAIN, John R.	War	A-202	1853
KANATZE, Nellie	Was	1-428	1882
KANE, John J.	War	B-369	1899
KANN, Joseph	Wil	1-267	1844
KARPE, Anchel	Mad	2-76	1897
KARR, Joseph	Ada	1-174	1818
KATZENAMER, Jacob	War	B-48	1874
KATZMEIR, Nicholas	War	A-263	1860
KAVANAUGH, Maggie	Coa(1)	1-221	1890
KAY, F. Marion	Tis	1-9	1887
KAYES, Michael	Yaz	B-178	1884
KEAN, John	Low	1-415	1879
KEARNEY, Edmund	Jef	B-204	1898
Oscar D.	Mad	A-454	1867
KEARSEY, John Kinchen	Mad	2-115	1898
KEATING, James	Ada	1-300	1823
KEEGAN, A. M.	Law	P.B-91	1838
KEEL, John	Laf	1-236	1873
KEELER, Oscar T.	Low	1-291	1870
KEELING, Edward A.	Mas	P.8-435	1852
KEEN, Elizabeth O.	War	A-72	1837
KEENE, Lawrence	Ada	4-355	1885
Margaret A.	Mon	I.6-305	1894
KEEP, Henry V.	Isa	C-137	1884
KEES, M. V.	Lin	1-51	1898
KEIRNAN, John	Ada	4-514	1890
KEITH, William B.	New	1-19	1879
KELLEHAR, Dennis	Ada	1-347	1825
KELLER, Thomas	Cop	AAA-287	1839
KELLOGG, Adam	War	B-352	1898
George W.	Ada	2-206	1840
Mary Ann	Wil	1-241	1841
Mason Bartlett	Isa	C-165	1900
KELLUM, Bowdoin	Hin	1-89	1837
KELLY, C. Clay	Att	C-320	1893
Chauncy S.	Wil	1-179	1837
George	Yal(1)	B-237	1897
James	Car(1)	A-43	1844
James	Jef	P.D-582	1847
James F.	Hin	1-171	1843
James G.	Yal(1)	B-196	1882
James I.	DeS	2-231	1884
John	Tun	1-264	1860
John E.	Hin	B-54	1860
Joseph	Yal(1)	B-2	1858
Laura V.	Att	C-320	1893
Littleton	Hin	1-241	1849
Mary Ann	Hol	1-415	1877
Obadiah K.	Hin	1-235	1849
Parthenia M.	Hin	B-325	1876
Patrick	Ada	1-48	1809

Peter	Ada	4-286	1883
Samuel D.	Hin	B-309	1875
T. C.	Lee	1-76	1883
William Sims	Yaz	B-198	1885
KEMP, John	Clk	1-45	1883
Simeon	Hol	1-91	1849
KEMPER, James	Nox	A-14	1838
KENDALL, James B.	Mon	I.8-209	1852
KENDRICK, J. W.	Pre	1-57	1884
KENIONS, Stephen	Ada	1-65	1811
KENLY, Phebe A.	Cla	B-196	1847
KENNAN, Thomas	War	B-209	1888
KENNEDY, Alfred	Chi(2)	1-55	1891
Eugene A.	Car(1)	A-134	1853
Jesse	Cly	1-7	1873
John	Lau	1-106	1874
John J.	Was	2-113	1899
Joseph	Mas	P.2-88	1840
Maggie	Was	2-26	1896
Stephen	Ada	3-9	1855
William P.	Jas	1-61	1870
KENNER, Daniel F.	Hin	1-209	1847
KENNON, Martha	Ran	1-154	1877
KENT, E. B.	Mot	1-51	1881
Elias J.	Ada	3-262	1865
Nancy	Car(1)	B-18	1886
Smith H.	Mot	1-56	1882
KER, Mary	Ada	3-211	1863
KERCHEVAL, James	Ada	1-159	1817
KERLIN, Mary V.	Jef	B-172	1890
KERR, John	Cho	A-26	1892
John	DeS	2-22	1870
John	Kem	A-15	1884
Miller	Tun	1-517	1869
William	Yal(1)	A-32	1841
KERSHAW, Francis R.	Was	1-21	1842
KERU, Henry	Ada	4-21	1873
KESBY, H. C.	Chi (1863-1872)-61		1864
KETHLEY, Bryan	Cop	A-80	1892
KETTERINGHAM, Francis	Ada	2-455	1853
KEY, Drusilla	Cla	B-287	1859
John D.	DeS	1-58	1853
Thomas J.	Pan(1)	B-227	1877
KEYES, Sylvesta C.	Cla	B-296	1860
William T.	Cop	AAA-283	1863
Joseph Meek	Car(1)	A-151	1857
KIBBE, Elizabeth K.	Ada	2-353	1848
KIBBEE, Tennessee	Mad	A-132	1849
KICKER, Archibald M.	Jef	P.C-487	1844
KIDD, Henry B.	Yaz	B-74	1877
John B.	Low	1-305	1871

Thomas	Hin	B–360	1885
William	Low	1–297	1870
KIERNERY, Solomon	Ben	1–62	1885
KILBORN, James B.	Hin	1–82	1837
KILCREASE, Mary T.	Cop	AAA–279	1846
KILGARIF, Bernard	War	B–382	1900
KILGORE, Althea Lois	Laf	1–268	1876
Benjamin	Chi (1863–1872)–44		1865
KILLEBREW, Edwin	Hol	1–86	1849
Henry B.	Coa(1)	1–91	1866
James S.	Coa(1)	1–53	1857
William B.	Coa(1)	1–109	1868
KILLIAN, Max	Isa	C–161	1899
KILLINGSWORTH, Anon			
W.	Jef	B–151	1880
Cidic N.	Jef	P.G–276	1857
James A.	Jef	P.G–279	1857
Jane	Jef	P.G–269	1857
Noel	Jef	A–111	1831
KILLOUGH, Jesse R. J.	Mas	P.15–553	1862
KILPATRICK, Atha	Pan(1)	B–119	1872
Joshua W.	Mon	1–148	1840
William	Cly	1–19	1876
KIMBALL, Leonard	Han	A–158	1885
KIMBLE, James	Yal(1)	B–199	1882
KIMBROUGH, Marmaduke			
D.	Car(1)	A–63	1848
KIMLEY, Samuel A.	Ada	2–65	1834
KINCAID, Andy	Yaz	B–145	1882
Carrie B.	Nox	C–22	1897
Celia	Yaz	B–155	1883
William A.	Nox	C–22	1897
KING, Anthony	Tal	A–327	1867
Edmund	Cop	AAA–277	1840
Elizabeth	Cla	B–179	1843
Elizabeth E.	Car(1)	A–57	1846
Hiram	Ran	1–240	1891
J. Munro	Hin	1–401	1857
James	Car(1)	A–20	1841
James	War	B–68	1877
James D.	Pan(1)	A–29	1847
John W.	Coa(1)	1–67	1859
John	War	B–212	1889
John D.	Ran	1–70	1865
Mikael	Tal	B–27	1871
Nancy H.	Cop	AAA–268	1857
Prosper	Ada	1–389	1827
Richard M.	Chi (1863–1872)–15		1863
Samuel	Ada	2–302	1845
Samuel	Ran	B.1–17	1840
William	Ada	1–45	1809

William	Ada	1-405	1806
William	Cla	A-31	1808
William	Jef	A-33	1818
William	Nox	A-245	1857
William A.	Hol	1-210	1859
William R.	Car(1)	A-450	1862
KINKADE, Robert B.	Car(1)	A-123	1854
KINNARD, David T.	Nox	B-59	1864
KINNEY, Catherine	Tun	2-228	1900
James	Tip	1-143	1888
KINSEY, Abraham	Ada	2 305	1845
KIRBY, Sarah	Car(1)	A-152	1857
KIRK, James	Yaz	A-14	1835
John	Mon	1-201	1838
John R.	Ada	2-168	1838
Susan	Ada	1-44	1809
Thomas J.	Yaz	B-291	1893
KIRKLAND, A.	Jef	A-106	1829
J. T.	War	B-220	1889
Jane	Jef	P.D-570	1849
KIRKMAN, Thomas	Yal(1)	B-111	1866
KIRKPATRICK, J. G.	Mad	A-403	1864
KIRKWOOD, Robert	Car(1)	A-517	1868
William	Car(1)	A-146	1858
William C.	Laf	1-356	1886
KIRSH, Allen D.	Ran	1-74	1865
KIRVEN, Susan E.	War	B-136	1882
KISTLER, Abraham	Pre	1-93	1890
KITCHEN, Eliza	Hol	3-43	1896
KITTREL, John	Pan(1)	A-104	1851
KIZER, John C.	Mas	P.13-147	1858
KLAUS, David	Sha	A-14	1891
KLEIN, Isaac	Lau	1-401	1899
John A.	War	B-144	1883
Madison C.	War	A-337	1863
Samuel Sr.	Low	2-228	1898
KLOTZ, Frank	Cop	A-15	1888
KNAPP, Cyrus S.	Hin	B-284	1873
KNAPPER, Daniel	Sha	A-1	1877
KNEELAND, John	Ami	1-258	1817
KNIGHT, Charles	Ada	3-32	1855
Isabella	Wil	1-108	1834
John C.	Yal(2)	1-117	1898
KNOTT, David A.	Tal	A-146	1853
KNOWLES, Lewis	Mon	1-221	1844
Samuel	Lee	1-99	1887
KNOWLLON, John	Cla	A-89	1819
KNOX, Absalom	Pan(1)	A-194	1855
Ambrose	Was	1-280	1860
Archibald	Ami	1-168	1816
Robert E.	Grn	A-55	1884

KNUDSON, S.	Pik	1-108	1898
KNUT, Lily Barret	Ada	5-213	1898
KOCH, C. D. T.	Han	A-242	1894
KOEHLER, Gottfried	Ada	3-161	1860
KOGER, Joseph	Nox	B-77	1866
Thomas J.	Nox	B-24	1862
KOHLMAN, Delphine	Cop	A-112	1896
KOLB, Milton	Low	1-521	1880
Newton	Low	1-464	1883
W. B.	Low	2-97	1895
KOONTZ, George			
Washington	Ada	4-95	1876
Mary R.	Ada	5-89	1895
KORBER, Louis	Ada	3-129	1859
William	Hin	1-277	1851
KOTHE, Karl	Wil	2-391	1881
KRAMER, Christian G.	Cop	A-105	1895
KRANKEY, Hines	Han	A-173	1887
KRAUSE, August	Wil	2-160	1859
KREBS, Marie D.	Jac	1-109	1892
Rene	Jac	1-109	1892
KRECKER, J. P. Jr.	Low	1-441	1880
John P.	Low	2-134	1896
KROUSE, Adrian	Clk	1-211	1899
T. J. Sr.	Clk	1-213	1899
KUHN, Alexander	War	B-228	1889
Jacob	Lea	1-118	1884
KUSEEKER, Andrew P.	Was	1-486	1890
KUYKENDALL, W. H.	Mon	I.1-125	1871
KYKENDALL, Anthony C.	Grn	A-111	1895
KYLE, Caroline	Ada	5-232	1899
Charlotte C.	Hol	3-17	1895
Christopher	Ada	1-419	1827
David	Hol	1-442	1881
Gideon	Cop	AAA-263	----
John	Mad	A-366	1862
Rufus C.	Tun	2-177	1899
LABAUVE, Felix	DeS	2-148	1879
LABENBERGE, Regina	Cla	3-183	1899
LABROUSE, Mathew	Lau	1-13	1858
LACAZE, Bernard	Ada	1-161	1816
LACEY, Abbie R.	Yaz	B-162	1883
LACK, Abner	Sco	A-314	1869
LACKEY, William	Lee	1-189	1897
William L. L.	Cla	3-59	1879
LACKLAND, John J.	Hin	B-201	1866
LACOCK, Sarah A.	Grn	A-81	1888
LACOSTE, Mary E.	Ada	4-93	1874
LACY, James	Jac	1-32	1884
John B.	Pon	1-152	1839

Nancy	Pre	1-29	1876
Stephen	Mas	P.2-578	1842
LADD, Jane E.	Low	1-456	1882
LADER, Leander	Han	A-145	1883
LADNER, Bazile Sr.	Han	P.(1853–1860)-530	1856
Carlos	Han	A-131	1881
Francois	Han	P.(1853–1860)-16	1853
LAFITTE, Auguste	Han	P.(1853–1860)-182	1853
LAFFITO, Clarice	Han	P.(1853–1860)-679	1857
LAGRONE, Adam	Mon	I.3-85	1878
Christiner	Nox	B-64	1865
William	Car(1)	A-104	1852
William	Chi(2)	1-95	1896
LAIRD, Martha C.	Mon	I.7-37	1898
Thomas H.	Mon	I.7-34	1898
LAKE, Anna Ernestine	Jef	B-197	1897
George A.	Jef	B-180	1894
William A.	War	A-306	1861
LAKEMON, Francis M.	War	A-343	1865
LAMAR, Mack	Ada	1-246	1821
LAMAS, Sarah	Jac	1-38	1885
LAMB, G. A.	Was	2-129	1900
John	Web	A-1	1874
Jonathan	Yaz	A-126	1848
Mary	Yal(1)	A-209	1852
Theopolus	Hin	B-339	1879
LAMBERT, A. B.	Lee	1-83	1884
John	War	A-203	1853
Samuel	Ben	1-32	1884
William	Mad	A-554	1873
LAMBETH, John S.	Mon	I.12-670	1857
William L.	Yaz	A-141	1851
LAMBRIGHT, George	Cop	AAA-260	1835
LAMBUTH, James William	Mad	2-20	1892
LAMKIN, David W.	War	B-127	1879
Martha E.	War	B-212	1887
LAMMEY, John	Laf	1-119	1856
John	Win	1-40	1866
LAMMOND, Hugh	Yaz	B-336	1897
LANCASTER, Hiram	Web	A-102	1893
LAND, A. B.	Kem	A-86	1900
David C.	Hin	1-374	1856
Mahuldah	Hol	1-175	1857
Martha	War	B-1	1868
LANDEN, D. C.	Mad	A-596	1880
LANDERS, Elizabeth	Jef	B-134	1875
John	Chi(2)	1-84	1899
M. E.	Tip	1-97	1881
LANDSFORD, James T.	Yal(1)	A-107	1845
LANE, Ann	Mas	P.8-365	1852

Edward M.	War	A-274	1860
F. A.	DeS	1-6	1852
Joseph	Laf	1-112	1856
Joseph E.	Mad	A-633	1885
Joseph I.	War (1823-1827)-102		1824
N. V.	War	B-332	1897
Thomas	Ami	1-125	1814
William	Cla	A-116	1821
LANEHART, Hansford	Wil	2-216	1863
LANEY, W. E.	Lee	1-132	1891
LANGDON, Keziah	Ada	3-101	1857
LANGFORD, David	Mad	A-15	1833
John T.	Yal(2)	1-76	1893
Lorenzo Dow	Yaz	B-280	1892
Martha	Yal(2)	1-114	1896
LANGHORN, James C.	Mad	A-64	1841
LANGLEY, W. G.	Jac	1-1	1876
Willis W.	Hin	B-246	1868
LANGSTON, John M.	Laf	2-72	1900
Joseph	DeS	1-304	1862
LANIER, Elizabeth P.	Low	1-445	1881
LANIGAN, Mary	War	B-184	1887
LANGFORD, Peter L.	Pan(1)	A-156	1853
LANZA, Dominique De La	Han P.(1853-1860)-156		1853
LAPE, John	Ada	1-161	1817
LATHAM, A. R.	PRi	1-4	1898
Abraham	War	B-51	1874
Edward	Han	A-141	1882
Lorenzo	Mad	A-75	1843
LATHROP, Fannie E. B.	War	B-287	1893
LAUDERBACK, Andrew	Cla	B-204	1849
LAUDERDALE, D. C.	DeS	1-414	1867
John G.	DeS	2-186	1882
William	Nox	B-45	1863
LAUDERMILK, Martha S.	Laf	2-3	1897
LAUGHERY, William	Ada	1-5	1803
LAUGHLIN, Alexander	Tal	A-224	1860
Florida Davis	War	B-253	1891
Mary Ann	War	B-46	1874
LAUPAT, John H.	Mas	P.4-109	1845
LAURENCE, Elizabeth	Cop	AAA-257	1856
LAVAZZA, Elizabeth	War	A-329	1865
LAVENDER, Robert S.	DeS	1-62	1853
LAW, William	Mad	2-82	1897
LAWHON, William	Hin	1-67	1836
LAWLER, Eli	Coa(1)	1-60	1858
LAWRENCE, H. N.	Low	1-555	1888
H. N.	Nox	B-354	1888
Horace	Laf	1-61	1851
John	Yal(1)	A-71	1839

Sarah Frances	Cly	1-117	1895
LAWS, Lot W.	Low	1-157	1864
LAWSON, Charles M.	War (1827-1832)-81		1827
Hugh A. H.	Mad	A-329	1860
William H.	Was	1-207	1855
LAYNE, Eleanor	Car(1)	B-2	1876
LAZUELY, J. J.	Sim	A-22	1872
LEA, Addison	Mon	I.15-157	1863
Calvin	Yaz	A-105	1846
Lewis V.	DeS	2-70	1872
William	Hin	1-11	1833
LEACHMAN, Robert E.	Lau	1-127	1879
LEAK, F. T.	Tip	1-5	1866
Martha J.	Ben	1-13	1870
LEAKE, William J.	Yaz	A-333	1867
LEAKIN, Mary L.	Ada	3-166	1861
LEARY, Patrick O.	War	A-366	1867
LEATHERBERRY, Susan W.	War	B-258	1891
William	War	A-357	1866
LEATHERMAN, Daniel	Wil	1-260	1843
Daniel J.	Wil	2-5	1846
George W.	Tun	2-4	1872
Nancy	Wil	2-252	1867
LEATHERS, Thomas P.	Ada	5-137	1897
LEAVEL, Emily S.	Ran	1-50	1863
LEAVELL, Mrs. M. L.	Laf	2-13	1898
Rhoda	Hin	B-167	1863
LEBLANC, Joseph J.	Pik	1-143	1900
LECORRE, Paul	Yaz	B-45	1875
LEDBETTER, H. V. M.	Isa	A-4	1846
Richard	Yaz	B-68	1877
Susan H.	Lee	1-151	1892
T. W. Jr.	Pre	1-94	1893
Tazwell W.	Pre	1-103	1896
LEDUC, Henry	Han	A-309	1897
LEE, A. J.	Hin	1-382	1856
A. J. Sr.	Kem	A-42	1891
Andrew	Tal	A-166	1855
Benjamin A.	War	B-52	1875
Elizabeth Mary	Mad	A-291	1859
George H.	Low	1-312	1871
Hattie M.	War	B-9	1870
J. P.	Yaz	B-311	1896
James	Lau	1-418	1900
James	Mad	A-92	1844
Lewis	Was	1-512	1893
Margaret N.	Tal	B-7	1868
Mary Ann	Sha	A-17	1892
Ransom	DeS	2-400	1894
Robert E.	Ran	B.1-178	1844

Sherrod	Hin	1-56	1835
LEECH, Elbert E.	Low	2-1	1889
James	Wil	1-150	1836
LEFLORE, Greenwood	Car(1)	A-473	1865
Louis	Hol	1-1	1834
LEFLWICH, Littleberry	Mas	P.5-88	1847
LEGG, Pleasant C.	Coa(2)	1-16	1893
LEGGETT, Absalom	Hin	1-65	1835
Margaret	Web	A-126	1898
Mary	Ada	4-144	1879
LEGRAND, Alexander	War	B-359	1899
LEHAN, Margaret	War	B-246	1890
LEHMAN, Mayor	Yaz	B-345	1897
LEIB, John Frederick	Pik	1-39	1891
LEIGH, A. C.	Yal(1)	A-180	1850
J. E.	Low	2-47	1891
James Henry	Pan(2)	A-57	1885
John T.	Yal(1)	A-160	1850
Richard H.	Yal(1)	A-112	1847
Robert E.	Low	1-111	1862
LEITCH, Fannie W.	Mad	A-579	1879
LELAND, Alice F.	Yal(2)	1-124	1899
LEMLE, Sarah	Ada	4-480	1889
LEMLY, Jane	Coa(1)	1-188	1886
LENNERD, C. L.	Att	C-350	1893
LENOIR, Naomi	Han	A-11	1866
William T.	Mar	A1-142	1845
LENYER, Moses	Tun	2-175	1899
LEONARD, Charles	Mas	P.11-249	1856
Israel	Ada	2-186	1839
Jacob	Mas	P.13-559	1858
Jonah	Lea	1-27	1859
Thomas S.	Tat	1-103	1888
LEROY, John	Cla	B-269	1857
LESLEY, James	Was	1-195	1838
LESSEL, John L.	Yaz	B-261	1891
LESSLEY, Samuel	Wil	1-171	1837
LESTER, James D.	Laf	1-304	1879
Leah	Mas	1-168	1900
Temperance	Att	B-362	1882
LESUEUR, Littlebury	Mas	P.2-441	1841
LESUUER, Penelope	Mas	P.10-191	1854
LEVY, Chapman	Att	A-176	1849
Felix	Hin	B-428	1894
LEWELLEN, Jesse	Mas	P.16-217	1864
LEWELLING, Stephen W.	Mas	P.10-391	1855
LEWENSTIEN, Leopold	Lau	1-378	1898
LEWERS, Thomas	DeS	1-355	1866
LEWIS, Alfred E.	Jac	1-41	1886
Benjamin	Yaz	A-147	1851
Cealia Ann	Clk	1-113	1890

Dabney F.	Wil	2-134	1857
Eleanor T.	Ada	3-273	1865
Elijah H.	Lea	1-7	1856
Francis	Ada	2-375	1850
Francis	Hin	1-248	1850
George W.	Ran	1-105	1868
Hugh	Mad	A-550	1873
J. P.	DeS	1-258	1860
James W.	Jac	1-45	1887
Jesse	Hol	1-53	1845
Joel	Hin	1-312	1853
John B.	Ran	1-144	1875
John C.	Pan(2)	A-142	1898
Lewis	War	B-281	1893
Mary	Yaz	A-351	1868
Millie	War	B-140	1882
Norah	War	B-119	1881
Prentiss	War	B-291	1893
Robert W.	Jac	1-52	1887
Sarah	Ran	1-57	1863
Theodore H.	Yal(2)	1-3	1878
Thomas I.	Low	1-190	1865
Wiley	Cho	A-17	1887
William	War	B-93	1878
LEY, William	Was	1-35	1843
LEYSER, Dave S.	Was	2-40	1897
LIDDELL, John	Ada	3-70	1856
Dr. W. W.	Car(1)	A-537	1875
LIGHT, George C.	Mad	A-322	1860
LIGHTCAP, Evelyn	War	B-89	1878
LIGHTSEY, Francis	Jas	1-78	1882
Richard T. H.	Jas	1-17	1862
LIGON, E. R.	Lee	1-185	1897
James L.	Ada	5-3	1892
Joseph	Yal(1)	A-298	1857
Joseph A.	Ada	4-293	1883
LIKENS, Thomas J.	Was	1-179	1853
LILE, Mary C.	Mon	I.3-401	1879
LILES, Joseph A.	Mas	1-19	1892
LILLYBRIDGE, Louis	Tal	A-304	1866
LINCECUM, Grabel	Nox	A-13	1837
LINDEMANN, Kale	Mad	A-518	1870
LINDENMAYER, Gothel	Wil	3-138	1895
LINDER, John A.	Hol	3-25	1895
LINDERMAN, Henry	Mas	P.4-59	1845
LINDLEY, Ammon	Lau	1-47	1864
LINDSAY, Nancy L.	Coa(1)	1-184	1883
Rachel E.	Att	B-240	1876
Sally	Mad	A-59	1841
LINDSEY, Joseph C.	Lea	1-13	1857
Robert R.	Lea	1-60	1865

LINEBARGER, F. H.	Tip	1-129	1886
LINN, Samuel	War	A-227	1856
LINTON, John	Ada	2-101	1834
LINTOT, William B.	Ada	2-127	1836
LIPFORD, John	Hol	1-7	1834
LIPSCOMB, Baker	Car(1)	A-103	1852
Jeffrey	Hol	1-460	1883
Jeffry	Car(2)	1-27	1881
LISCHER, Margaret S.	Cla	3-76	1882
LITTLE, C. F.	Low	2-225	1896
John	Car(1)	A-193	1860
Nancy	Pan(1)	A-211	1855
Peter	Ada	3-80	1856
LITTLEFIELD, Cornelia			
L.	DeS	1-405	1866
LITTLEJOHN, William	Uni	1-38	1895
William B.	Yaz	B-95	1878
LITTLETON, Green	Low	2-118	1895
LIVELY, William T.	Tat	1-77	1885
LIVERETT, John C.	Yal(1)	B-87	1863
LIVINGS, Catherine	PRi	1-2	1899
LIVINGSTON, James	Mad	A-113	1846
James	Yaz	A-143	1848
Peter Van Burgh	Cla	A-152	1825
LLOYD, David	Mon	I.7-498	1852
Edward	Mad	A-470	1868
Elizabeth	Cop	AAA-247	1859
J. O.	Cop	A-106	1896
Richard	Mar	A2-7	1884
William W.	Cop	AAA-252	1839
LOBDELL, Jonathan C.	Cla	B-223	1852
LOCK, William H.	Low	1-235	1867
LOCKARD, Charles O.	Pre	1-107	1897
Moses	Car(1)	A-8	1837
LOCKE, Andrew Jackson	Lef	A-46	1871
Benjamin R.	Mad	A-96	1845
Francis	Tat	1-82	1885
M. F.	Tat	1-251	1900
S. B.	Mad	A-393	1863
Samuel B.	Mas (1838-1839)-130		1838
Sue M.	Coa(2)	1-49	1898
W. B.	Pan(1)	B-196	1876
LOCKETT, Almira			
Margaret	Mad	A-531	1873
R. A.	Nox	B-176	1876
T. C.	Nox	B-323	1887
William B.	Nox	B-340	1889
LOCKHART, John	Mas	P.9-290	1853
Jno. J.	Coa(1)	1-228	1891
M. I.	Car(1)	A-72	1849
Minerva T.	Hol	3-33	1895

Samuel	Mas	P.15–66	1860
Samuel T.	Car(1)	A–174	1858
Thomas	Hol	1–227	1860
William T.	Mas	P.17–166	1866
LOCKRIDGE, Robert P.	Mas	P.7–56	1849
LODER, Vincent	Ada	1–399	1828
LOFTIN, Isaac S.	Att	D–244	1900
LOFTIS, Powell	Low	1–391	1876
LOFTON, Samuel T.	Chi (1863–1872)–158		1867
LOGAN, John W.	Mas	19–118	1869
Mary W.	DeS	1–115	1856
Thomas C.	Mad	A–397	1863
Tylor	Laf	1–335	1884
LOGUE, F. M.	War	B–357	1899
LOMAX, Peter	Cla	3–85	1883
LOMBARD, Ephraim H.	Ran	1–101	1868
John	Ada	1–465	1827
LONG, Elizabeth A.	Low	1–253	1867
Esther C.	DeS	2–225	1884
Francis M.	Nox	C–80	1899
Isaac	Ada	1–161	1817
J. B.	Cho	A–6	1882
John J.	Yal(1)	A–243	1854
Sherrod	Cla	3–82	1882
Short	Yal(1)	A–217	1852
William H.	Mas	P.18–113	1867
LONGAKER, Samuel	Ada	2–261	1843
LONGBRIDGE, Mary Catherine	Jas	1–92	1892
LONGSTREET, James	Nox	A–54	1843
LOONEY, John L.	Chi(1)	1–83	1887
LOPER, Susan A.	Jas	1–115	1897
LORD, Frances	Hin	1–275	1851
George J.	Han	A–147	1883
LORING, Isreal	Cla	B–179	1844
LOTT, Aaron	Car(1)	A–135	1856
Aaron	Car(1)	A–445	1862
Elisha	Mad	A–340	1860
Elizabeth J.	Mad	A–508	1870
James E.	Car(1)	A–542	1875
Margaret	Car(1)	B–9	1879
LOURY, H. C.	DeS	2–335	1891
LOVE, Austin	DeS	2–388	1894
B. B.	Car(1)	A–448	1862
D.	Low	1–337	1873
David	DeS	1–431	1868
David	Nox	A–61	1837
David Alexander	Yaz	A–134	1850
Emily B.	DeS	2–319	1889
Harriet Julia	DeS	2–43	1872
John D.	Tal	A–294	1862

Millon R.	Nox	B-102	1870
Mrs. S. E.	DeS	2-326	1891
Samuel	Mot	1-36	1880
William K.	DeS	2-115	1876
LOVELESS, William F.	Nox	B-9	1862
LOVELL, Joseph	Ada	3-381	1869
W. S.	War	B-382	1900
LOW, James	Mas	P.10-299	1855
Martha A.	Cop	A-101	1895
LOWE, Mrs. A. M.	Mad	A-283	1859
Figures	Mad	A-171	1852
Jesse	Pan(1)	B-220	1877
John Sr.	Mad	A-7	1832
John B. Sr.	Cop	AAA-244	1858
Stephen	Mad	A-163	1851
Willis	Hin	B-64	1861
LOWENBURG, Isaac	Ada	4-462	1888
LOWENHAUPT, Isaac	War	A-344	1866
LOWERY, Peter	Cho	A-16	1886
LOWREY, John W.	Tip	1-176	1894
Mark Perrin	Tip	1-126	1886
LOWRY, Henderson	Hin	B-469	1899
Robert	Ami	1-95	1813
Robert	Pre	1-43	1880
William	Isa	A-28	1847
William	Mad	A-76	1843
LOYD, Fred	War	B-146	1884
Mary	War	B-274	1893
LUBENFELD, Lewis	Win	1-165	1896
LUCAS, Abraham B.	Yal(1)	A-309	1857
James B.	Wil	2-30	1848
John C.	Att	C-3	1887
John R.	Hin	1-158	1831
Mary	Car(1)	A-54	1832
Peter W.	DeS	1-459	1870
Robert	Ada	1-386	1826
William	DeS	2-374	1893
William	Mas	P.8-124	1852
LUCKETT, Andrew J.	Mad	A-245	1857
Francis S.	Mad	A-557	1873
Gustus	Mad	A-195	1853
James	Cla	B-159	1838
Nancy Mildred	Mad	A-566	1875
Oliver A.	Mad	2-144	1900
LUCKY, David	Yal(1)	A-43	1838
LUCY, Edward A.	Ran	B.1-11	1833
Edward W.	Ran	1-71	1865
LULL, Frances V. A.	Low	1-477	1884
James S.	Low	1-318	1872
LUM, Ann	War	B-13	1869
Erastus	Cla	A-349	1837

William	War	A–204	1853
LUMPKIN, Elizabeth	Mas	P.16–208	1864
William	Mas	P.2–157	1841
LUNA, L. L.	Ben	1–73	1897
LUND, Benjamin	Yal(1)	B–153	1869
LUNDIN, Charles F.	Mon	I.6–253	1893
LUNDY, Mary Norman	DeS	2–192	1882
W. L.	DeS	2–357	1892
LUSBY, J. C.	Was	2–138	1900
Sarah E.	Mon	I.3–46	1878
LUSE, Deborah	Ada	1–402	1822
Nathan H.	Yaz	A–102	1846
LUSK, Martha	Laf	1–138	1859
Robert	Yal(1)	A–271	1855
LUSTER, Eliza A.	Hin	B–474	1899
Henry	Hin	B–456	1898
LUTTIES, James	Chi (1863–1872)–62		1865
LYLE, Mary N.	Ada	4–353	1885
Matthew D.	Lau	1–319	1893
LYLES, Martha L.	Mot	1–5	1873
LYNCH, Alice V.	Car(2)	1–64	1892
Antonio	Yaz	A–343	1867
Montgomery	DeS	2–254	1885
Sedley M.	Hin	1–437	1858
LYNE, James	Wil	1–204	1839
Eliza Alice	DeS	2–176	1881
LYON, C. W.	Cly	1–86	1889
Edward	Ada	1–459	1829
Margaret	Hin	1–188	1846
Nicholas	Jas	1–2	1858
Stephen H.	DeS	1–116	1856
LYONS, Andrew E.	Ada	2–337	1847
Aurora	Ada	3–17	1855
Joseph B.	Ada	2–141	1837
Joseph B.	Ada	2–404	1851
Thomas	Nox	A–57	1826
MAAS, Albertine	Lau	1–344	1894
Charles	Mad	A–563	1875
Leopold	Mad	A–576	1878
MABBELL, Gideon	Jef	B–173	1890
MABRY, B. T. E.	Hin	B–142	1861
J. H.	Att	D–64	1898
James	Att	D–171	1899
James L.	Tat	1–123	1890
Nancy	Mad	A–238	1856
V. A.	Att	B–474	1885
MACKEY, Amanda	Jac	1–161	1896
John	Coa(2)	1–6	1892
John B.	Coa(1)	1–255	1892
L. C.	Coa(1)	1–172	1885

Samuel	Cla	3–47	1878
MACKIN, Elizabeth	Ada	4–194	1881
MACLIN, William W.	War	A–19	1831
MACON, Jacob M.	Nox	B–11	1862
MACOUILLARD, Guillome	Han	A–89	1874
MACQUILLEN, Joseph R.	Isa	C–54	1862
Martha A.	Isa	C–50	1861
MACRERY, Dickinson	Ada	2–453	1853
MADDEN, J. Hugh	Ada	2–167	1838
John	Hin	1–167	1843
MADDOX, Adderton	Cla	3–122	1890
Samuel W.	Cho	A–23	1891
MADDUX, John E.	Pan(1)	B–336	1880
Mary A.	Hin	B–443	1895
MADISON, Eliza	Yaz	B–386	1899
MADLOCK, Jennie	Pan(1)	B–499	1899
MAGEE, A. B. Jr.	Hin	B–386	1888
Euphemia	Cov	1–8	1894
Felix	Laf	1–187	1868
James	Ada	4–210	1878
James	Pan(1)	B–35	1867
Mary J.	Coa(1)	1–112	1868
T. N.	Yal(1)	B–142	1870
Thomas A.	Fra	A–12	1891
MAGGATT, Sarah	War	B–28	1873
MAGOUN, Calvin B.	Wil	1–185	1837
MAGRUDER, Eliza L.	Ada	4–120	1877
Elvira H.	Hol	1–127	1853
Joseph M.	Cla	B–306	1865
Lucy	Mad	A–185	1853
Priscilla	Jef	P.B–575	1835
Susanna Prescilla	Cla	A–220	1830
Thomas	Mad	A–199	1854
William	Mad	A–158	1850
MAGUIRE, Frank	Coa(1)	1–93	1866
Patrick	Laf	1–68	1850
MAHAN, Archimidens	Nox	A–246	1857
James W.	Lau	1–41	1863
Samuel	Ada	1–39	1808
William H.	Hin	B–420	1892
MAHON, Patrick	Low	1–486	1885
MAHORNER, Matthias	Nox	B–113	1872
MAIR, Abram	Low	1–371	1875
Cornelia W.	Lau	1–260	1889
MAIRS, William H.	Pan(1)	A–3	1845
MAJET, Nicholas	Yal(1)	B–25	1859
MAJUR, John G.	Lea	1–80	1876
MALANE, William	Hol	3–41	1896
MALARD, Louisa	Lau	1–237	1888
MALCHETT, Edward	Hol	1–135	1853
MALLORY, Jesse	Yal(1)	A–314	1858

Johnson	War	A–217	1854
Turner	Cop	AAA–231	1850
MALOM, Thomas	Yaz	B–75	1877
MALONE, Isham C.	Lau	1–226	1886
Jane	Mon	I.17–59	1863
Samuel B.	Low	1–151	1863
Thomas J.	Mas	1–22	1893
William G.	Mas	P.17–236	1866
William P.	Laf	1–53	1851
MAN, George W.	Was	1–120	1849
MANAHAN, R. M.	Tat	1–217	1897
MANASCO, James W.	Mon	I.17–57	1863
MANDEVILLE, Henry D.	Ada	4–142	1879
MANEESE, Mary A.	Nox	B–296	1885
MANEY, James	Mad	A–532	1873
MANGUM, Lucy	Ada	3–446	1870
MANIFALD, Margaret	Was	2–96	1899
MANLEY, Joseph Wilson	Laf	1–113	1856
MANN, Claibourn	Nes	A–48	1857
Jabez	Cly	1–36	1879
Jeremiah D.	Mon	I.18–32	1865
Richard	Tis	1–18	1888
W. B.	Lea	1–184	1899
MANNEY, Michael	Tip	1–67	1873
MANNING, Ashley B.	Yaz	A–332	1867
George Felix	Mon	I.9–525	1853
Martin J.	Tun	2–45	1877
Sarah F.	Mon	I.4–407	1883
Silas	Cla	A–45	1813
Sophia	Mon	I.8–205	1852
MANNOCCI, Ferdinando	Ada	5–258	1900
MARBLE, Elizabeth M.	War	A–250	1858
MARCH, James G.	Tip	1–89	1879
Lucinda	Tip	1–102	1882
MARCHBANKS, Mary A.	Mon	I.3–1	1878
William Burton	Mon	I.21–56	1871
MARDIS, Abner	Ada	3–11	1855
MARE, Henrietta	Laf	1–77	1852
MARION, Job V.	Laf	1–143	1861
Mary	Chi(1)	1–58	1886
Patric	Cop	A–136	1899
MARK, Benard	Jac	2–25	1900
MARKHAM, James	Lin	1–49	1898
MARKS, Marcus A.	Lin	1–20	1894
MARLET, P. M. L.	Ada	1–21	1815
MARLOW, Joseph	Hol	1–233	1860
S. A.	Cop	A–17	1888
MARNAN, Patrick	Ada	2–90	1835
MARR, Alexander	Mas	P.9–148	1853
James D.	Mas	P.2–109	1840
John	Mas	P.3–295	1844

125

Nancy G.	Hin	1-385	1856
MARRON, John	Ada	4-564	1891
MARSALIS, James	Pik	1-2	1882
MARSH, George W.	War	B-144	1884
Louisa	Lau	1-334	1894
Marlin	Tip	1-98	1881
Samuel	Car(1)	A-15	1839
William	Mas	P.8-392	1851
William Daniel	Clk	1-17	1873
MARSHALL, Charles C.	Tal	A-102	1849
Harry S.	Ada	3-269	1866
J. E.	Web	A-130	1898
James W.	Mon	I.19-546	1865
John G.	Mon	I.4-104	1879
Letitia	War	B-196	1888
Levin R.	Ada	3-459	1871
Martin	War	B-315	1895
Samuel	Ada	2-267	1843
MARTIN, Alexander S.	Hol	1-304	1865
Andrew L.	Mas	P.2-586	1842
Andrew L.	Mas	P.5-564	1849
Andrew L.	Mas	P.16-302	1865
Ann Mariah	Car(1)	B-71	1900
Anna M.	Jef	P.D-508	1849
Annie L.	Tis	1-65	1893
Benjamin F.	Cop	A-54	1891
Charles	Ada	1-162	1817
Cornelius	War	A-158	1847
Edward J.	Hin	1-99	1838
Edward James	Hol	3-91	1898
Ellen	War	B-350	1898
George W.	Tal	A-154	1854
Harrison L.	Mad	A-7	1831
Jackson	Mot	1-98	1890
Jackson	Tal	A-310	1866
James G.	DeS	2-152	1879
James W.	Cla	3-196	1900
John	Ada	1-324	1825
John	Han	A-95	1876
John	Mad	A-377	1862
John D.	DeS	1-385	1866
John J.	Car(2)	1-38	1887
John M.	War	A-142	1844
Joshua L.	Nox	A-236	1856
Mary E.	Cla	3-61	1879
Nancy	Cop	AAA-235	1863
Nancy	Pre	1-24	1874
Philip	Tip	1-60	1873
Priscilla	Pan(1)	A-420	1861
Richard	Yaz	B-266	1891
Sarah A.	Nox	B-309	1886

Sarah H.	Cla	B-332	1871
Thomas	Low	1-275	1870
Thomas J.	Hin	B-181	1865
Thomas J.	Was	1-458	1883
Thomas J. Sr.	Hin	B-344	1883
Thomas N.	Chi(1)	1-63	1886
William	Att	2-576	1866
William G.	Laf	1-177	1857
MARTINEZ, Hannah Jane	Han	A-288	1896
MARTZ, Alice	Mad	2-124	1899
MARYE, Madie M.	Cla	3-113	1889
MASCWELL, Elizabeth R.	Low	1-360	1874
MASON, A. T.	Ben	1-68	1895
C. J.	Jas	1-72	1877
George	Nox	A-21	1839
Harrison	Hin	B-409	1890
John	Pan(1)	B-462	1890
John	War	A-212	1854
Mary B.	Ada	4-455	1888
Thomas	Ada	4-425	1887
MASSENBURG, Benjamin Harrison	Hin	1-35	1834
MASSEY, Allen Alenzo	Tat	1-263	1900
David	Mad	2-14	1893
David	Mad	2-34	1894
Emily E.	Cop	AAA-242	1857
J. B. Sr.	Tat	1-68	1884
J. H.	Mon	I.7-63	1899
James M.	Tat	1-159	1893
John B.	Mad	A-635	1885
Jonathan P.	Mas	P.17-558	1867
M. S.	DeS	2-143	1879
Nathaniel	Hin	1-154	1830
Susan	Yaz	B-172	1884
Susan E.	War	B-136	1882
MATCHETT, Edward	Hol	1-33	1842
MATHENY, Charles	Cop	AAA-238	1833
MATHEWS, Anna R.	Car(2)	1-23	1880
Catharine A.	Hin	B-458	1898
George	Ada	1-86	1813
James Allen	Ada	1-464	1829
James T.	Car(1)	A-437	1862
Mary E.	Mon	I.7-54	1899
Michael	Hin	1-149	1823
Robert L.	War	A-253	1859
T. C.	Pan(2)	A-8	1881
MATHIAS, Samuel W.	Laf	2-45	1900
MATTHEWS, Andrew	DeS	1-407	1865
Catharine	Lee	1-173	1897
Elisha M.	Laf	1-332	1884

127

James Alverson	Mas	1-92	1896
John E.	Tat	1-84	1885
John J.	Car(1)	A-443	1862
Kitty	Low	1-82	1861
Mary A.	Cop	A-77	1892
Olivia C.	Low	1-427	1879
Peter M.	Laf	1-284	1878
Richard A.	Low	1-12	1858
Robert F.	Low	2-245	1899
Stephen	Hol	1-13	1838
T. E.	Cop	A-128	1898
William E.	Car(1)	A-425	1860
MATTINERS, Mary	Hin	B-228	1867
MATZNER, Leopold	Kem	A-75	1899
MAUCHERE', Margaret	Ada	1-83	1812
MAULDIN, Ransom L.	Yal(1)	B-151	1872
MAUPIN, Robert C.	Mon	I.15-258	1860
MAURY, James H.	Cla	B-345	1874
Reubin	Mas	1-6	1892
MAUSS, Samuel	Low	1-354	1872
MAXEY, J. W. G.	Lee	1-28	1877
Napoleon	Ran	1-139	1875
Robert	Ran	1-127&133	1874
MAXWELL, Eleanor	Car(1)	A-38	1832
Elizabeth R.	Low	1-360	1874
John H.	Pan(1)	B-341	1880
Margaret	DeS	1-307	1862
Thomas E.	DeS	2-471	1898
Thomas S.	DeS	1-102	1855
Viney	Tat	1-214	1896
MAY, A. T.	Hol	1-104	1851
Aron B.	Chi(1)	1-3	1874
Joseph	Chi(1863-1872)-118		1865
Joseph	Nox	B-40	1863
Letitia H.	Lau	1-179	1882
Philip	Jef	A-119	1833
William	Nox	A-42	1842
William	Sim	A-68	1894
MAYBERRY, Abram	Jef	P.B-5	1836
MAYER, Adrian N.	Mas	P.19-249	1869
Mrs. J. C. P.	Wil	3-51	1888
MAYES, Daniel	Hin	B-135	1861
Haman B.	Cop	A-52	1891
Robert B.	Yaz	B-188	1885
W. D.	Yal(1)	B-145	1870
MAYFIELD, Elisha B.	Hol	1-417	1877
Isaac	Mad	A-181	1853
James H.	Mad	A-243	1857
William Sims	Tal	B-14	1869
MAYHAW, Casnell	Tun	2-141	1896
MAYHEW, George			

Washington Sr.	Grn	A-1	1872
Sarah	Grn	A-102	1893
MAYNARD, Maggie	Coa(1)	1-226	1891
MAYO, John W.	Att	C-275	1891
MCADORY, James	Att	C-107	1867
James	Jas	1-102	1896
Martha A.	Att	C-288	1892
Williamson	Att	2-309	1863
MCAFEE, Appalouise L.	Ran	1-160	1879
Francis	Ada	2-60	1834
Joseph	Ran	1-36	1861
Madison	Hin	B-155	1862
MCALEXANDER, Edward	Tun	1-476&556	1870
MCALISTER, Elizabeth	Ada	3-62	1856
William G.	Ada	4-14	1872
MCALLISTER, B. C. S.	Tip	1-185	1894
Barnabus G.	Lee	1-134	1890
Elizabeth A.	Cly	1-63	1883
Hector	Cla	A-96	1820
Mrs. S. F.	Mon	I.7-56	1898
William	Yaz	A-63	1842
MCALLUM, Martha	Kem	A-78	1899
MCALPEN, Alexander	Cla	A-130	1823
MCALPINE, Edwin R.	Cla	B-305	1862
John R.	Cla	3-154	1894
Sarah	Law	P.B-46	1837
William R.	Cla	B-262	1856
MCANULTY, William O.	Mas	P.12-48	1856
MCARTHUR, Marseline	Han P.(1853-1860)-412		1855
Patrick	Lee	1-183	1897
MCBEE, Silas	Pon	2-418	1845
MCBRIDE, Daniel	Tip	1-65	1873
John	Hol	1-326	1868
Joseph	Web	A-42	1899
William	Mad	A-564	1871
MCCAA, David	Jef	B-133	1871
MCCABE, James	Ada	4-474	1889
James	Jef	P.D-98	1847
Jane	War	B-370	1899
Patrick	Jef	B-10	1859
Thomas	War	B-230	1889
MCCAFFERTY, C.	Cho	A-55	1898
MCCAIN, J. S.	Hol	3-68	1898
Mary	Tal	A-118	1848
Monroe	Lef	A-69	1880
William	Laf	1-274	1868
MCCALEB, David	Cla	B-207	1850
Frances L.	Cla	3-91	1884
Indiana	Cla	B-293	1860
Jonathan	Cla	B-228	1853
Martha Jane	Ada	5-294	1900

William	Cla	A-49	1813
MCCALEP, Lewis H.	Tal	B-42	1875
MCCALL, Janet Harris	Yal(1)	B-11	1858
John	Hin	1-101	1838
MCCALLA, Martha			
Elizabeth	Tis	1-107	1899
MCCALLISTER, Mary C.	Mon	I.2-479	1876
MCCAMPBELL, Margaret			
J.	Car(1)	A-529	1873
MCCANN, John	Tun	2-38	1876
Robert C.	Yaz	B-284	1893
MCCARDLE, Cornelia A.	Cla	3-137	1892
MCCARLEY, Eliza	Nox	C-1	1896
John C.	Att	C-130	1889
MCCARTNEY, Charles	Mas	P.3-133	1841
Henry I.	Tun	1-164	1856
MCCARTY, Daniel	Clk	1-174	1895
Daniel	Jas	1-111	1897
Edward	Clk	1-41	1882
Mary Ann	Lau	1-350	1895
Nancy A.	Jas	1-72	1876
Owen	War	A-219	1855
William	Low	1-103	1862
MCCASKILL, Ann E.	Car(1)	B-10	1879
MCCAULEY, James	Car(1)	A-497	1867
John	Mad	A-256	1857
Samuel J.	Mas	P.18-79	1867
Susannah	Ada	3-67	1856
MCCAULLA, James	Car(1)	A-497	1867
MCCAVELL, James	War	A-10	1830
MCCLARY, Daniel	War	B-59	1875
MCCLEARY, Abram	War	A-11	1827
MCCLELLAN, George	Ada	1-355	1823
MCCLENDON, Joel	Grn	A-13	1876
MCCLURE, R. E.	Ada	4-587	1892
MCCLURG, Susan M.	Car(2)	1-3	1875
MCCLUSKEY, Elizabeth			
C.	Mot	1-71	1884
MCCLUSKY, Agnes	Mad	A-542	1873
MCCOMB, Joseph R.	Tal	A-52	1844
Susan	Cla	B-307	1865
MCCONAGHY, Martha E.	Jac	1-46	1883
MCCONCHIE, James	Ada	3-291	1866
MCCONN, John W.	Low	1-175	1865
MCCORCLE, Elizabeth			
L.	Pan(1)	A-401	1860
MCCORD, Hugh B.	Tip	1-142	1888
J. T.	Laf	2-44	1899
S. E.	Yaz	B-241	1890
MCCORKLE, Eli	Pan(1)	A-118	1852
Isaac B.	Jef	B-135	1875

Patrick	Laf	1-353	1886
S. E.	Laf	1-299	1879
Sarah C.	Pan(1)	A-242	1856
Stephen	DeS	1-148	1857
MCCOWN, James	DeS	1-39	1852
MCCOY, Helen	Ada	2-429	1852
James	Ada	2-204	1840
James H.	Ada	2-409	1852
Samuel	Tis	1-60	1893
MCCRACKEN, Ephraim	Yal(1)	A-206	1852
George	Ada	1-178	1819
James Lyle	Cop	A-160	1900
MCCRARY, Margaret C.	Car(2)	1-4	1876
MCCREADY, John	Wil	1-174	1837
MCCRORY, Thomas	Pre	1-122	1898
MCCULLAR, Oliver	Yal(2)	1-47	1885
MCCULLOUGH, John	Lee	1-64	1881
Sallie	Laf	1-434	1893
MCCUNE, John T.	Low	1-130	1862
William A.	New	1-65	1858
MCCURDY, Ann	Ada	1-341	1825
MCCURY, James	Ada	1-88	1813
MCCUTCHEN, James	War	B-132	1882
John C.	War	B-156	1886
Lucy A.	War	B-183	1885
William	War	B-56	1875
MCDADE, George Z.	DeS	1-390	1866
James D.	DeS	1-16	1852
MCDANIEL, Absalom	War	A-1	1829
Ambrose	War	A-16	1831
Henry	New	1-11	1876
James D.	DeS	1-446	1869
John	Fra	A-5	1885
R. A.	Chi(2)	1-27	1884
Stephen	Mad	A-683	1892
William A.	Tal	B-33	1863
MCDERMOT, Francis	Wil	2-240	1866
MCDONALD, Allen	Cop	A-70	1890
Allen	DeS	2-421	1895
Allen	Nes	A-63	1861
Archibald	Nes	A-99	1876
Elizo E.	Jas	1-37	1858
Ellen	Coa(1)	1-196	1887
Flora	Kem	A-10	1883
George	Jas	1-89	1889
Hugh	Nox	A-144	1850
James	Lea	1-192	1900
John	Nes	A-78	1865
John Wilbur	Chi(1)	1-113	1893
John Wilber	Web	A-99	1893
Marina	Jef	B-175	1892

Mary	Win	1-25	1862
Thomas	Pre	1-71	1888
W. B.	Jas	1-71	1876
William	Clk	1-24	1874
Willis	Jef	P.B-522	1839
MCDONOUGH, Michael	Mon	I.14-319	1859
MCDOUGALD, Charles	Jef	P.F-462	1856
MCDOUGALL, Ellen	Ada	4-216	1882
Nicholas	Cla	B-217	1851
MCDOW, Mary	Mas	P.5-682	1849
MCDOWELL, Joseph	Hin	1-426	1858
Maria E.	Mas	P.13-66	1857
MCDUFF, Archibald	Ada	1-22	1803
MCELHENY, Richard N.	Mad	A-85	1844
MCELLIGOTT, Johanna	War	B-256	1891
MCELRIN, Aquilla	Pik	1-129	1899
MCELROY, Charles	Lau	1-194	1883
MCELWEE, James	Cla	A-26	1806
MCEWEN, Cyrus	Laf	1-323	1883
Eliza M.	Mas	1-14	1892
Margarette E.	Laf	1-420	1896
MCFADDEN, Abigail	Ada	2-292	1844
MCFADYEN, John A.	Mas	P.16-331	1865
MCFARLAND, David	Cla	A-107	1821
Mrs. J.	Mon	I.4-411	1883
John	Yaz	B-140	1882
Robert	Ada	1-413	1828
Thomas J.	Yal(2)	1-126	1900
MCGEE, Henry L.	Tat	1-6	1874
J. C.	Pre	1-77	1889
Joseph	Hol	1-147	1855
Martha A.	Hol	1-373	1873
Mary H.	Clk	1-27	1876
W. A.	Cly	1-81	1887
William	War	B-316	1895
William A.	Hol	1-177	1857
William P.	Att	D-142	1899
MCGEHEE, A. F.	Tat	1-152	1892
MCGEHEE, Edward F.	Pan(1)	B-311	1879
Hugh	Pan(1)	A-231	1855
J. W.	Car(1)	A-477	1865
James B.	Pan(1)	B-27	1866
John C.	DeS	1-142	1857
John S.	Pan(1)	B-69	1870
Micajah	Wil	2-383	1880
Willis	Nox	B-350	1890
MCGILVARY, Mary F.	Cla	3-124	1891
MCGILVERY, Thomas	Gre	1-14	1894
MCGINLY, Patrick F.	Yaz	B-26	1873
MCGINNIS, Mary J.	Cop	A-85	1892
MCGINSEY, William	Mad	A-22	1834

MCGINTRY, John	Yal(1)	B-217	1890
MCGINTY, Bridget	Ada	5-153	1897
MCGIVNAY, Hugh	Ben	1-7	1869
MCGONAN, Robert	Clk	1-2	1872
MCGORRAN, Catherine			
Q.	Mas	1-52	1895
MCGOWAN, Turence	Ran	1-93	1866
William	Mas	P.8-98	1852
MCGOWEN, Hugh	Hin	1-414	1857
MCGRADY, Thomas	Laf	1-128	1859
MCGRAW, Cornelius	Laf	1 115	1857
Cornelius	Laf	1-130	1859
Patrick H.	Ada	4-168	1880
Uriah	Ada	1-308	1824
MCGREW, Caroline	Cla	B-249	1855
MCGUFFEE, B. V.	Hin	B-465	1899
MCGUIRE, Frank	Coa(1)	1-93	1866
Richard	Coa(1)	1-10	1845
MCILVUNE, John	Yal(1)	A-17	1836
MCINERNEY, John	Han	B-50	1900
MCINNIS, D. W.	Sim	A-90	1899
Harriet Malinda	Cop	A-40	1890
John	Gre	1-27	1899
John	Jac	1-2	1876
Mary	Lau	1-185	1883
Sarah J.	Cov	1-14	1899
MCINTIRE, G. C.	Lef	A-98	1887
MCINTYRE, Duncan	Mas	P.4-158	1845
MCINTOSH, Daniel	Nox	B-250	1881
Daniel M.	Lea	1-58	1865
James	Ada	1-172	1809
John G.	Sim	A-73	1896
M. M.	Chi(1863-1872)-33		1864
Mary Ann	Nox	B-277	1882
William	Ada	1-173	1818
MCINTYRE, Duncan	Mas	P.4-158	1845
Hugh	Ada	1-187	1818
John C.	Ran	1-137	1875
Margaret	Cla	3-123	1891
William J.	Tip	1-204	1899
MCIVER, Donald James	Chi(1863-1872)-178		1868
MCJUNKIN, Susan D.	Chi(1)	1-31	1880
MCKAY, Daniel	War	A-43	1834
Elias M.	Mad	A-28	1836
John	Ran	1-318	1900
Letitia	Lau	1-246	1888
Richard	Ada	1-400	1828
Susan	Att	2-508	1865
Samuel	Mad	A-104	1846
MCKEE, B. P.	Qui	1-19	1899
Elizabeth S.	Mas	1-110	1897

John	Yaz	A-299	1864
MCKEEVER, Candis	Cla	3-84	1884
MCKELLAN, Dugald	Low	1-98	1862
MCKENNIE, Michael	Pan(1)	A-244	1857
MCKENZIE, Donald	DeS	2-435	1896
Hector A.	DeS	2-107	1875
John	Lau	1-234	1888
L. T.	Ben	1-42	1888
MCKEOWN, Hugh B.	Mon	I.19-79	1865
MCKERNAN, John	Yal(1)	A-20	1839
MCKIE, James M.	Laf	1-142	1861
MCKIERNAN, Charles	Ada	1-60	1810
MCKINNEY, Ira	Pan(1)	A-191	1855
J. W.	Mon	I.6-86	1891
John B.	Tis	1-101	1899
Sarah W.	Tis	1-23	1890
MCKINNIE, Louisa R.	Pan(1)	A-196	1855
MCKINSTRY, William	Hol	1-353	1871
MCKLIN, David O.	Pan(1)	A-433	1863
MCKNIGHT, John C.	Jas	1-53	1867
MCKOWN, Daniel	Ada	1-53	1810
MCKOY, Patsy	Hol	1-339	1869
MCLANAHAN, Elijah	Low	1-478	1884
MCLANATHAN, Charles			
Wellington	Jac	1-162	1897
MCLARTY, A. L.	Laf	1-281	1877
MCLAUGHLIN, Duncan	Ada	1-39	1808
James C.	Laf	1-225	1872
John	Ada	1-383	1826
John	Ada	2-156	1837
Laughlin	Yal(1)	A-269	1853
MCLAURIN, D. A.	Sim	A-25	1884
D. D.	Jas	1-85	1887
Duncan	Lau	1-367	1897
Duncan A.	Sim	A-29	1884
Hugh L.	Smi	1-2	1893
J. R.	Lau	1-228	1886
Oivella	Ran	1-296	1890
MCLEAN, Amelia A.	Cla	3-125	1890
E. A.	Cla	B-202	1849
E. R.	Lef	A-78	1883
James D.	Car(1)	A-40	1843
MCLENDON, Lewis M.	Kem	A-33	1888
William	Jas	1-27	1858
MCLENNON, Susan M.	DeS	2-102	1875
MCLEOD, Duncan C.	Lef	A-32	1859
John	Nox	A-278	1859
Malcomb	DeS	1-182	1858
Melecent Rachel	Jac	1-11	1881
Neal	Nox	B-368	1891
W. D.	Hol	3-46	1896

William M.	Nox	A-258	1858
MCLIN, David O.	Pan(1)	A-433	1863
MCLINDON, Mattie	Kem	A-2	1881
MCMAHAN, Nancy	Mad	A-275	1858
Timothy	Mad	A-649	1887
MCMANNUS, John Henry	War	B-102	1879
MCMANOMY, James	Car(1)	A-29	1842
MCMANOUS, Fanny	Ran	B.1-247	1845
MCMANUS, Burrell	Lee	1-146	1893
MCMATH, Ambrose F.	Car(1)	A-430	1861
Elijah	Car(1)	A 194	1860
John H.	Car(1)	B-1	1876
William A.	Car(1)	A-149	1857
MCMILLAN, Alex A.	Att	B-95	1872
John	Mon	I.12-214	1856
William	Att	B-233	1876
MCMILLON, Dugall	Laf	1-109	1856
MCMORRIS, John J.	Wil	2-250	1867
MCMULLEN, Patrick	New	1-156	1896
James	Att	A-282	1859
MCMULLIN, Sarah F.	Yal(2)	1-75	1892
MCMURRAN, John T.	Ada	3-298	1867
Mary L.	Ada	4-570	1891
MCNABB, James	Ran	B.1-18	1823
James Y.	Ran	B.1-557	1850
Jessie J.	Mas	1-121	1897
MCNAIR, Lorenzo D.	Hin	B-332	1878
MCNAMARA, Johanna	Yaz	B-419	1900
John	Yaz	B-41	1875
MCNAMEE, Thomas W.	Chi(1)	1-61	1886
MCNEAL, Albert T.	Yal(1)	A-88	1844
Ezekiel P.	Tun	2-157	1898
G. B.	Nes	A-130	1893
MCNEELEY, James	Wil	1-275	1844
MCNEELY, James	Hin	1-185	1844
John	Wil	2-407	1882
MCNEER, John	Hol	1-150	1855
MCNEES, Delila	Nox	A-220	1855
S. B.	DeS	2-28	1870
MCNEIL, Elizabeth	Cop	AAA-223	1854
John	DeS	1-334	1865
John	Jas	1-77	1881
John	Lef	A-2	1848
Samuel	Nes	A-84	1865
MCNEILL, Albert F.	Car(1)	A-481	1866
Alexander	War	A-99	1839
Eliza S.	Ada	1-352	1825
John A.	War	B-105	1879
John H.	Mot	1-104	1891
John P.	Ada	1-353	1825
Louisa	Car(1)	A-143	1857

Malcolm	Coa(1)	1–154	1885
Pryor	Ada	1–352	1825
William	Hin	B–53	1860
MCNULLY, John	Wil	1–124	1835
MCNULTY, Mathew	Ada	2–338	1847
Robert	Car(1)	A–464	1864
MCNUTT, Joseph P.	War	A–48	1834
MCPHEETERS, Laura W.	Ada	4–567	1891
MCPHERSON, Archibald	Jef	P.G–177	1857
Daniel G.	Jef	P.D–446	1849
James J.	Cly	1–31	1878
John	Ada	1–393	1827
John	Jef	P.C–23	1840
Sarah A.	Cly	1–71	1885
MCQUEEN, Henry H.	Lau	1–132	1880
Mary E.	Lau	1–339	1894
MCRAE, Argolus A.	Ada	2–432	1853
Duncan	Ran	1–38	1861
J. H.	War	B–233	1889
Kenneth	Ran	B.1–310	1847
Margaret	Hin	1–34	1830
Murdock H.	Hin	B–170	1863
Mary H.	Grn	A–26	1878
MCRAY, Alexander	Hin	1–318	1853
MCREE, E. M.	Lin	1–13	1895
N. E.	Clk	1–72	1884
MCSMIE, William M. R.	Grn	A–124	1897
MCSWINE, John	Yal(1)	A–263	1855
William M. R.	Grn	A–124	1897
MCVEY, Andrew	War	A–218	1854
Elizabeth	Hin	B–55	1861
MCVOY, Allen P.	Cla	3–181	1899
Elizabeth	Hin	B–55	1861
MCWALKER, Mary	Pan(1)	B–325	1880
MCWILLIE, Ann	Mad	A–89	1844
Catherine A.	Mad	A–528	1873
MEACHUM, R. G.	Tat	1–252	1900
MEADE, Cowles G.	Yaz	A–128	1849
Evilene	Hin	B–436	1893
Frances C.	Hol	1–313	1866
Sarah F.	Yaz	A–296	1865
MEANS, David J.	Grn	A–7	1875
Hannah	Mas	(1838–1839)–121	1838
J. K.	Lee	1–117	1889
John Coulter	Ada	5–266	1900
MEANY, Thomas	War	A–354	1866
MEDLIN, Jackson Sr.	Tip	1–87	1878
MEEHAN, A. M.	War	B–292	1894
MEEK, Alexander B.	Low	1–194	1866
Betty	Mad	2–131	1899
Eliza	Att	B–163	1874

Frank	Low	1–552	1888
George Washington	Car(1)	A–78	1850
James	Tal	A–49	1844
James	Wil	1–175	1837
Kays	Mas	P.13–57	1857
Rufus	Mas	1–88	1896
Samuel	Car(1)	A–109	1833
William E.	Att	B–382	1883
William M.	Mas	P.16–291	1865
MEESE, James I.	Mad	A–251	1857
Sophia	Lau	1–405	1900
MEIERS, Regina	War	B–318	1896
MELLARD, Thomas	Law	P.B–73	1838
MELLEN, Ann S.	Yaz	A–176	1854
George F.	Yaz	B–64	1877
William P.	Ada	3–264	1866
MELLON, Thomas A.	Hin	B–431	1894
MELTON, Jessee C.	Hol	1–430	1879
John T.	Low	1–126	1862
MELVIN, Grayson	Ada	2–15	1832
Samuel T.	Han	B.1–185	1844
MENEFEE, John L.	War	A–98	1839
MERCER, Amos	Clk	1–103	1888
Eliza Jane	New	1–74	1882
William Newton	Ada	4–42	1874
MEREDITH, Elisha	Nes	A–60	1861
Frederick	DeS	1–7	1852
Thomas	Ami	1–83	1812
William A.	War	A–362	1867
MERIMAN, Joseph W.	Laf	1–350	1885
MERITT, Reimond	Ada	1–97	1813
MERIWEATHER, Charles S.	DeS	2–32	1871
Douglas	Car(1)	A–6	1837
John N.	Tal	B–38	1874
Valentine Harn	DeS	1–201	1858
MERREL, Jesse S.	Ran	1–303	1896
MERRELL, Ayres P.	Ada	4–299	1883
Peter	Nox	A–29	1840
MERRILL, Jane Surget	Ada	4–72	1866
Susan M.	Lee	1–142	1891
MERRITT, Jane E.	DeS	2–77	1873
MERRIWETHER, William P.	Chi(2)	1–3	1883
MESHOW, James	Laf	1–1	1843
MESSINGER, George	War	A–330	1865
George Wm. Bacon	Isa	C–58	1863
METCALF, Elizabeth	Wil	1–5	1830
Ilai	Ada	1–372	1824
James	Yal(1)	A–61	1842
William N.	Yal(1)	A–253	1854

METCALFE, Bela	Ada	1–293	1823
Helen C.	Ada	5–239	1899
James	Ada	3–321	1867
Volney	Ada	2–421	1853
MEZEIX, Claudius	Ada	3–228	1865
MHOON, Junius	Sha	A–20	1895
MICKLE, D. A.	Mot	1–138	1897
John B.	Tal	B–10	1868
MICON, Julia			
Fauntleroy	Mas	1–171	1900
MIDDLEBROOKS, Sophrona			
Jane	Okt	1–46	1898
MIDDLETON, Benjamin			
H.	Cop	A–130	1898
H. W.	Pan(2)	A–5	1881
Malcom C.	Mon	I.5–183	1886
Saul	Cop	A–94	1894
William	War	A–282	1860
MIERS, Edward	Mot	1–65	1883
MILAM, Jarvis	Mas	P.7–82	1849
Jos. R.	DeS	1–305	1862
MILES, Alexander	Pan(1)	A–371	1858
Jack	Yaz	B–293	1894
Mary J.	Yaz	B–316	1896
Orange S.	Ada	4–295	1883
MILES, W. R.	Hol	3–89	1900
MILLER, Aaron	Cop	AAA–233	1867
Abram W.	Tat	1–174	1891
Alexander	Cly	1–25	1877
Calvin	Pan(1)	B–352	1881
Calvin J.	Ben	1–23	1879
Catherine	War	B–238	1890
Charles P.	Tip	1–71	1875
Charlotte	Ada	3–369	1869
Charlotte	Ada	3–388	1870
Christopher	Ada	3–13	1855
Collins W.	Wil	1–295	1845
Daniel C.	Ada	2–111	1835
Duncan	Coa(1)	1–7	1844
E. H.	Mas	1–24	1893
Edward H.	War	B–92	1878
Emily	Wil	2–219	1864
Frederick	Hin	1–381	1856
George	Car(2)	1–7	1875
Harry	Yaz	B–254	1891
Harvey	Was	1–321	1861
Henry I.	Hol	1–179	1857
I. W.	Wil	1–169	1837
John	Isa	C–152	1890
John B.	Ada	2–205	1840
John C.	Was	1–9	1840

John E.	Gre	1–5	1889
John G.	Coa(1)	1–119	1877
Lewis	Car(1)	A–40	1843
Lewis C. H.	Hol	1–37	1842
Mary	Ada	5–43	1893
Mary C.	War	B–34	1873
Mary J.	Yaz	A–352	1869
Nancy J.	DeS	2–257	1884
Robert	Was	1–270	1859
Robert J.	War	B–37	1874
Rosa C.	DeS	2–515	1900
Samuel G.	Cla	B–318	1862
Samuel P.	Pan(2)	A–41	1884
Sarah	Ada	2–5	1832
Sarah M.	Hin	B–258	1869
Thomas K.	Lea	1–142	1888
Thomas M.	Ada	2–419	1852
Washington	Ada	5–191	1898
William	Cla	A–29	1806
MILLIKEN, John	Cla	B–185	1845
MILNER, John T.	Jac	2–7	1898
MILLS, A. E.	Jef	P.B–112	1836
Caledonia R.	Mon	I.2–12	1874
Charles	Hin	1–208	1847
Charlotte	Yaz	A–274	1861
Elizabeth	Pan(1)	B–5	1864
Ellen	Hin	B–101	1865
Eveline B.	Ada	4–405	1886
William D.	Tal	A–8	1835
William H. H.	Yaz	A–281	1862
MILLSAPS, Jasper	Mon	I.2–60	1873
MILTON, Jesse M.	Pre	1–37	1876
MIMS, Drury	Mas	P.15–228	1861
MIMMS, Jesse	Jef	A–99	1828
Jesse A.	Hin	1–234	1849
Susan K.	Hin	B–358	1884
William M. C.	Low	1–39	1859
MINGA, Mrs. N. J.	Low	2–263	1900
MINOR, Ann	Cla	B–311	1863
John	Ada	2–17	1832
Katherine	Ada	2–278	1844
Major Stephen	Ada	1–23	1816
Rebecca Arin	Ada	4–428	1887
Robert	Isa	C–138	1885
Stephen B.	Cla	A–103	1821
MINTER, B. W. M.	Mad	A–47	1839
MISSENGER, Anthony	Mot	1–157	1899
MITCHELL, A. J.			
Dallas	Mad	A–229	1855
Asa H.	Jef	B–16	1859
Belinda F.	Grn	A–145	1898

Bell W.	Laf	1–366	1887
Benjamin F.	Lau	1–26	1861
Clarinda	Att	D–52	1895
David	Ada	1–8	1803
David	Ada	1–224	1820
Edward	War	A–37	1834
Frank	Mas	1–171	1900
Green	Hin	B–372	1885
J. C.	Cop	AAA–229	1863
J. L.	Yaz	B–113	1880
James Edwin	Lau	1–39	1863
James P.	Tal	A–31	1843
James S.	DeS	1–275	1861
Jesse T.	Cly	1–73	1886
John	Jef	B–70	1862
John Irvin	Jef	B–109	1870
John M.	Han	A–279	1895
M. A.	Tun	2–198	1900
Malissa Arcola	Cop	A–92	1893
Mary A.	Clk	1–117	1891
Mary E.	Hol	3–1	1894
Mattie R.	Uni	1–35	1895
Samuel	Att	B–352	1881
Sarah	Ada	1–230	1821
Sarah	Wil	2–91	1854
Sarah S.	Coa(2)	1–23	1894
Sidney	Pan(1)	B–144	1873
William C.	Yal(1)	B–190	1883
MITH, John	Ada	2–189	1839
MIXON, Alexander	Chi(1)	1–5	1875
William	Cly	1–61	1883
MIXSON, Richard B.	Low	1–188	1865
MIZE, F.	Laf	1–361	1886
MOBLEY, Fountain W.	Yaz	A–272	1861
MOCK, Benjamin	Ada	5–96	1895
MOFFAT, Harriet S.	Chi(1)	1–49	1883
MOHEAD, Jesse C.	Car(1)	A–188	1859
MOHUNDER, Thomas P.	Tip	1–43	1870
MONAHAN, John J.	DeS	2–247	1882
MONASCO, J. W.	Mon	I.17–57	1862
MONCHET, Jacques			
Henri	Ada	2–51	1831
MONDAY, Samuel	Tip	1–42	1870
MONEY, Pierson	Car(1)	B–46	1893
Triphena	Car(1)	A–523	1870
Upton	Car(1)	A–465	1863
MONHOLLAND, Moses	Yaz	A–116	1848
MONK, William B.	Nox	A–127	1849
MONROE, Jennett	Hin	1–93	1837
Thomas	War	B–389	1900
MONTGOMERY, Amelia			

Farra	Cla	3–41	1877
David F.	Okt	1–17	1888
F. P.	Was	2–56	1897
Ferdinand	Tun	2–42	1876
Hugh	Jef	B–114	1870
James McElwain	Mas	P.2–6	1839
John	Jef	A–73	1821
John H.	Tal	B–19	1869
Joseph	Cla	A–158	1825
M. E.	Ada	3–341	1868
M. H.	Tip	1–162	1889
Olivia T.	Hin	B–390	1887
Robert	Mad	A–561	1873
S. H.	War	A–219	1855
Samuel	Ada	1–434	1825
Samuel	DeS	1–264	1858
William	Jef	P.D–295	1848
MONTROY, John B.	Coa(1)	1–256	1894
MOODY, Elmira	War	B–272	1892
George V.	Cla	B–320	1866
M. W.	Low	1–502	1885
Nathaniel P.	Cla	B–247	1853
William H.	DeS	1–357	1866
MOOELY, Elizabeth F.	Tip	1–27	1868
MOON, John	Mon	1–257	1849
T. J.	Mon	I.5–558	1890
William A.	Ran	1–80	1865
William S.	Chi(1)	1–77	1886
MOONE, William A. Sr.	Ran	1–49	1863
MOORAN, Alva William	Hin	B–179	1865
MOORE, A. Barry	Mad	A–162	1851
Alfred	Car(1)	A–188	1859
Alfred G.	Hin	1–87	1837
Allen	Web	A–39	1885
Archie	War	B–169	1886
B. W.	Hol	1–382	1875
Bartholomew Figures	Lau	1–134	1880
Brittain	Nox	A–9	1837
Brittain	Nox	A–189	1853
Bryant	War	B–366	1897
C. C.	Hin	1–319	1853
C. Y.	DeS	2–482	1898
Charles	Mad	A–128	1848
Charlotte	Ada	3–223	1865
Delaney	Lea	1–116	1884
Edward	Ada	3–44	1855
Edward	Lau	1–208	1886
Elizabeth	Mas	P.4–48	1845
Elizabeth Malinda	Mad	A–618	1882
Ellen C.	Wil	2–55	1850
Ellen L.	Lef	A–104	1890

George Henry	Hol	1–300	1864
George W.	DeS	2–88	1874
Henry	Cov	1–12	1897
Jacob K.	Yal(1)	B–184	1879
James	Ada	1–426	1829
James	Hol	1–449	1882
James	Mon	I.19–111	1865
James C.	Ran	1–214	1885
James S.	Mas	P.10–39	1854
Jefferis H.	Cla	A–56	1814
John	Coa(1)	1–131	1879
John B.	Mas	P.2–43	1840
John G.	Nox	A–109	1848
John L.	Tis	1–6	1887
John Taylor	Cla	3–52	1879
John W.	Mon	I.3–79	1878
Joseph	Cla	A–198	1827
Joseph	Web	A–143	1900
Joseph A.	Hin	1–366	1855
Joseph F.	Laf	1–316	1882
Louisa	Car(1)	A–203	1860
Mrs. M. P.	Laf	1–425	1896
Mary	Cop	AAA–225	1852
Mary	War	B–391	1900
Mary Virginia	Was	1–463	1886
Mellison A.	DeS	2–224	1884
Michael	Ada	1–4	1803
Moore	Yal(1)	A–231	1853
Nancy	Low	1–174	1864
Nathaniel	Hin	B–238	1867
Nelson	Lau	1–283	1892
Osborn J.	Mot	1–128	1896
Peyton P.	Hin	B–226	1862
Robert	Ada	1–428	1829
Robert	Cla	A–76	1818
Robert A.	Mas	1–153	1899
Russell	Mad	A–597	1880
Sarah M.	Isa	C–160	1893
Sarah M.	Ran	1–293	1893
Susannah B.	War	A–247	1858
T. R.	Mad	A–572	1876
Thomas	Pan(1)	B–170	1875
Thomas J.	Mad	A–53	1839
Tom B.	Tat	1–248	1900
William	DeS	1–382	1866
William	Jef	A–69	1820
William	Mas	1–177	1900
William W.	Laf	1–107	1856
William W.	Low	1–568	1889
Zenobia P.	Mas	1–30	1893
MOOREHEAD, G. S.	Tip	1–33	1868

MOORHEAD, Mary A.	Yal(2)	1-60	1890
MOORING, Henry	Mas	P.4-47	1845
James	Mas	P.12-333	1857
MOORMAN, Benjamin	Car(1)	B-34	1890
MOREAU, Madeline			
Jeann	Han	A-96	1877
MOREHEAD, Samuel			
Judson	Cop	A-50	1891
MOREHOUSE, Clara E.	Ada	3-52	1856
MORGAN, Albert P.	Ada	4-11	1871
B. G.	Ben	1-65	1895
Benjamin	Jas	1-23	1860
Dock	Hol	3-55	1898
E. F.	Att	D-174	1899
Elisha	Hol	1-42	1843
Gilbert	Ada	2-213	1840
J. B.	DeS	2-349	1892
J. H.	Ben	1-35	1882
Jacob	Tip	1-56	1871
James W.	Hol	3-106	1900
James W.	Laf	1-41	1843
John M.	Low	1-405	1877
Joseph S.	DeS	1-181	1858
Louisa C.	Low	2-82	1894
Mary M. L.	Was	2-112	1899
Nathan L.	Mon	I.19-12	1865
Thomas	Hol	3-103	1900
William	Ada	1-6	1803
William	Yal(1)	A-73	1842
MORISON, George	Hin	B-323	1876
MORLET, E.	Jac	1-108	1892
MORNINGSTAR, Adarn	Wil	2-54	1850
MORRAH, Ellen R.	Ran	1-126	1873
MORRIS, A. C.	DeS	2-71	1872
Catharine	Ada	3-210	1863
Christopher S.	Hin	1-264	1851
Doctine	Jas	1-14	1861
Edmund	War	A-307	1862
Elizabeth	Wil	2-170	1861
Ezekiel	Low	1-35	1859
Helen L.	Was	2-18	1895
John	Car(1)	A-440	1862
John	Lef	A-143	1898
John S. Sr.	Nox	A-106	1848
John T.	DeS	1-320	1864
Jordan	Car(1)	A-201	1858
Levi L.	Car(1)	A-19	1841
Margaret L.	Low	1-506	1885
Mayberry	Wil	1-229	1840
Nathan	Hol	1-92	1849
Nathan D.	Ran	1-44	1862

Preston	Nes	A-89	1868
Robert L.	Ran	1-84	1866
Simeon	Pik	1-5	1882
Spencer	Ada	4-566	1891
Susan	Wil	2-113	1856
Thomas	Low	1-28	1859
William	Hin	1-261	1850
MORRISON, Angus	Hin	1-224	1848
Daniel	Hin	1-377	1856
Jesse W.	Hin	B-145	1861
John	Ran	1-187	1883
R. W.	Car(1)	A-420	1859
Roderick	Hin	1-338	1854
William N.	Laf	1-144	1862
MORROW, John	Hol	1-431	1879
MORSEN, Delilah	War	B-318	1895
MORSON, William	Hin	1-144	1841
MORTEN, Elisha	Ben	1-60	1888
MORTON, Alexander B.	Mas	P.12-225	1857
Abraham B.	Mas	P.10-55	1854
Benjamin W.	Hol	1-422	1878
John	Low	1-346	1873
Joseph W.	Yaz	A-297	1864
Loring	Ada	1-355	1825
Nancy	Ada	4-204	1882
Samuel	Ada	1-364	1826
Solomon	Yaz	B-136	1881
MOSBY, Eliza G.	Was	1-336	1862
William B.	Coa(1)	1-136	1879
MOSELEY, Arthur	Yaz	A-58	1841
Eliza F.	Kem	A-38	1890
H.	Pan(2)	A-120	1895
J. R.	Was	1-345	1865
Joseph R.	Yaz	B-57	1876
Pleasant	DeS	2-181	1881
William A.	Kem	A-30	1887
MOSELY, Hartwell	War	A-287	1860
James C.	War	A-332	1865
Joseph	Hin	1-316	1853
Arthur	Cla	B-353	1866
Campbell	Tun	2-154	1898
G. B.	Coa(2)	1-44	1897
MOSLY, Ann	War	B-239	1890
MOSS, Harry	Yaz	B-183	1884
J. L.	Low	1-554	1888
Joseph	Hin	1-143	1841
MOTLEY, Allen	Low	2-10	1890
Mrs. E. T.	Tun	2-30	1875
MOTTLEY, Mrs. E. T.	Tat	1-17	1875
MOUCHET, John Baptiste			
Henry	Ada	1-443	1829

144

MOUNTCASTLE, George			
E.	Mas	P.4-567	1847
MOWER, Joseph Z.	Mad	A-9	1832
Milo	Ran	1-34	1861
William B.	Hin	B-37	1860
MUCE, William L.	Yal(1)	B-103	1863
MUDD, L. E.	War	B-159	1886
MULDOON, Charles	War	B-362	1899
MULHOLLAN, Henry	Ran	1-174	1882
MULHOLLAND, Charles			
H.	War	B-326	1896
MULLIGAN, Patrick	Yal(2)	1-38	1884
MULLIKIN, Johnathan			
Isom	Laf	1-345	1885
MULLIN, William H.	Att	B-475	1885
MULLINS, George H.	Mon	I.17-245	1863
MUNDELL, Abijah H.	Cla	A-225	1831
Andrew	Cla	A-69	1817
MUNDILL, Joseph M.	Ada	1-487	1829
MUNIS, Mary	Han	A-265	1894
MUNIZ, Ann	Han	A-62	1870
MUNN, Osburn	Mas	1-56	1894
MUNNELEE, Mary A.	Lee	1-103	1887
MURCHISON, John	Hin	1-42	1834
Simon	Hin	B-374	1885
MURDOCK, Abram	Low	1-547	1888
Esther	Cla	B-182	1844
Francis	Cla	B-156	1838
Grace A.	Low	1-432	1880
Elizabeth	Car(1)	A-117	1852
John	Cla	A-178	1827
Mary	Yaz	B-217	1887
MURFREE, Mathias B.	Mad	A-200	1853
MURGRAVE, Richard L.	Mas	P.19-639	1871
MURLAGH, Edward	Han	A-236	1893
Thomas	Mad	A-593	1879
MURPHEY, Alexander G.	Tal	B-28	1873
James B.	Ada	1-394	1827
John	Ada	2-143	1837
MURPHY, Alexander	Mon	I.1-107	1869
Ann	Mad	A-574	1878
Annie E.	Mon	I.5-27	1884
Cornelius D.	Qui	1-11	1897
Cornelius D.	Sun	1-39	1900
Daniel	Wil	1-90	1833
Daniel W.	Mad	A-268	1858
Elizabeth A.	Tat	1-144	1889
Frank	War	B-387	1900
J. S.	Mad	A-579	1879
James	Wil	2-238	1866
James M.	Mon	I.4-29	1879

John	Nox	C-73	1898
John	Pan(1)	A-47	1848
Joseph G.	Hin	B-272	1870
Mary	Cla	B-194	1846
Mary Smith	Tal	A-211	1859
Mathew	War	B-10	1870
Miles	Yaz	B-143	1882
Patrick	Ada	4-367	1885
R. M.	Hol	1-456	1882
Stephen	Coa(1)	1-52	1857
MURRAY, Alexander	Ada	1-119	1814
Charles G.	Chi(2)	1-13	1883
James	War	B-352	1898
John R.	Cla	B-249	1854
Judith	Ada	1-206	1820
Judith	Ada	1-219	1820
Robert S.	Yal(2)	1-42	1885
MURRELL, Onslow G.	Hin	1-448	1859
MURRY, M. H.	DeS	2-336	1891
Marshall H.	DeS	2-493	1899
Penny	DeS	2-423	1895
Robert	Mad	A-318	1860
MURXEY, Robert	Ran	1-127	1874
MUSE, T. M.	Yaz	B-285	1893
MYERS, Absalom	DeS	1-328	1865
George H.	Jac	1-39	1885
George H.	Jac	1-169	1897
Isaac	Ran	1-26	1860
John	Law	P.B-142	1841
Mary Ann	Law	1-4	1877
Mena	Jac	1-170	1897
Mina	Jac	1-50	1888
P. J.	Per	1-25	1890
Phillip	Hin	B-74	1864
Susan Amanda	Nox	B-326	1888
NABORS, S. O.	Hol	3-44	1896
NAGLE, Mary Ann	War	B-324	1896
NAIL, Elisha	Nes	A-7	1838
NAILER, D. B.	War	B-243	1889
Jefferson	War	A-293	1861
Mary C.	War	B-330	1896
Theresa	War	B-123	1880
NALL, Berry	Hol	1-409	1875
John	Yaz	A-1	1830
NANCE, James H.	Tip	1-133	1887
Mary A.	Hol	3-53	1897
Terrel	Tip	1-91	1879
NAPIER, Sarah M.	Mad	A-65	1842
NARBON, Joseph	Hin	B-68	1861
NASH, Madison G.	Mad	A-220	1854

Mariah G.	Coa(1)	1-49	1856
Reuben B.	Low	1-425	1879
William	Mad	A-214	1853
NASON, Richard	Yal(1)	B-96	1864
NASSAUER, H.	Cly	1-124	1897
NAUERTH, John Michael	Hin	1-173	1844
NAVRA, Abraham	War	B-237	1890
NEAL, Emeline M.	Mad	A-632	1884
John	Pre	1-64	1879
Robert	Car(1)	A-416	1859
T. J.	Qui	1-4	1890
William W.	Mas	P.12-228	1857
NEARING, Milly	Laf	1-32	1848
NEARMAN, Frank	Yaz	A-174	1854
NEBLETT, Benjamin R.	Mas	1-115	1897
NECKLE, R. H.	Pan(2)	A-105	1894
NEEL, George Thomason	Pan(1)	A-287	1857
Susan L.	Att	B-474	1885
NEELEY, Ezekiel C.	DeS	1-207	1859
Jacob	Ran	1-216	1887
Jane M.	Cla	B-343	1873
NEELY, John J.	Mas	P.19-487	1870
Mary A.	Chi(2)	1-16	1884
Samuel	Yaz	A-78	1846
Samuel Sr.	Cop	AAA-211	1834
W. W.	War	B-3	1869
NEIHYSEL, Philip	Ada	3-438	1870
NEILSON, Charles			
Purvis	Was	2-1	1894
W. W.	Low	1-264	1869
William S.	Laf	1-387	1892
NELMS, Charles	Lee	1-29	1876
Charles G.	DeS	1-400	1866
Charles G.	Mas	P.15-511	1862
Martin	Car(1)	A-36	1843
Murphy	DeS	2-402	1893
NELSON, Achilla	Lau	1-221	1886
Alice M.	DeS	2-275	1886
B. F.	Cop	A-67	1892
Catharine N.	Cla	B-324	1867
Charles W. F.	Yaz	A-82	1845
Christian	Cop	AAA-216	1835
Eliza	Car(1)	B-61	1898
Emelia	Pan(1)	A-54	1848
George W.	Pan(1)	B-60	1869
John Albert	Laf	1-291	1879
John H.	Ada	4-560	1891
Levi	Hin	1-253	1850
Lucretia L.	Pan(1)	B-467	1891
Margaret	Ada	1-215	1812
Mary E.	Cop	A-35	1889

Matthew	Nox	B-222	1879
Nancy W.	Pan(1)	B-66	1868
Peter	Ada	1-205	1820
Peter	Han	A-161	1886
Sarah A.	Lau	1-252	1889
Thomas	Isa	A-159	1852
Thomas	Yaz	A-66	1838
William	Cla	B-255	1856
William	Laf	1-329	1884
William R.	Tip	1-8	1866
NERREN, Nancy	Laf	1-351	1885
NESBITT, Mary	DeS	1-2	1851
Thomas	DeS	2-295	1888
NESMITH, Daniel B.	Hol	1-394	1876
Frances C.	Cop	A-6	1887
NETTER, Elizabeth	Ada	5-104	1896
NETTERVILLE, Charles	Wil	2-45	1849
Margaret E.	Wil	2-48	1849
NETTO, Florentine	Han P.(1853-1860)-634		1857
NEVALS, Martin	Jef	P.B-253	1838
NEVIN, John A.	Lin	1-39	1896
NEVITT, Charlotte L.	Ada	3-141	1860
John B.	Ada	3-295	1867
NEW, Walter W.	Hin	1-423	1858
NEWBERRY, Sina B.	Yal(1)	B-225	1892
NEWELL, Charles Story	Cop	AAA-219	1860
NEWELL, George B.	Wil	2-114	1856
George B.	Wil	1-16	1831
James	Att	A-227	1859
Sarah T.	War	B-353	1898
Silas B.	DeS	2-183	1882
William	Wil	1-91	1833
NEWMAN, Alexander F.	War	B-19	1872
Benjamin	Jef	A-29	1818
Clarinda	Jef	P.D-97	1847
Eugene	War	A-195	1852
Ezekiel	Ada	1-490	1831
Isaac	War	A-108	1841
James C.	War	B-235	1890
Josiah	Car(1)	A-432	1860
Laura C.	War	B-235	1890
Mary J.	Yal(1)	B-241	1900
Reuben	War (1827-1832)-93		1828
Sally	War	A-9	1830
Sarah	Wil	2-327	1877
Sarah R.	War	A-187	1851
Simeon	Jef	A-86	1825
Simeon B.	War	A-369	1865
Thomas R.	War	A-147	1845
Uriah	Car(1)	A-15	1839
NEWSOM, David	Yaz	B-154	1883

John S.	Pan(1)	A-291	1858
Mrs. M. N.	Pan(2)	A-158	1900
NEWSUM, Sarah	Mas	P.3-61	1843
NEWTON, Edgar W.	Mad	A-548	1873
Ellen	Law	1-5	1883
Isham	DeS	1-126	1855
Martha H.	Jef	B-168	1888
Mary	Uni	1-7	1883
NICAISE, Edmond	Han	A-297	1896
NICHOLLS, Mary D.	Ada	5-28	1893
NICHOLS, Abigail G.	Ada	3-102	1857
Amariah	Mad	A-38	1837
Andrew	Mas	P.19-183	1869
Charles M.	Ada	3-41	1855
Henry	Hin	1-5	1833
James	Sha	A-13	1885
Joseph	Ada	4-591	1892
Mary	Mas	1-1	1892
Riley	Mon	I.6-585	1896
Sarah	Hin	1-17	1833
NICHOLSON, Eliza			
Eveline	Mad	A-165	1851
Eliza J. P.	Pik	1-73	1896
George	Pik	1-78	1896
Isaac W.	Nox	A-293	1861
John Hacker	Han	A-75	1870
John M.	New	1-81	1888
Salena A.	Pik	1-83	1896
William F. I.	Wil	1-2	1825
NIELSON, William W.	Low	1-87	1861
NILES, Charles	Mas	P.11-56	1855
Jason	Att	C-404	1894
NIPPER, Jordan	DeS	1-342	1865
NIX, A. F.	Pre	1-96	1895
NOA, Elizabeth	Mad	A-553	1873
NOBLE, Alfred	Mad	A-48	1838
E. Fenwick	Cla	3-96	1886
Isaac	Jef	P.D-9	1847
John L.	Hol	1-9	1837
NOBLIN, Linie	Okt	1-56	1900
Nancy	Web	A-119	1898
R. H.	Hin	B-459	1897
S. D.	Web	A-115	1897
NOEL, Mrs. F.	Mad	2-114	1898
Laura V.	War	B-242	1892
NOLAND, Pearce	War	A-239	1857
Phillip	Wil	1-161	1836
Thomas	Hol	1-356	1871
William	War	A-222	1855
NOONAN, Patrick	Mad	A-410	1862
Thomas	Yaz	A-152	1852

NORFLEET, Dudley	Mas	1-41	1894
William B.	Mad	A-60	1840
NORL, Leland	Hol	3-39	1896
NORMAN, Beulah	Cop	A-65	1891
Elijah	Ada	1-301	1823
Louisa	Lin	1-5	1894
Madison G.	Cop	A-28	1889
Martha A.	Cop	A-140	1900
Thomas D.	Mad	A-632	1884
NORMENT, Elizabeth	Wil	2-23	1847
NORREL, John B.	Jef	A-85	1825
Maria Ann Mary	Ada	1-357	1825
NORRIS, Eli	Att	2-370	1864
John	Mas	P.7-199	1849
M. E.	Clk	1-78	1885
Mary	Jef	P.C-195	1842
NORTON, Amelia E.	War	B-16	1870
Charles M.	Ada	1-315	1824
Henry W.	Chi(1863-1872)-185		1869
John H.	Hin	1-443	1859
Mortimer O. H.	Han	A-73	1872
NORWOOD, Elias Warren	Ran	B.1-264	1845
John	Sim	A-16	1876
NORELL, Edward	Mas	P.13-513	1858
NOWELL, Thomas N.	Ran	1-323	1900
NOWLIN, David	Web	A-24	1878
NOYES, Elizabeth	Ada	3-148	1860
NSSERY, Elizabeth Ann	Tun	2-184	1899
NUNALLY, James B.	Mas	P.10-457	1854
NUNNALLY, Dorothy J.	Mas	P.15-530	1862
NURSE, Samuel	Was	2-60	1897
NUTT, Collin	Jef	A-61	1820
Haller	Ada	3-266	1866
Rittenhouse	Hin	B-73	1862
Rush	Jef	P.B-252	1837
NYE, Lucy A.	Yaz	B-215	1887
OAKES, E. H.	Att	C-43	1887
OAKLEY, Fielding	Mad	A-30	1836
Thomas	Hin	B-67	1861
OAKS, Mary	Yaz	B-157	1883
OAR, Massey	Ran	1-112	1869
OATES, Jacob	War	A-358	1866
OATIS, Francis Tucker	Cop	A-6	1887
O'BANNON, John	Grn	A-77	1887
O'BRIEN, James	Ada	5-283	1900
Mary J.	Coa(1)	1-116	1871
OBRIEN, Sarah	Jac	2-22	1899
OBRYANT, L. R.	Pan(2)	A-31	1883
OBUN, Mary S.	Ada	4-585	1892
OCALLAGHAN, J. P.	Lee	1-74	1883

ODENEAL, Milton	Low	1-475	1884
Rosamond W.	Low	1-403	1877
ODENHEIMER, John	DeS	1-241	1858
ODOM, Frances	Jef	P.D-99	1847
Ransom	DeS	2-244	1885
ODONNELL, Patrick	Yaz	A-288	1865
O'FERRALL, John J.	Ada	5-225	1899
Patrick	Ada	5-35	1893
OFFUTT, Henry A.	Mad	A-79	1843
OGDEN, Ann M.	Ada	3-336	1868
Edmund	Yaz	A-32	1836
Elias	Ada	2-299	1845
Jane W.	Hin	B-379	1882
John	Ada	1-319	1824
Rebecca	Wil	1-201	1839
Robert N.	Han	A-224	1894
Robert T.	Wil	1-234	1840
Rufus William	Ada	3-21	1855
William D.	Yaz	A-136	1850
O'HARA, Thomas C.	Ada	4-201	1881
O'HARRA, Timothy	Ada	1-345	1824
OHILTON, William	Nes	A-20	1848
OHINER, Mary			
Magdaleine	Jef	B-144	1877
O'KEEFE, Dennis			
Joseph	War	B-202	1888
Katie	War	B-231	1889
OLD, Robert T.	Mad	A-27	1836
OLDENBURG, Susan	DeS	2-96	1875
OLDHAM, J. William	Coa(1)	1-26	1850
James	Coa(1)	1-75	1859
Moses	Coa(1)	1-104	1867
Oliver M.	Att	D-65	1898
O'LEARY, Henrietta			
E.	Mad	A-286	1859
OLIPHANT, James H.	Hol	1-28	1836
OLIVARI, Eugenia	Han	A-205	1892
OLIVE, Fabius J.	Mad	A-175	1852
James	Hol	1-189	1858
OLIVER, David Terrel	DeS	1-370	1866
Dionysius	Pan(1)	A-107	1851
Mrs. H. J.	Car(1)	B-50	1896
Joseph F.	Lau	1-359	1896
Mrs. M. T.	DeS	2-116	1876
Shelton	DeS	1-410	1866
Simeon	DeS	2-90	1874
Simeon	DeS	2-131	1877
Thomas W.	Pan(1)	A-161	1853
William	Cop	A-58	1891
OLLIVER, C. A.	Cly	1-58	1883
OLMSTEAD, D. G.	Was	1-375	1867

ONEAL, Emberson	Tun	1–240	1860
O'NEAL, James	Car(1)	A–501	1867
ONEAL, Lycurgus E.	Jef	P.F–492	1856
Sarah A.	Mot	1–43	1880
ONEIL, Charles E.	Lau	1–328	1893
O'NEIL, James	Ada	4–436	1888
O'REILLY, Patsey	Yaz	B–405	1899
Philip	Yaz	A–3	1833
O'REILY, Michael	Mad	A–445	1867
Michael D.	War	A–154	1846
John	Yaz	A–161	1846
ORMOND, Benjamin			
Franklin	Lau	1–399	1898
ORNE, Richard E.	Pan(1)	B–46	1866
O'ROURKE, Felix	Han	A–66	1872
ORR, Christopher	Lee	1–1	1867
James	Ada	4–333	1884
Jane F.	War	B–325	1896
Jones K.	Tal	A–184	1857
Simon	Nox	B–124	1872
ORRICK, M. E.	Coa(1)	1–107	1867
Nicholas Cromwell	Mad	2–93	1897
OSBORNE, William W.	War	A–91	1838
OSBURN, Lennie S.	Cop	A–152	1899
Louisa	Hin	B–388	1887
Ozias	Cop	A–32	1889
Samuel H.	Hin	1–110	1839
O'SHEA, Timothy	War	B–264	1892
OSTEEN, Abram C.	Tat	1–161	1893
Nancy	Cop	AAA–209	1869
Simeon	Hin	1–339	1854
Thomas S.	Jef	B–101	1867
OSMUN, Benejah	Ada	1–122	1815
OTEY, Martha A.	Hol	1–336	1869
OTT, John G.	Mad	A–103	1843
OTTLEY, John K.	Low	1–429	1880
OUSLEY, Nixon	Att	B–151	1874
Rachel Ella	Hol	3–42	1896
Welden	Yaz	B–133	1881
OUTLAW, Clara Eliza	Okt	1–22	1884
OVERAKER, George	Ada	1–202	1816
OVERLY, George W.	Sim	A–65	1890
OVERSTREET, B.			
Chelton	Hol	1–78	1848
OWEN, Andrew T.	Laf	2–1	1896
B. H. Sr.	Att	C–577	1897
B. T.	Hol	1–365	1872
Edward	Mas	P.3–511	1845
Ellen J.	Cla	3–151	1893
Eugene B.	Mad	A–562	1874
Fleming B.	Hin	B–178	1865

Henry	Mon	I.6–109	1891
Isabella R.	Pre	1–99	1895
J. E.	Ben	1–80	1899
John	Laf	1–5	1840
John	Mas	P.16–285	1865
John	Tal	A–92	1847
Robert	DeS	2–45	1872
Silas Jr.	Laf	1–376	1889
Silas Sr.	Laf	1–320	1883
Stephen F.	Hol	1–474	1885
Susan	Mas	P.9–291	1853
T. B.	Hol	3–113	1900
William	Laf	1–158	1865
William	Laf	1–168	1865
William E.	Att	D–109	1898
OWENS, Henry S.	Cop	A–124	1897
James	Hin	1–14	1833
James	Hol	1–103	1851
James M.	Tun	2–32	1876
James W.	Hin	B–274	1872
Middleton E.	Okt	1–32	1897
Norfleet	Laf	2–10	1898
Rebecca	Cla	B–334	1871
S. S.	Pre	1–40	1878
Thomas	Cla	B–327	1868
Thyrza Ann	Sim	A–39	1886
William	Mad	A–61	1841
OZMORE, John W.	War	A–103	1840
PACE, A. C.	Hol	3–104	1900
Bennett R.	Lau	1–361	1896
Elijah H.	War	B–65	1876
Mrs. G. S.	Lau	1–384	1899
L. D.	Mad	A–389	1863
Royal	War(1823–1827)–181		1825
PACKS, Elisha	War	A–103	1840
PADRICK, Ann B.	Hol	1–259	1861
PAGE, George H.	Coa(1)	1–62	1859
J. G.	Okt	1–40	1898
Mollie	Yaz	B–189	1885
William Jefferson	Ada	4–380	1885
PAGR, Emma W.	Ada	3–444	1871
PAINE, Eliza J.	Ada	4–65	1874
James A.	DeS	2–368	1893
R. W.	Sco	A–128	1867
Robert	Mon	I.6–457	1895
PAKLEN, John J.	Hol	3–99	1900
PALESK, Charles G.	Ada	1–201	1820
PALLEY, John	Mon	1–155	1840
PALMER, Ann	Yal(2)	1–37	1883
B. M.	Cly	1–115	1892

Hasting D.	Att	B–306	1879
Isham	Hin	1–120	1839
J. Monroe	Ran	1–313	1900
Lucy J.	Att	B–510	1885
Randolph	Tip	1–39	1869
Richard S.	Hin	1–157	1831
Samuel	War	B–389	1900
PANKEY, Stephen	Hol	1–167	1857
PANNELL, D. A.	Uni	1–6	1883
PANNILLS, Joseph	Ada	1–69	1811
PAQUINETT, Romanta J.	Yaz	A–134	1849
PARCHMAN, George W.	Chi(2)	1–80	1898
Martha	Mon	I.19–142	1865
PARHAM, Harrison	Mon	I.15–339	1860
John T.	Hin	1–108	1838
Sarah	Car(1)	A–494	1866
PARISH, Anderson	Yaz	A–149	1852
E. A.	Yal(1)	B–240	1898
PARK, John L.	Mon	1–145	1840
PARKER, Alexander	Ada	2–3	1832
Burwell	Hol	1–48	1844
Christopher Adams	Ada	2–133	1836
David R.	Cop	A–93	1893
Dicie	DeS	2–31	1871
E.	Clk	1–193	1895
Henry	Mas	P.19–125	1869
James D.	Jas	1–6	1851
James M.	Coa(1)	1–31	1852
John	Nes	A–81	1865
John G.	Ran	1–107	1868
Joseph J.	Jac	1–9	1878
Maria	Ada	4–32	1872
Mary	Ada	4–226	1882
Rebecca	Ada	2–270	1843
Rhasa	Ada	4–97	1876
Richard	War	A–121	1841
Sophia	Ada	1–409	1828
Thomas Jefferson	Mad	2–88	1897
William	Lef	A–1	1845
William E.	Hol	1–151	1855
Zalmona	Ada	2–73	1834
PARKES, Nancy	DeS	2–285	1887
Samuel	Yal(1)	B–55	1861
PARKINSON, Emily J.	Cla	3–138	1893
PARKISON, G. W.	Pan(1)	B–493	1899
PARKMAN, Elizabeth	Hin	B–376	1887
James	Hin	B–382	1887
PARKS, George N.	Isa	B–81	1854
M. M. H. E.	Uni	1–68	1900
PARNELL, P. A.	Pik	1–30	1887
PARR, B. W.	Cla	B–186	1845

Henry	War	A-24	1833
PARRAMORE, Redding	Tal	A-106&116	1849
PARROTT, Ruth	Wil	1-274	1844
PARSONS, Mrs. D. L.	Mad	2-75	1897
James	DeS	1-252	1860
PARTEE, Georgia M.	Pan(1)	B-303	1879
PARTIN, Barnabas	Wil	2-100	1855
PARTON, Alex M.	War	B-176	1886
Charles	Mon	I.10-356	1854
PASLAY, Austin	Pan(1)	B-231	1878
PASSMORE, Ellis P.	Mad	A-52	1839
PATE, Annanian	Car(1)	A-184	1859
Charles A.	Car(1)	A-469	1864
James H.	Car(1)	A-444	1862
Jefferson C.	Car(1)	A-181	1859
Joel H.	Car(1)	A-81	1850
John Frank	Yal(2)	1-9	1875
Lotts S.	Tip	1-182	1893
William H.	Pre	1-4	1870
PATILLO, Robert H.	Pan(1)	A-25	1847
PATRICK, C. A.	Wil	2-361	1880
Ellis	Ran	1-294	1894
Henry	Ada	2-145	1837
Mattie	Wil	3-64	1887
PATTEN, Mary E.	Hin	B-450	1897
PATTERSON, Andrew I.	Hol	1-120	1852
George C.	Mad	A-30	1839
Giles J.	Nox	C-112	1899
James W. H.	Ada	5-194	1898
John	Ada	1-441	1829
John	Cla	A-122	1822
John	Tal	B-56	1878
John	War	A-36	1834
Judith Ann	War	B-270	1892
Martha	Ada	5-155	1897
Sarah	Hol	3-79	1899
W. H.	Yaz	B-389	1899
William	Nox	B-155	1874
William M.	Mot	1-154	1899
PATTIE, John	Ada	1-440	1829
PATTISON, Jane E. C.	Cla	3-25	1874
PATTON, Adaline A.	Car(1)	A-74	1849
Francis P.	Cla	B-237	1853
James T.	Laf	1-156	1865
James W.	Pan(1)	A-177	1854
John	Hol	1-274	1862
John B.	Pan(1)	A-6	1845
Leanna L.	Ran	1-24	1860
Robert	Cla	B-191	1846
Robert S.	Cla	3-67	1881
Samuel	Laf	1-17	1847

155

PATTY, Francis Marion	Win	1-168	1896
Georgia	Win	1-179	1899
J. W.	Nox	B-287	1883
Kate Foote	Nox	B-344	1890
PAUL, Peter	Ada	1-425	1829
PAULK, James	Chi(1)	1-33	1881
PAVELL, Becky	Was	1-473	1888
PAXTON, Andrew J.	Was	2-130	1900
John Galaten	Was	1-283	1860
PAYNE, Adaline	Mas	1-94	1896
Cubberson B.	DeS	1-99	1855
Felix A.	Coa(2)	1-41	1895
John H.	DeS	1-31	1852
Jordan	DeS	2-188	1882
Jordan A.	DeS	2-358	1893
P.	DeS	2-383	1894
T. D.	Chi(1)	1-85	1887
Thomas	Pon	2-332	1844
W. A.	Lau	1-270	1890
William M.	Low	1-392	1876
PAYRO, Gregorio	Han	A-191	1890
PEACOCK, Thomas E.	Grn	A-31	1878
PEALE, Alexander	War	A-128	1842
Jacob	War	A-361	1867
PEARCE, Charles E.	Pan(1)	A-254	1857
Elizathan	Att	B-370	1882
Zeberdee	Pan(1)	B-394	1884
PEARSON, Charles W.	Cla	3-193	1899
Jane	Yal(1)	B-118	1866
John	Yal(1)	A-223	1851
John W.	New	1-53	1884
William	Mas	P.4-652	1847
PEARY, Joseph	Pan(1)	B-271	1878
PEASE, Henry H.	Yaz	A-54	1841
PEASTER, John	Win	1-107	1888
Michael	Yaz	A-233	1860
PEAVY, Archibald	Cop	AAA-206	1858
John Wesley	Mon	I.7-67	1899
PEDEN, Henry	Yaz	A-60	1841
PEEBLES, Alpha	Mot	1-12	1867
Berlin	DeS	2-333	1891
George	Car(1)	A-95	1838
Lennie V.	Att	D-111	1896
Martha P.	Hin	B-168	1863
Mary J.	DeS	2-376	1893
William	Car(1)	A-179	1857
PEED, John	Car(1)	A-115	1844
PEEL, Albert	Mas (1838-1839)-124		1838
John Coffee	Mas	P.10-244	1854
Pernelia Jane	Tis	1-22	1889
Thomas J.	Mas	P.15-552	1862

Volney	Mas	P.4–180	1846
PEELE, Thomas	Tal	A–187	1858
PEELER, Anthony	Att	2–503	1865
Jesse	Tip	1–135	1887
PEEPLES, Amanda	Web	A–20	1877
PEETE, Thomas	Tal	A–187	1858
PEGRAM, G. G.	War	B–286	1893
James W.	Yaz	A–88	1846
PEGUES, Alexander H.	Laf	1–211	1872
Charlotte J.	Laf	1–321	1883
Emily	Mas	1 28	1893
Malachi	Mas	P.5–86	1847
Malachi M.	Laf	1–213	1872
Rebecca Ann	Laf	1–418	1889
Thomas E. B.	Laf	1–261	1875
PEIRCE, Irvin	Jef	B–86	1865
PELHAM, Thomas D.	Was	1–287	1860
PENDER, Joseph J. B.	Coa(1)	1–111	1868
PENDLETON, Rea	Hin	1–67	1836
PENN, Charles	War	A–348	1866
PENNEY, William	Coa(1)	1–194	1884
PENNINGTON, Edward M.	Jef	A–70	1821
Susannah	Ran	1–301	1895
William R.	Mas	P.10–76	1854
PENNY, W. T.	Was	1–317	1861
PENON, William	Mas	P.15–37	1860
PENRICE, Francis R.	Was	1–12	1841
Joseph B.	Was	1–167	1852
PENRY, Jonathan	Nox	B–44	1863
PEPPER, S. J.	Yaz	B–101	1878
PERCY, Francis George	Was	1–487	1890
John Walker	Was	1–339	1864
LeRoy P.	Was	1–428	1873
Nannie I.	Was	2–57	1897
Thomas G.	Was	1–23	1842
W. A.	Was	1–479	1889
PERDUE, Cora	Han	A–304	1896
William W.	Wil	1–26	1833
PERICOLE, Angelique	Han	A–119	1880
PERKINS, Asa Soule	Yaz	A–174	1854
Betsey	Nox	A–193	1854
Calvin	Low	1–154	1863
Early P.	Pan(1)	A–73	1850
George	Ada	1–302	1823
Isaac H.	Mad	A–143	1850
J. R.	Lin	1–12	1895
John Sr.	Low	1–221	1866
John B. F.	Ada	2–365	1849
John R.	Mas	P.17–57	1866
Joseph	Ada	1–280	1823
Lelia	Tun	2–125	1891

Nathaniel	Ada	1–362	1825
Reese	Win	1–88	1878
Stringer	Nox	A–45	1842
Thomas G.	Ran	1–60	1863
PERRANNI, Louis	War	A–298	1861
PERRAULT, Armand L.	Ada	4–347	1885
Elizabeth M.	Ada	5–126	1897
PERRION, Banister	DeS	1–412	1867
PERRY, Barnabus	Ada	1–49	1809
Eliza	Ada	2–46	1833
Evin	Tat	1–40	1880
Jacob	Hin	1–14	1833
Jasper F.	Jas	1–41	1862
John	Wil	3–5	1883
Josiah	Cly	1–34	1879
Mrs. M. S.	Hol	1–402	1876
Mrs. N. J.	Mon	I.6–84	1891
O. H.	Yal(1)	B–137	1868
Pauline G.	Hol	1–461	1883
Rix	Mas	P.5–31	1847
Robert C.	Hol	1–181	1858
William	Nes	A–34	1854
Zadock	Yal(1)	A–171	1850
PERRYMAN, David G.	Hin	B–88	1864
PERSON, John	Yal(1)	A–1	1834
Joseph	Car(1)	A–35	1837
PESCOD, William	War	A–78	1837
PETERS, Henry R.	Mon	I.7–93	1851
John	Ada	1–301	1823
John	Ada	5–276	1900
Lucy	Mas	P.3–40	1835
Mathew L.	Was	1–402	1875
Richard H.	Mon	I.1–389	1872
Samuel I.	Han	P.(1853–1860)–460	1855
PETERSON, John T.	Lau	1–238	1887
Robert T.	DeS	2–365	1893
William	Win	1–13	1862
PETIT, Jules	Jac	1–18	1882
PETRIE, Lemuel W.	Hin	1–280	1852
William	Ran	B.1–22	1841
PETTES, Edward	War	B–180	1886
PETTIBONE, Annie R.	Wil	2–396	1882
PETTIS, John	Mad	A–31	1837
William D.	Laf	1–300	1879
PETTIT, Alexander	Cla	B–178	1843
PETTY, Abner T.	DeS	1–38	1853
Gilbert	Low	1–362	1874
James S.	Coa(1)	1–64	1859
John	Nes	A–116	1882
PETTYGREW, James H.	Car(1)	A–412	1860
PEVEY, Little Berry	Law	1–3	1885

PEYTON, Ellen	Hin	B-438	1894
Louisa R. B.	Car(1)	A-23	1841
PHELAN, James	Mon	I.3-614	1880
PHELLS, Betsy	Wil	3-32	1883
Newton J.	Web	A-22	1878
PHELPS, W. G.	Was	1-516	1894
Wilbourn	Tal	A-10	1835
PHILBRICK, Benjamin	Coa(1)	1-4	1842
Charlotte C.	Wil	1-3	1831
PHILIPS, Mrs. E. R.	Yaz	B-22	1872
William	Mas	P.4-193	1845
PHILLIP, James	Hin	1-103	1838
PHILLIPS, Anna E.	Ada	2-307	1845
Bennett S.	Pan(1)	A-102	1851
Carmelite	Ada	1-446	1829
Dabney B.	Yal(1)	B-176	1878
Elizabeth Ann	Mas	P.7-10	1849
Emily L.	Mad	A-575	1878
Haywood	Yaz	B-250	1890
Jenken	Cla	A-212	1829
John	Ran	B.1-7	1829
John S.	DeS	2-27	1870
Joseph	Cla	A-354	1837
Laura A.	Ada	3-386	1870
Mrs. M. A. E.	Nox	C-52	1898
M. N.	Pan(1)	B-298	1879
Margaret E.	Pan(1)	A-340	1859
Martha	Nox	C-33	1897
Martha C.	Hol	1-351	1871
Matilda R. A.	Att	B-308	1880
Peter H.	DeS	1-420	1867
Richard S.	Hol	1-171	1857
Richard W.	Jef	B-174	1875
Samuel W.	DeS	1-131	1856
Sarah	Hin	1-181	1844
Solomon C.	War	A-5	1830
PHILLNICK, Orlando			
Davis Hamilton	Wil	2-121	1857
PHIPPS, Jesse	Ada	2-95&103	1835
Mary A.	Yaz	B-72	1877
Montgomery B.	Yaz	A-165	1854
PICKENS, Ezekiel	Car(1)	A-427	1861
Israel W.	Hol	1-324	1867
John	Jef	P.B-254	1836
PICKETT, Mary	Yaz	A-106	1848
Micajah	Yaz	B-361	1898
Sarah C.	Yaz	B-179	1884
Seaborn B.	Hol	1-217	1859
PIERCE, Sarah	Low	1-292	1870
Wiley P.	Ran	1-249	1892
PIGG, Wilson	Cop	AAA-202	1846

PILKENTON, Temperance

Jane	Low	2-248	1899
PILLOW, William R.	Lef	A-101	1889
PILMORE, Catharine	Ada	3-215	1865
PINSON, Richard A.	Cly	1-13	1874
PIPER, Robert	Ada	5-184	1898
PIPES, Abner	Ada	1-1	1802
Levi	Ada	3-190	1862
Mary	Ada	2-435	1853
Mary W.	Ada	5-16	1892
Winsor	Jef	A-11	1808
PITCHFORD, Augustus	Hol	1-114	1852
Frederick	Ada	4-569	1891
PITMAN, Jane	Cop	AAA-196	1857
PITTMAN, Daniel R.	Yal(1)	A-304	1857
Enos	Mot	1-122	1896
J. G.	Coa(1)	1-186	1885
J. W.	Web	A-124	1898
Robert	Car(1)	A-13	1838
Silas	Hin	1-415	1857
PITTS, H.	Uni	1-66	1900
John H.	Ada	3-144	1860
Phebe	Yal(1)	A-94	1845
PLANCHEL, Georges	Han	A-260	1894
PLATT, Nannie E.	War	B-388	1900
PLUMMER, Ann	Jef	B-195	1896
Hagen M.	Jac	1-189	1898
Robert	Jef	B-171	1890
POE, Anderson	Web	A-95	1892
James C.	Laf	1-111	1856
Laura Ann	Web	A-97	1893
William G.	Laf	1-122	1858
POINDEXTER, George	Hin	1-331	1854
Jane	Nox	A-198	1854
POINTER, Monroe	Pan(1)	B-454	1890
POITEVANT, Eliza J.	Han	A-285	1896
John	Yal(1)	A-234	1853
POLK, Charles T.	Low	2-104	1895
James	Tun	1-459	1869
James R.	Yal(1)	A-148	1849
L. G.	Tal	B-117	1898
Thomas	Low	1-171	1864
W. P.	Pre	1-89	1892
William	Mas	P.18-29	1867
POLKINGHORNE, Henry	Ada	2-374	1850
POLLARD, William	Tip	1-74	1876
POLLOCK, Thomas C.	Ada	4-330	1884
POND, Benjamin F.	Mon	I.7-74	1900
POOL, Craven P.	Hin	1-134	1840
John H.	Ran	1-31	1861
Sarah	Mon	I.7-564	1851

W. W.	Low	1-491	1885
POORE, John	Pan(1)	A-134	1852
POPE, Elias F.	Pan(1)	B-75	1870
George W.	Yal(1)	A-115	1847
J. B.	Pon	1-8	1899
John	Mas	P.18-139	1867
P. B.	Yaz	B-138	1881
Sampson	Yaz	A-90	1846
William H.	Was	1-149	1848
Willis	Low	1-21	1858
POPKINS, Eds Folkes	Ada	3-488	1871
PORTER, Alexander B.	Pan(1)	A-9	1846
Charles	Pan(1)	B-14	1864
Flavell M.	Car(1)	A-9	1837
George W.	Tal	B-23	1870
Gracy	Hin	1-369	1855
Henry	Cop	AAA-185	1839
James M.	Att	B-511	1885
Jeremiah	Hol	1-113	1852
Joseph Benjamin	Pan(1)	B-471	1891
Mrs. M. E.	Lau	1-421	1900
Nancy G.	Lau	1-207	1885
Richard R.	Yal(2)	1-82	1894
Samuel T.	Uni	1-46	1896
Waitus	Chi (1863-1872)-100		1865
William	Hin	1-40	1834
William B.	Pon E.(1844-1848)-209		1847
William J.	Tal	A-227	1859
William S.	Tat	1-19	1876
POSEY, Ben Lane	Han	A-177	1888
Carnot	Wil	2-201	1864
Carnot	Yaz	B-165	1884
Elizabeth	Wil	2-33	1848
Jane	Yaz	B-328	1897
John B.	Wil	1-197	1838
Stanhope	Wil	2-145	1859
POSTLEWAITE, Emily	Ada	4-328	1884
Samuel	Ada	1-348	1823
POTTER, Caleb	Hin	1-203	1847
Gustavus	Tun	1-488	1869
POTTES, Edward	War	B-180	1886
POTTICARY, William	War	A-350	1866
POTTS, John W.	Pan(1)	A-257	1857
Rocinda R.	Pan(1)	A-362	1859
Rosanna	Mad	2-71	1896
POUNCEY, Robert R.	Wil	2-227	1865
POUNDERS, Daniel	DeS	2-293	1888
William	DeS	1-349	1865
POWEL, Mary A.	Tun	2-94	1888
POWELL, Amel	Cop	AAA-182	1834
Ansel	Hin	1-58	1835

161

Austen	Mad	A-684	1892
Elizabeth	War	A-73	1837
J. W.	DeS	2-146	1879
John	Grn	A-98	1893
John G.	Mad	A-311	1860
Martha	Gre	1-20	1898
Mary	War	B-62	1875
Mary E. Harwood	War	B-370	1899
R. D.	Low	1-375	1875
Roderick	War	A-104	1840
Thomas	Mas	P.17-295	1866
Thomas	War	A-197	1853
Valentine	Jas	1-43	1865
W. A.	Cly	1-11	1874
William	Grn	A-130	1898
William T.	Mad	A-239	1856
Williamson	Tat	1-92	1886
POWER, John	Pan(1)	A-98	1850
Sinah	Pan(1)	B-23	1860
Thomas	Mas	P.3-191	1843
POWERS, Benjamin	Yaz	A-185	1855
Isaac	Cla	B-284	1859
James D.	Hol	3-50	1886
Lewis B.	Tal	A-111	1847
Martin	Tun	1-43	1847
Patrick	Hin	B-416	1892
Polly	Cla	A-195	1827
Susan Catherine	Yal(1)	B-92	1863
POYTRESS, S. H.	Yal(1)	A-307	1857
PRATER, William K.	Wil	2-309	1875
PRATT, Henry	Nox	A-253	1858
James P.	DeS	2-149	1879
William	Tal	A-6	1835
Willoughby L.	Ada	1-312	1823
PRELASCO, Cyprian	Ada	1-240	1821
PRESCOTT, Abel	Cla	A-268	1833
Jesse Jackson	Cop	AAA-193	1844
Lavina	Yal(1)	B-223	1884
PRESTIDGE, Elizabeth	Law	P.B-48	1837
PRESTIGE, Robert	Law	P.B-96	1839
PRESTON, Susan	Ran	1-28	1860
Zenas	Isa	C-142	1885
PRESTRIDGE, James	Yaz	A-199	1855
PREWETT, Abner	Mon	P.1-249	1872
Lemuel	Mon	1-215	1844
PREWITT, Archibald	Jas	1-12	1862
Joseph	Jef	B-77	1865
Rhoda E.	Cho	A-1	1881
PRICE, Allen P.	Sim	A-95	1900
Alsey C.	Mas	P.4-420	1846
Amos	Yaz	A-213	1858

Armead	Laf	1–309	1880
Edwin H.	Pan(1)	A–1	1845
Elizabeth	Mas	P.4–4	1844
H. V.	Was	1–449	1886
Henry	Ada	1–251	1822
I. R.	Jas	1–47	1864
John	Mar	A1–182	1847
Joseph Sr.	Cop	AAA–188	1856
Lydia	Ada	1–409	1828
Thomas	Nox	C–60	1898
Washington	Laf	1–98	1855
William	Hol	1–81	1848
PRICHARD, B. L.	Mad	A–453	1867
E. S.	Tat	1–223	1898
Emily P.	Mad	A–669	1890
Francis	Mad	A–479	1868
Harriet	Fra	A–9	1886
PRICHERD, James S.	Mad	A–277	1858
PRIDDY, Banister S.			
Sr.	Tal	B–51	1876
PRIESTLEY, James	Mad	2–83	1897
PRIMM, Angeline	Wil	2–372	1880
PRIMUS, Charles	Mad	A–594	1879
PRINCE, Bayliss E.	Cla	A–144	1825
Catherine S.	Cla	B–294	1860
Francis	Tal	B–89	1890
Robert	Jef	A–26	1817
W. Berry	Car(1)	B–44	1893
PRITCHARD, Richard	Ada	4–114	1876
PRITCHETT, George K.	War	A–325	1866
Henry M.	Yaz	A–200	1855
PROBST, J.	Mad	A–365	1862
PROCTOR, Ann H.	Hol	1–484	1887
PROPST, Allen H.	Low	2–160	1896
PROSSER, Thomas Henry	Wil	1–213	1839
PROVINE, Samuel F.	Yal(1)	A–111	1847
PROWELL, James W.	Low	2–198	1898
PRUITT, Mary	Jas	1–65	1874
PRYOR, Adam Alexander	Mas	P.15–529	1862
Emma	Web	A–69	1889
Green	Cla	B–257	1855
Green	Mas	P.9–171	1853
James M.	Hol	1–350	1871
Mary A.	War	A–241	1857
R. S.	War	B–178	1886
Sam H.	Mas	1–180	1897
PUCKETT, John	Hin	1–149	1823
PUGH, Henry	Yaz	A–36	1838
Mary A.	Mas	P.4–83	1845
PULLEN, Robert H.	Hol	1–281	1863
PULLIAM, Jane Davis	Mas	1–16	1892

Mandy	Chi(2)	1–82	1898
Mary	Mon	I.4–111	1881
Theophelus W.	Laf	1–10	1845
Thomas	Hin	1–68	1836
PULLIN, John T.	DeS	2–500	1900
PUREY, F. M.	Mas	P.17–399	1866
PURNEL, Albert	Lau	1–214	1886
PURNELL, Harrison	Ada	2–377	1850
John	Car(1)	A–56	1835
Levi	Ada	2–91	1835
M. T.	Car(1)	A–451	1862
Martin A.	Car(1)	A–483	1864
Micajah T.	Car(1)	A–76	1849
PURSSELL, Edmund	Hol	1–99	1850
PURVES, George S.	Han	A–256	1894
PURVIS, Bandge	War	A–112	1841
Edward W.	Yaz	A–291	1864
Gilbert Johnson	Hin	1–48	1835
James P. J.	Hin	1–66	1836
John	War	A–184	1850
John W.	Yaz	B–44	1875
Silas	Yaz	B–131	1881
PUTNAM, Joseph W.	Han	A–312	1898
PYLE, George N.	War	B–60	1875
QUARLES, John	Win	1–54	1869
Sarah A.	Tal	B–98	1891
QUEGLES, Joseph	Ada	1–460	1820
QUILLING, Moses	Cla	A–23	1806
QUIN, Hugh	Chi(1863–1872)–21		1864
QUINE, Abram	Wil	1–113	1834
James	Wil	2–39	1849
Mary	Wil	2–99	1854
Nancy	Wil	2–209	1863
William	Wil	1–187	1838
QUINLAN, Margaret			
Rebecca	DeS	2–125	1876
QUINN, William	Tat	1–180	1893
RABB, Alexander I.	Low	1–25	1859
Jack	Low	1–457	1882
John R.	Coa(1)	1–145	1856
Peter T.	Ada	2–146	1837
William	Yaz	B–242	1890
RAGAN, Harriet M.	Hin	B–333	1878
Thomas	Ada	1–31	1808
William	Mas	P.15–337	1861
RAGLAND, Arthur S.	Hin	1–200	1847
John D.	Nox	B–177	1872
Nathaniel	DeS	1–234	1859
Samuel E.	Laf	1–412	1894

W. S.	Laf	1-379	1889
William	Ran	1-114	1869
RAGSDALE, David W.	Mon	I.7-193	1851
Edward	Cla	A-298	1834
Howell	Cla	A-60	1815
L. A.	Lau	1-231	1887
Mary	War	A-102	1839
Samuel	Cla	A-132	1823
Sarah A.	Lau	1-249	1889
RAIL, John	Cla	B-176	1843
RAILEY, F. C.	Grn	A-75	1887
James	Ada	3-153	1860
Matilda S.	Ada	3-299	1867
RAINES, Mary	DeS	1-127	1856
William Newby	New	1-114	1892
RAINEY, Barzillai G.	Tun	2-105	1888
Frank W.	Han	A-215	1893
James	Hin	1-299	1852
John W.	Att	C-455	1894
William F.	Mon	I.19-244	1867
RALEY, Patsey Auston	Grn	A-10	1875
RALL, George	Lea	1-4	1855
RALSTON, George	Ada	4-572	1891
RAMPLEY, William M.	Pre	1-115	1898
RAMSEY, John G.	Yal(1)	A-279	1855
RAMSOUR, Jonas	Mas	P.12-437	1857
RAND, Ada Elizabeth			
Norfleet	Mas	1-103	1896
H. O.	Mas	1-7	1892
RANDLE, Isaac W.	Mon	I.5-232	1887
Mattis	Lef	A-92	1886
Peyton	Car(2)	1-36	1886
Thomas G.	Chi(1)	1-91	1858
RANDOLPH, A. J.	Wil	1-183	1838
Amy B.	War	B-146	1884
Annie Eliza	Pan(1)	B-329	1880
David W.	Yaz	B-283	1892
Elizabeth B.	Low	1-434	1880
F. C.	Pan(1)	B-322	1879
Freeman	Pan(1)	B-148	1874
Peter	Wil	1-42	1832
Richard	Low	1-37	1859
Whitinel S.	Pan(1)	B-50	1867
RANKIN, Christopher	Ada	1-370	1826
James A.	Laf	1-150&167	1862
RANSAMON, E.	Yaz	A-157	1852
RAOUL, James	Wil	1-132	1835
RAPALZE, June	Ada	1-305	1823
RASBERRY, Sarah	Mon	I.10-358	1854
RASCOE, H. E.	Laf	1-341	1885
RASCOR, Jane			

Elizabeth	Laf	2-18	1899
RATCHFORD, Mary	Ada	5-55	1894
RATCLIFF, Henry	Yaz	A-124	1849
Henry L.	Yaz	A-201	1855
Samuel N.	Yaz	B-149	1883
RATLIFF, James	Yaz	A-25	1836
Samuel C.	Mad	A-116	1847
Simpson	Hin	1-43	1834
RAVLIN, Elizabeth	Nox	B-166	1875
RAWLINGS, A. D.	Ada	4-385	1887
Susan	Ada	2-320	1846
Susan P.	Ada	3-276	1865
RAWLS, Benjamin	Per	1-1	1889
Claudeus	War	A-52	1835
Elizabeth	War	A-241	1857
John T.	Chi(2)	1-31	1886
William R.	Lea	1-123	1885
RAY, Henderson	Yal(1)	B-211	1888
James J.	Mad	2-4	1892
Valentine C.	War	A-69	1837
W. S.	Cho	A-38	1894
William	Cop	AAA-175	1855
RAYBOURN, W. C. A.	Laf	1-310	1879
RAYBORN, Noah	Laf	1-171	1863
RAYBURN, Phillip	Tal	B-52	1876
RAYMOND, A. H. Sr.	Lee	1-55	1881
Nathan E.	Wil	2-40	1849
RAYNE, R. W.	Jac	1-65	1890
REABEN, Fannie C.	Pik	1-43	1892
READ, John D.	Hin	1-337	1854
Lydia	Ada	1-260	1820
Thomas H.	Mas	P.3-166	1843
REAGAN, Cecelia	Hin	1-298	1852
REAGH, John	Ada	1-51	1810
REASONOVER, Jeremiah	DeS	1-30	1852
REASONS, Duncan			
Stuart	Yal(1)	A-119	1847
REAVES, Lawson D.	Hin	1-258	1850
Nathan R.	Coa(1)	1-130	1879
RECORD, John W.	Mas	P.15-74	1861
RED, Ephraim L.	Hol	1-88	1849
George	Hol	1-39	1842
REDD, William J.	War	A-88	1838
REDDING, Wyatt M.	Grn	A-34	1878
REDDISH, Joel B.	Ada	2-117	1835
REDDITT, Mary E.	Car(1)	B-25	1882
Peter E.	Car(1)	A-113	1853
REDDY, Jane E.	Jef	B-212	1900
REDEEMER, Moses	Ada	4-500	1889
REDFRAME, Samuel B.	Ben	1-10	1875
REDMOND, Green	Hol	3-94	1899

Hubbard	Hol	3-49	1897
Winnifred	Mad	2-40	1895
Y. W.	Hol	1-470	1885
REDUS, Aaron	Mon	I.13-646	1858
Thomas	Mas	P.3-338	1844
REDWINE, Jesse M.	Laf	1-15	1846
REECE, Charles A.	Pre	1-14	1873
Edward J.	Lau	1-371	1897
REED, Ann S.	DeS	1-56	1853
Elijah	Tip	1-95	1880
Henderson	Yaz	B-375	1898
Hilliard I.	Pan(1)	A-31	1847
James	Cho	A-40	1895
L. E.	Cho	A-32	1893
Margaret A.	Jef	P.B-255	1838
Mary	Ada	3-229	1865
P.	Tis	1-70	1893
Reubin	Pon	2-316	1844
Robert	Uni	1-10	1884
Thomas	Ada	4-563	1891
Thomas	Nox	A-6	1836
Thomas B.	Jef	A-108	1829
REEDER, Thomas Y.	Pan(2)	A-160	1900
REESE, Elizabeth	Mad	A-685	1892
James M.	Yal(1)	B-105	1865
Maria	Pik	1-23	1886
REEVES, John D.	Low	2-106	1895
Stephen Stapleton	Ada	5-297	1900
REGAN, Charles K.	Cla	3-190	1899
J. R.	Yaz	B-176	1884
Joseph	Cla	3-44	1878
Mary A.	Yaz	B-370	1898
Phebe	Cla	B-158	1838
William S.	Mar	A2-5	1874
William Span	Mar	A2-12	1890
REID, Amos I.	Jas	1-58	1870
Jane	Wil	1-95	1833
John B.	Uni	1-41	1896
John M. T.	Low	2-12	1890
Joseph	Mad	A-122	1847
Nancy T.	Mad	A-263	1857
REINFROW, Marck	Cop	AAA-179	1851
REINHARDT, Michael	Mas	P.8-412	1852
REIS, Briant	Lea	1-178	1897
REMBERT, Jane	Cop	AAA-172	1876
RENFROE, James	Hin	1-301	1852
Marcus H.	Tat	1-59	1883
RENSON, Ren	Hol	1-18	1839
REUSS, Francis	Ada	2-188	1839
REYNOLDS, Anderson	Hol	1-237	1860
Ann	Mon	I.7-59	1898

Charles	War	B-364	1899
Charles C.	War	B-260	1891
George K.	Ran	1-46	1863
Ira	Ada	1-416	1828
Joel	Hin	B-307	1875
Reuben O.	Mon	I.5-389	1882
Reuben O.	Mon	I.7-64	1899
Sarah	Mas	1-114	1897
William A.	Nox	A-99	1847
RHEN, Sarah O.	Tal	B-60	1880
RHINE, Isaac	Mas	1-138	1898
RHOADES, E. M.	Mas	1-27	1893
RHODES, J. P.	Lef	A-103	1889
L. D.	Ran	1-218	1887
Tholemiah	Cla	A-304	1835
William L.	Hin	1-367	1855
RHYMES, Little John	Hin	B-156	1862
RHYNE, Elizabeth	Hol	1-411	1877
Jno. S.	Hol	3-4	1894
Simon P.	Hol	1-169	1857
RICE, Ada Dickins	Pan(1)	B-413	1885
Ancil C.	Mas	1-122	1897
Charles	Jef	P.E-91	1850
George R.	Cly	1-129	1896
Harriet Malvina	Mas	P.15-541	1862
Mary J.	Tal	B-64	1881
RICHARDS, Benjamin	DeS	1-184	1858
David	Ada	1-488	1830
Edward P.	Low	2-131	1895
John	Ada	1-420	1826
L. B.	Nox	C-37	1898
Nathan	Mad	2-90	1897
Samuel B.	Ada	1-194	1817
Sarah	Ada	4-128	1878
Thomas	Cop	AAA-169	1841
William Hogan	DeS	1-451	1869
William L.	Yaz	A-48	1839
RICHARDSON, Alvah	Pik	1-53	1894
Henry	Sha	A-21	1895
Henry	Tat	1-11	1875
Lee	War	B-300	1894
Levi	Pan(2)	A-74	1890
Martha	Wil	1-36	1832
Mary Ann	DeS	2-321	1890
Mary D.	Ada	4-228	1882
Ransom	Lau	1-346	1895
Robert R.	Wil	2-283	1874
RICHEY, William J.	Okt	1-43	1898
RICHMOND, John C.	Laf	1-295	1879
Thomas Y.	Cla	3-192	1899
RICKETTS, Temperance	Yaz	B-321	1896

RICKEY, William J.	Okt	1-43	1898
RICKS, Benjamin S.			
Jr.	Yaz	B-403	1899
Eliza A.	Mad	2-142	1900
RIDDLE, Joseph	Wil	1-298	1845
Ruth B.	Tip	1-171	1890
Willey J.	Tip	1-169	1890
RIDGELEY, Josh	Lef	A-166	1900
RIDGEWAY, Mary	Lau	1-281	1891
RIDINGS, David	Mon	I.7-137	1899
RIDLEY, Henry	Mad	A-32	1835
RIDLING, John	Laf	1-6	1845
RIEHM, Louis	Jac	1-105	1892
RIGBY, Emily	War	B-356	1898
Thomas	War	B-215	1889
RIGGAN, Helen E.	Yaz	B-307	1896
Jeremiah	Mon	I.17-110	1862
RIGGIN, John J.	Hin	1-411	1857
RIGGS, Lafayette	Low	1-166	1864
RILEY, J. C.	DeS	2-361	1893
James	Mas	P.7-598	1851
Jane	Hol	1-317	1864
Joseph	DeS	2-291	1888
Mary Newton	Chi(2)	1-51	1890
Sarah	Hol	1-68	1845
Sarah	Hol	1-182	1858
William	Yaz	B-148	1882
RIMES, William	Cop	AAA-130	1834
RIMMER, James D.	Att	B-316	1880
James D.	Att	B-354	1881
Richard	Mad	A-269	1858
William	Att	2-320	1864
RING, William	Nox	A-245	1857
RINGO, Robert Mathis	Yal(1)	B-52	1861
RIST, Dorethe	Pik	1-135	1900
Katie	Wil	3-108	1893
RITCHEY, Daniel	Cla	A-48	1813
RITCHIE, Eliza	Cla	B-319	1865
RIVES, Charles A. B.	Mas(1838-1839)-246		1839
Elizabeth	Hin	1-228	1848
James H.	Nox	B-170	1875
Leona S.	Nox	C-68	1898
Mary W.	Was	1-447	1883
Robert G.	Nox	B-410	1894
William M.	Hin	1-231	1849
RIZER, Robert	Mas(1838-1839)-135		1838
ROACH, Alexander M.	Yaz	B-249	1890
Benjamin	Ada	2-325	1847
Benjamin Jr.	Ada	3-384	1870
James	War	A-267	1860
James F.	Ada	3-168	1861

John	Yal(1)	B-172	1877
ROBB, John	Pon E.(1844-1848)-387		1848
Julia A.	Jef	B-159	1884
Margaret	Ada	1-92	1808
Robert Burns	Hin	B-476	1899
Samuel	Jef	A-121	1830
William	Jef	A-101	1827
ROBBINS, Duncan	Ran	1-133	1873
ROBERTS, Allen	Hin	1-1	1832
F. A.	Chi(2)	1-68	1895
Griffin	Mon	I.8-395	1852
Isaac	Hin	B-302	1874
James	Hin	1-271	1851
James H.	Hol	1-207	1859
John	Ada	1-4	1802
Joseph L.	Ada	2-441	1853
Wilson W. G.	Lef	A-29	1857
Winfred	Ada	1-314	1822
ROBERTSON, A. B.	DeS	2-474	1898
Benjamin F.	Cly	1-52	1880
David F.	DeS	1-360	1866
Drury	Laf	2-66	1887
Elizabeth	Hin	1-113	1839
George H.	Hin	B-335	1879
Hiram D.	Hin	B-194	1866
J. C. N.	DeS	2-153	1880
J. D.	Mar	A2-14	1891
James	Ada	3-219	1865
James A.	Pan(1)	B-203	1876
John	Hin	1-3	1832
John J.	Jef	B-103	1868
Joseph	Hin	1-148	1823
Leanah	Isa	C-1	1858
Nancy M.	Chi(1)	1-28	1880
Reuben K.	Ada	3-58	1856
Rosetta	Chi(2)	1-69	1895
William	Cla	B-174	1843
William	Hin	1-182	1843
Young	Cop	A-47	1891
ROBINSON, A. B.	Car(1)	A-170	1858
A. B.	Tal	A-197	1857
Elam	Low	1-339	1873
George	Hin	B-477	1897
George B.	Cop	AAA-167	1851
Henry Combs	Lau	1-111	1874
J. L.	DeS	2-273	1886
J. S.	Lef	A-65	1879
John	Cla	A-223	1831
John	Jac	1-10	1880
John	Nox	A-281	1859
John	Mad	A-599	1880

Josiah A.	Pan(1)	B-22	1866
Lydia E.	DeS	1-424	1867
Malissa	Ada	4-409	1886
Mary	Nes	A-9	1846
Mary J.	Mot	1-144	1898
Mose	Pik	1-174	1900
Moses H.	Chi(1)	1-50	1884
Raymond	Hin	1-71	1836
Reddrick	Cla	B-194	1846
Sarah	Ada	2-114	1835
Seth	Cla	A-54	1814
William	Car(1)	A-76	1849
William M.	Hin	1-178	1844
ROBIRA, Joaquin	Han P.(1853–1860)–360		1855
ROBISON, Alexander	Cop	A-125	1897
Margaret	Cop	A-127	1897
ROBSON, John	Ada	3-60	1856
ROBY, Francis E.	Nox	B-19	1862
Francis M.	Low	1-184	1865
William W.	Nox	A-249	1857
ROCCA, Giovani B.	Ada	4-415	1887
ROCCO, George	Yaz	A-353	1869
ROCHE, P. J.	War	B-384	1900
ROCHELLE, Amanda C.	DeS	2-329	1891
W. W.	DeS	2-325	1890
ROCHESTER, Caroline	Ada	4-166	1880
RODERY, Washington	Mas	P.18-128	1867
RODES, V. H.	Lef	A-63	1879
RODGER, Jane	Ada	5-87	1895
RODGERS, Amy	Win	1-150	1895
James S.	Mas	P.17-406	1866
John	DeS	1-137	1857
Lemuel	Mas	P.3-111	1843
Robert	Yaz	A-50	1839
ROGERS, A. G.	Hol	1-425	1878
Absalom	Mad	A-458	1867
Benjamin	Wil	2-184	1862
Caroline Ellen	Tat	1-80	1885
D. W.	Yal(2)	1-129	1900
Egbert T.	Jac	1-172	1897
Elizabeth	Pan(1)	A-374	1859
Enos	Lef	A-126	1897
George W.	Cop	A-21	1888
Green M.	Mad	A-282	1859
Hugh	Mad	A-4	1828
J. E.	Tip	1-173	1893
Mrs. J. McD.	Lau	1-348	1895
Jackson	War	B-240	1890
James	Cop	M.A-180	1826
James	Pan(1)	A-366	1859
John	Cop	AAA-159	1834

Lida	Okt	1-31	1894
M. E.	Clk	1-57	1884
Stephen	War	A-3	1830
Thomas J.	Yal(2)	1-21	1882
William S.	Hol	1-293	1864
ROGILLIO, Eliza	Ada	4-374	1886
ROGILLIS, Emanuel	Ada	3-202	1862
ROGUEVELT, Louis	Jac	1-58	1890
ROINCE, Franciose	Ada	1-93	1813
ROLLING, Ophelia E.	Han	B-28	1899
ROMANE, William S.	War	A-185	1850
ROOK, John	Mas	P.15-173	1861
ROOS, Marion	Ada	5-110	1896
Samuel	War	B-257	1891
ROOTES, Cypressa C.	Pan(2)	A-17	1881
ROPEL, Stephen W.	DeS	1-436	1868
ROPER, Louisa M.	Ada	2-383	1850
Solomon B.	Mas	P.4-86	1845
ROSAMOND, Frances	Att	2-85	1861
Richard	Att	A-593	1861
Samuel	Att	2-150	1862
Samuel E.	Att	A-532	1860
Sarah E.	Hol	1-438	1881
T. A.	Att	C-48	1887
Thomas A.	Yal(1)	B-63	1862
ROSE, Elizabeth	Ada	4-206	1882
Enoch	Ada	1-84	1812
Enoch	Mad	A-81	1843
Ferrell	Web	A-134	1898
Matilda	Was	1-496	1892
Thomas	Ada	3-201	1862
W. H.	Lef	A-54	1877
ROSEMBAUM, Isaac	Lau	1-167	1881
ROSNEBAUME, David	Lau	1-303	1892
ROSNEY, John R.	Laf	1-409	1893
ROSS, A. B.	Cla	B-165	1840
Alexander	Ada	1-23	1806
Allison	Jef	P.B-175	1834
Ann	Car(1)	A-27	1842
B. W.	Mas	P.19-119	1869
David	Tal	B-34	1874
F. M.	DeS	2-432	1896
Francis	Nes	A-94	1871
Isaac	Jef	P.B-1	1836
James D.	Mad	A-16	1833
Jasper	Tal	B-6	1867
John	Cla	A-3	1804
John I. W.	Jef	B-211	1898
Marion S.	Mad	A-523	1871
Martin C.	Coa(1)	1-30	1851
Mary Ann	Ada	2-277	1844

Miles F.	Yal(2)	1-19	1881
Minerva A.	War	B-161	1886
Richard	Att	B-231	1876
Robert Love	Lau	1-236	1888
Robert Love	Lau	1-289	1892
S. E.	For(2)	1-6	1900
Samuel T.	Jef	P.C-795	1846
Sarah	Cla	A-22	1806
W. C.	Nox	C-141	1900
William	Yaz	B-196	1885
ROSSBECK, Christian	Ada	3-250	1866
ROSSEL, Toulmon H.	Mas	P.3-453	1844
ROSSKIN, Isaac	Cla	A-261	1833
ROTHCHILD, Martin	Wil	3-193	1900
ROULETT, A.	Mas	P.19-463	1870
ROUNDS, Charles	Ada	4-187	1880
ROUNSAVILLE, Joel	Laf	1-20	1848
ROUSH, John	Cla	A-159	1826
ROUSSEAN, C. M.	Cop	A-18	1888
ROUSSEL, Bernard	Jac	1-31	1884
ROUTH, Job	Ada	2-86	1834
Job	Cla	3-85	1883
ROW, Edmond	Tal	A-13	1835
Mary Ann	Wil	3-1	1883
ROWAN, Ida M.	Jef	B-166	1886
John A.	Was	1-52	1843
Mary	Ada	3-205	1863
S. A.	Pon	1-20	1900
Samuel	Lee	1-219	1900
Sarah	Ada	2-77	1834
T. J.	Mon	I.7-61	1898
William	Ada	2-71	1834
William W.	Wil	2-133	1858
ROWELL, Jonathan E.	Jas	1-79	1884
ROWLAND, D. R.	Tip	1-75	1876
Jane	Mad	A-605	1881
William	Pan(1)	A-216	1855
ROWLETT, John W.	DeS	2-177	1881
ROWT, Marietta	Hin	B-297	1874
ROWZEE, James M.	Pan(1)	A-334	1859
ROY, Margaret	Mot	1-69	1884
ROYALL, John M.	Yaz	A-167	1854
ROZELL, Claiborne W.	Coa(1)	1-50	1857
Yerby P.	DeS	2-190	1882
RUBON, Ephraim	Ada	1-85	1812
RUCKER, C. C.	Tip	1-68	1874
Emiline M.	Tip	1-178	1894
Jonathan	Ada	4-69	1874
Peter	Ada	2-290	1844
RUCKS, James	Was	1-332	1862
James T.	Coa(1)	1-128	1878

RUFF, Rebecca	Nox	B-253	1881
Reuben	Nox	B-258	1881
RUFFIN, James	Pan(1)	A-33	1847
James D.	Pan(1)	B-417	1886
Thomas	Pan(1)	B-259	1878
RULE, Ann C.	Hol	1-134	1853
John S.	Hol	1-224	1860
RUM, Adam	Jef	A-76	1822
RUNDELL, Amos	Cla	B-171	1842
Joshua	Cla	A-63	1815
Seth	Cla	B-161	1839
RUNDLE, Margaret B.	War	B-383	1900
RUNNELS, Ellis J.	Ran	1-251	1893
Hardin D.	Mad	A-55	1839
RUSHING, Mrs. B. C.	Lau	1-258	1889
Signiora B.	Lau	1-186	1883
William	Isa	C-42	1861
RUSHTON, James	Wil	2-242	1866
RUSSEL, Alexander	War	A-341	1865
Fergus	Mad	A-595	1880
RUSSELL, Alexander	New	1-88	1890
Arnold	Yaz	B-37	1873
Elijah M.	Car(1)	A-52	1844
Elizabeth T.	Low	1-170	1864
Ephraim	Ran	1-146	1876
Isaac	Lau	1-147	1875
Martin E.	Mad	A-288	1859
Mary C.	Ada	4-365	1886
Nealy	Mad	2-148	1900
RUST, Hyde	Wil	3-198	1900
RUTHERFORD, John			
A. H.	Pan(1)	B-97	1871
RUTLAND, Edmond J.	DeS	1-352	1866
Harrison	DeS	2-298	1888
Stephen W.	DeS	1-325	1865
W. Henry	Mad	2-30	1894
William	Mad	A-620	1882
RUTLEDGE, Caroline C.	Tis	1-47	1891
RYAN, Cornelius	War	B-71	1877
Michael	War	A-250	1858
Robert	Ada	3-104	1857
Robert	Hin	B-205	1857
RYLAND, Joseph D.	Cly	1-18	1877
SACKETT, Porter	Ada	2-160	1837
SACOCK, Mary F.	Grn	B-1	1900
SADDLER, E. M.	Tis	1-40	1890
SADLER, Augustus	Mad	A-205	1853
Mariah E.	Chi(2)	1-5	1883
S. A. M.	Mon	I.6-560	1897
William	War	A-333	1865

SAGE, Travis	Mas	P.11-204	1855
SAGNY, Charles	Mas	P.19-431	1870
SAILER, Israel	Mas	1-101	1896
SAIRD, J. S. R.	Cop	A-129	1897
SALAMAN, Jacob S.	Lau	1-354	1896
SALE, John B.	Mon	I.2-265	1876
Oswald B.	Cla	A-313	1834
SALLE, M. Aunlius	Mas	P.9-143	1853
SALLIS, J. G.	Att	C-576	1897
John	Att	2-486	1865
SALTZER, Henry	Ada	2-217	1840
SALZIGER, Henry G.	Was	1-435	1883
SAMPLE, Caroline A.	Hol	1-190	1857
George I.	Sun	1-2	1889
Harriet	Hol	3-52	1897
Isaac	Hol	1-105	1851
James	Hol	1-124	1853
Samuel	Hol	1-192	1858
SAMPSON, James J.	Clk	1-16	1873
Mary H.	Hol	1-122	1852
SANBORN, Phineas	Yal(1)	A-40	1841
SANDEFER, J. M.	Low	2-275	1900
James K. P.	Hol	1-348	1871
Lowry	Hol	1-185	1858
SANDENON, Daniel P.	Mas	P.11-90	1855
SANDERFER, F. M.	Qui	1-9	1897
SANDERS, A.	Kem	A-88	1900
Adison H.	Nox	B-81	1867
B. W.	Hol	1-36	1842
Benjamin Franklin	DeS	1-79	1852
Bernhard	Car(1)	B-57	1893
Charles	Ada	4-558	1891
Davis H.	Wil	2-82	1854
Enoch B.	Att	B-236	1876
Henrietta M.	Mon	I.23-8	1871
Henry	Car(1)	A-18	1841
Hugh	Mad	A-186	1853
Isaac	Lea	1-36	1863
J. W.	Car(1)	A-507	1868
John	War	A-178	1849
Joshua	Mas	P.10-56	1854
L. M.	Lea	1-71	1874
Lucretia	Wil	2-116	1856
Margaret	Car(1)	A-485	1865
Mary	Mad	A-42	1838
Micajah	Lea	1-110	1882
Sallie M.	Grn	A-92	1891
Uriah R.	Mas	P.12-444	1857
W. J.	Att	B-93	1872
W. P.	Lea	1-151	1891
William	Cla	3-81	1882

175

SANDERSON, Catharine			
B.	Mas	P.12–334	1857
Elijah	Low	1–199	1866
Eliza	Ada	3–308	1867
Hugh H.	Chi(1)	1–41	1882
SANDFORD, Julia A.	Was	1–401	1875
SANDIDGE, James M.	DeS	1–323	1863
SANDIFER, James C.	Cop	AAA–143	1857
John	Cop	AAA–148	1854
SANDMYER, Marian			
Lester Prisbury	Mad	2–101	1898
SANDOS, Wilhelmina	Ada	1–245	1821
SANDS, Mahala	Mas	1–146	1898
Susan A.	Low	1–186	1865
SANFORD, Asay	Low	1–537	1887
Robert J.	Pan(1)	A–428	1862
SARAZIN, Lucretia	Ada	2–311	1845
SARGENT, Fannie E.	Hol	1–437	1880
Mary	Ada	2–272	1844
Mary V.	Nox	B–227	1879
Winthrop	Ada	1–207	1818
SARRAZIN, Paul Justin	Jac	1–117	1892
SARTOR, James T.	Mon	I.14–266	1859
Mary	Mon	I.4–341	1882
SARVARIN, Simon	Ada	1–384	1826
SATTERFIELD, Emma K.	Was	1–448	1885
William E.	Was	1–429	1880
SATTERWHITE, James S.	Pan(1)	A–76	1850
SAUCIER, Jacques	Han	P.(1853–1860)–319	1855
Martina P.	Han	A–198	1891
Victoire	Han	A–273	1895
SAUNDERS, Abraham	Wil	2–136	1858
Benjamin F.	Coa(1)	1–110	1868
Hubbard	Han	A–115	1879
John	Tal	B–91	1890
John S.	Tal	B–80	1884
Oliver P.	Grn	A–32	1878
Thomas	Cop	AAA–152	1835
Thomas	Tun	1–559	1871
Turner	Mon	I.9–271	1853
William H.	Mon	I.6–436	1895
SAVAGE, William R.	Mad	2–51	1896
SAVOY, Samuel	War	A–133	1842
SAWMAN, David	Mas	1–27	1893
SAWYER, William A.	Ada	3–271	1866
SAXON, Joshua	Cla	A–67	1817
SAYLE, David T.	Yal(1)	A–246	1854
SAYNE, William H.	Mas	P.7–556	1851
SCALES, B. A.	Lee	1–66	1881
Peter	Mas	P.16–9	1863
SCARBOROUGH, Lucy G.	Att	B–515	1886

Mary L.	Att	C-575	1897
SCHICK, Ellen	Chi(2)	1-66	1894
SCHILLING, Stephen	Cla	3-172	1895
SCHIRCK, Abraham	Lin	1-52	1898
SCHLETT, Louisa	Ada	5-32	1893
SCHLEY, George	Laf	1-202	1866
SCHMALING, Joseph	War	B-169	1885
SCHMITT, Andrew	Sun	1-8	1892
Andrew	Yaz	B-230	1888
SCHOBS, Julia	Mad	A-388	1862
SCHOLAR, Abner	Mad	*	1837

* Available only at the Canton Public
     Library, Canton, MS.

SCHONINGER, Elise			
Adrienne	Ada	3-71	1856
SCHOTT, John P.	Ada	2-442	1853
SCHUCK, Sarah	Lin	1-50	1899
SCHUMPERT, Mary	Lee	1-5	1869
SCHUYLER, Philip A.	Was	1-266	1859
SCHWARTZ, Christian	Ada	4-506	1890
Jacob	Wil	3-118	1893
John C.	Ada	4-508	1890
SCOFIELD, Abraham	Ada	4-441	1888
SCOTT, Abram M.	Wil	1-86	1833
Alfred	Web	A-67	1888
Burrell	Yaz	A-345	1867
C. W.	Laf	1-314	1881
C. W.	Mad	A-613	1881
Charles	Hin	B-131	1861
Edward	War	A-194	1852
Elias	Mad	A-303	1859
Gabriel	Yaz	A-9	1835
Griffin L.	Jef	B-70	1863
H. P.	Isa	C-162	1899
Hetty	Mas	P.3-450	1844
Horace	Was	1-431	1882
Isaac	Jef	P.D-733	1851
Jacob H.	Hin	1-77	1836
James	Han	A-104	1877
James	Hol	1-72	1847
James	Lef	A-99	1888
James A.	Lea	1-120	1884
James K.	Jef	P.C-287	1843
Jane	Jef	P.E-473	1853
Jane C.	Hin	B-59	1860
John 2/9	Cla	A-207	1829
John F.	Ada	3-334	1867
John L.	Jef	B-131	1873
John R.	Mas	P.3-167	1843
Joseph	DeS	2-93	1874
Joseph T.	Lea	1-21	1858

Mrs. L. C.	Cop	A-83	1892
Leonard	Yaz	A-97	1846
M. F.	Kem	A-66	1897
Mary Jane	Ada	4-411	1887
Michel B.	Yaz	A-250	1865
N. F.	Tat	1-116	1889
N. R.	Uni	1-29	1892
Osborne	Jef	B-147	1877
P. J.	Kem	A-23	1886
Peter E.	War	A-124	1841
Richard	Mad	A-386	1862
Robert	Ben	1-8	1871
Robert	Wil	2-300	1875
Robert	Yaz	A-110	1848
Robert T.	Laf	1-81	1852
Ruth	Cla	B-252	1855
S. G.	Mad	A-427	1865
Samuel	Jef	B-63	1862
Samuel	Mad	A-641	1886
Samuel H.	Web	A-34	1882
Smith	Kem	A-63	1896
T. J.	Fra	A-17	1900
Thomas S.	Yal(1)	A-2	1834
Virginia A.	Coa	1-52	1899
William	Cla	A-137	1823
William Parker	Yaz	A-329	1866
SCROGGINS, Joannah	Lau	1-292	1892
SCRUGGS, Drury	Ada	1-250	1822
James L.	Mas	P.19-302	1870
Marcus F.	Mas	1-42	1895
SCULLY, L.	Lau	1-310	1893
SEAGRIST, Jacob	Jef	A-41	1820
SEAL, Jacob J.	Han	A-85	1873
SEALE, Beaufort	Nes	A-71	1863
D. L.	Yaz	B-374	1898
SEALS, Elvira A.	Wil	2-6	1846
SEARS, George E.	Han	B-26	1899
SEATS, Asbury	Ada	3-389	1870
SEGAR, James M.	Hol	1-316	1864
SEGREST, Bardee	Cla	3-111	1889
Sarah	Cop	AAA-156	1865
SEIBE, Henry	Hin	1-152	1834
SEIMER, Henry	Mad	A-510	1870
SEIP, Frederic	Ada	1-180	1818
SELLARS, John	Jef	A-40	1820
SELLERS, Abraham	Cop	AAA-139	1872
Benjamin D.	Cop	A-1	1886
Thomas	Was	1-41	1843
Thomas George	Okt	1-38	1899
SELLS, Thomas	Clk	1-209	1899
SELSER, Henry	Ada	2-217	1840

Isaac N.	Hin	1-351	1855
SELTZER, M. A.	Pon	1-10	1900
SEMMES, Alphense			
Thomas	Mad	2-38	1895
Susan	Mad	A-558	1871
SEMPLE, Isabella	Wil	2-278	1874
Mary	War	B-385	1900
SERIBER, John Stephen	Jef	A-83	1824
SESSIONS, Charles R.	Ada	3-31	1855
Nancy	Ada	2-254	1842
Richard	Ada	1-365	1825
SESSOMS, Adelade	Tat	1-75	1885
SESSONS, James	Mas(1838-1839)-210		1839
SETTLE, Edward D.	Cla	B-245	1854
Mary Isabella	Tis	1-63	1893
SEWELL, James	Att	A-227	1859
Joshua K.	Hin	1-10	1833
SEYMS, Charlotte	War	B-218	1889
SHACKELFORD, Charles			
C.	Mad	A-575	1878
G. W.	Hol	3-88	1899
James R.	Car(1)	B-31	1891
John	Hol	3-30	1895
Philadelphia	Jef	B-150	1868
T. H.	Chi(2)	1-61	1893
T. M.	Yaz	B-244	1890
SHAEFFER, Clarissa	Low	1-519	1886
George	Low	1-511	1886
SHAFFER, J. T.	Web	A-132	1898
SHAIFER, Elizabeth H.	Cla	B-323	1867
SHAMBURGER, G. H.	Lau	1-369	1897
William	Car(1)	A-37	1843
SHANAHAN, Timothy	Cla	3-26	1876
SHANDS, Wilson Lee	Pan(1)	B-488	1898
SHANNON, Anne			
Parmelia	Lef	A-62	1878
E. D.	Mon	I.10-575	1854
John	War	A-196	1852
Madison T.	Cla	3-185	1899
Mary	Wil	1-22	1832
William Sr.	Yaz	B-243	1890
SHARINAN, Endorus L.	Lau	1-363	1897
SHARKEY, Allen	Car(1)	A-24	1841
John W.	Lea	1-50	1865
Patrick	Hin	B-61	1861
Sophia	Hin	B-479	1900
SHARP, Clarissa	Ada	4-83	1875
E. B.	Jon	1-1	1894
Elisha Hunter	Low	1-1	1858
Elizabeth J.	Low	2-54	1891
Francis	Kem	A-65	1897

James M.	Low	1-142	1863
John	Nox	C-121	1899
John A.	Laf	1-244	1874
John M.	Yaz	A-264	1863
Mary	Yaz	B-185	1885
Sumner M.	Hin	1-111	1839
Thomas I.	Low	1-179	1865
SHARPE, Josiah	Car(1)	A-459	1864
SHARPLEY, W. B.	Mon	I.5-468	1888
SHATTUCK, Andrew P.	Chi(2)	1-20	1884
SHAW, Alexander	DeS	1-259	1860
Henry Basil	Ada	4-67	1869
James M.	Yal(2)	1-15	1881
Rufus D.	Laf	1-147	1866
Sarah Simpson	DeS	1-422	1867
Sarah Stinson	DeS	1-60	1849
Smith	Chi(1)	1-134	1898
Wiley	Win	1-93	1878
William H.	Laf	1-354	1881
SHAY, John	Cla	B-329	1868
SHEARIN, Joseph	Yal(2)	1-40	1884
SHEEGOG, Mary	Laf	1-198	1871
SHEEHAN, Cornelius	Lau	1-322	1893
SHEELEY, William G.	Tal	B-20	1870
SHELBY, Isaac H.	Coa(1)	1-23	1850
Mary D.	Wil	2-105	1855
P. B.	Was	2-123	1900
Robert Prince	Isa	B-39	1854
SHELEY, A. C. N.	Tal	B-72	1883
SHELL, Francis A.	Chi(1863-1872)-98		1865
SHELLEY, Sallie H.	Cly	1-83	1889
SHELLY, Nancy B.	Att	D-70	1898
SHELTON, Ann	Nox	B-224	1879
James	Pan(1)	B-94	1871
Peter	Tal	A-25	1839
Rebecca J.	Hin	B-366	1885
Sarah	Nox	A-266	1858
SHENK, Elizabeth	Pan(1)	B-34	1867
SHEPARD, A. P.	Hol	1-423	1878
SHEPHARD, Martha	Hin	1-409	1857
C. M.	Wil	2-73	1852
Margaret A.	Wil	2-87	1854
R. C.	Yaz	B-394	1899
SHEPPARD, Charles P.	Car(1)	A-127	1855
Isaac	Hol	1-387	1876
John	Mon	1-214	1844
SHERARD, Gabriel	DeS	1-336	1865
Samuel Garvin	War	B-322	1896
SHERICK, William G.	Jef	P.C-154	1842
SHERIFF, Isabella	Han	A-25	1867
SHERIN, Henry	Car(1)	A-163	1857

SHERMAN, Cora	Grn	A-48	1882
Edward T.	Grn	A-36	1879
Henry B.	Grn	A-47	1882
Jacob J.	Low	2-129	1895
SHERREN, Nancy	Law	P.B-111	1839
SHERRICK, Joseph	Mad	A-171	1852
SHERROD, Albert	DeS	1-187	1858
Charles F.	Low	1-508	1886
SHIELDS, Agnes S.	Ada	3-258	1866
Benjamin	Cla	A-320	1836
Catherine	Ada	4-459	1888
John R.	Coa(2)	1-36	1895
Mary C.	Ben	1-37	1885
Sarah	Mad	A-281	1859
Victoire	Ada	3-48	1855
SHILLING, Jacob	Ada	1-31	1808
Polser	Ada	1-34	1808
SHINAULT, William	Pre	1-120	1898
SHINDS, Anthony C.	Tat	1-21	1877
SHINN, Warren S.	Pan(1)	B-49	1867
SHIPP, Bartley	Mas	P.8-411	1852
Coleman	Hol	1-38	1842
Cynthia R.	Coa(1)	1-129	1879
George	Ada	3-7	1854
Josiah	Mas	P.3-148	1843
Mrs. M. A.	Hol	3-18	1895
Thomas	Hol	1-164	1856
William	Ada	2-67	1834
SHIRLEY, James J.	Hin	1-293	1852
L.	Cly	1-82	1888
SHIVERS, W. R.	Sim	A-20	1880
SHOCKNEY, Abijial	War	A-273	1860
SHOEMAKER, Martha	Clk	1-82	1885
T. W.	Clk	1-138	1892
SHOFFNER, Henry	Ben	1-63	1893
SHORT, Mary	Low	1-3	1858
Monroe	Pan(1)	B-384	1883
SHOTWELL, Nelson J.	Coa(1)	1-135	1879
SHRACK, Joseph K.	Att	D-49	1897
SHRIEK, Ambrose S.	Cla	B-330	1869
SHROCK, David F.	Lea	1-23	1856
SIBLEY, David	Isa	C-157	1893
Thomas H.	Yaz	A-61	1842
SIDDALL, M. S.	Tip	1-150	1889
SIDEBOTOM, John	Ada	1-66	1811
SIDEBOTTOM, John H.	Ada	4-305	1882
SIDES, Henry C.	Hin	1-355	1855
SIGMIN, John	Mas	P.4-58	1845
SIGNAIGE, A. J.	Ada	3-330	1867
SIKES, Mary Ann	Jef	B-145	1877
SILLA, A. O.	War	B-259	1891

SILLARD, Amelia	Ada	3-236	1865
SILLAVEN, James A. Sr.	Mon	I.2-468	1879
SILLERS, John	Jef	P.B-523	1840
SILLIMAN, John I.	Mad	2-12	1893
W. C.	Lau	1-282	1891
SILLY, Tyra	Cla	3-52	1879
SIMMES, Catharine	Mad	A-655	1888
John	Mad	A-438	1866
Jonathan	Coa(1)	1-105	1867
SIMMONS, A. W.	Mad	A-313	1860
Albert V.	Yal(2)	1-68	1891
Benjamin	Ada	1-80	1812
Bennett	Pan(2)	A-14	1881
E. F.	Tis	1-53	1892
Elias	Att	2-185	1867
Emily Mandeville	Yal(2)	1-48	1886
Eveline	Hin	B-471	1899
Eveline	Hin	B-481	1900
Henry	Cop	AAA-136	1839
James S.	Hol	1-272	1862
John	Yaz	B-127	1881
John N.	Yal(1)	B-120	1866
Nancy	Yaz	B-191	1885
Samuel B.	Hol	1-295	1864
Sarah P. E.	Hin	B-417	1893
Thomas	Yal(1)	B-4	1858
SIMMS, Mary	War	B-390	1900
Thomas	Mad	A-374	1862
SIMON, Reuben	Mad	A-228	1855
SIMONDS, Ephraim	Cla	A-357	1837
Laura P.	Cla	B-160	1838
SIMONTON, William	Mas	P.3-261	1844
SIMPSON, Adam D.	Mad	2-105	1898
Albert	Low	2-22	1890
Archabald	Nox	A-102	1847
Charles	Lau	1-375	1898
Hugh M.	Mad	A-19	1832
James	Mad	A-612	1881
James	Tip	1-59	1872
John	Ben	1-50	1890
John F.	Jon	1-2	1895
Mary	Mad	A-109	1847
Robert	Mad	A-644	1886
Thomas	Ran	1-135	1875
SIMS, Ann	Low	2-187	1897
B. A.	Coa(1)	1-92	1866
Billy	Hin	B-263	1869
C. F.	Wil	3-181	1899
Elizabeth	Laf	1-85	1853
Henry	Jef	A-38	1819

J. J.	Yaz	B-182	1884
James	Cla	A-107	1821
John	War	A-5	1830
John	Wil	2-97	1854
John H.	Hin	B-44	1860
John H.	Wil	2-203	1863
Leroy	Mas	P.11-433	1856
Micajah	Nox	A-1	1834
Nathan	Hin	1-290	1852
Robert	Mad	A-19	1832
Virginia P.	Chi(2)	1-39	1884
William	Laf	1-56	1851
William H.	Hin	B-176	1863
William McD.	Cla	3-71	1882
Zechariah	Att	C-144	1889
SINCLAIR, E. D.	Laf	2-15	1899
John	Ran	1-7	1859
SINDAUER, Adam	War	A-251	1858
SINES, James	Mad	A-560	1874
SINGLETON, Ann J.	Cla	B-186	1845
Eliza Y.	Mad	A-619	1882
John G.	Cla	A-358	1838
Otho R.	Lea	1-143	1889
Otho R.	Mad	A-658	1889
Thomas T.	Yaz	A-276	1860
SISLOFF, Jane	Lef	A-112	1893
SISTRUNK, Samuel M.	Cop	AAA-124	1860
SITTON, John B.	Cho	A-43	1895
John B.	Win	1-153	1892
SIVINGSTON, James	Yaz	A-143	1848
SKIDMORE, Crosby S.	Mad	A-380	1862
Thomas	Coa(1)	1-170	1885
SKINNER, Adderton	Cla	B-189	1845
Caroline M.	Was	1-490	1891
Kinson	Jas	1-73	1876
Mary L.	Tip	1-194	1895
N. C.	Was	2-98	1899
Richard	Jef	P.B-254	1837
T. E.	Chi(2)	1-49	1889
SKIPWORTH, George G.	Hin	1-307	1853
SLACK, Nancy	Yal(1)	B-20	1859
SLATE, Henrietta C.	Laf	2-42	1899
John	Laf	1-342	1885
Peterson J.	Laf	1-263	1875
SLATER, Frederick	Wil	2-230	1865
James F.	Hin	1-373	1856
SLAUGHTER, James S.	Nox	B-32	1863
Stanton	Nox	A-13	1837
William H.	Mad	A-133	1849
SLAY, Daniel	Ran	1-179	1883
David	Hin	B-240	1868

SLEDGE, Amos P.	Pan(1)	A-122	1852
SLEDGE, George W.	Car(1)	A-202	1860
Leonidas S.	Pan(1)	B-113	1872
N. R.	Pan(1)	B-363	1881
SLEEN, Silas	Ran	1-1	1858
SLOAN, Esther J.	Jas	1-116	1899
John A.	Mon	I.2-633	1877
Miss R. B.	DeS	2-498	1899
W. B.	Tat	1-236	1899
SLOCOMB, Samuel B.	Ada	2-69	1834
SLOCUM, Isaiah G.	Tat	1-259	1900
SLOCUMB, J. G.	DeS	2-310	1889
Joseph Riley	Mas	P.17-46	1865
Junius G. Jr.	DeS	2-256	1885
Mary E.	Mas	1-123	1897
W. T.	Mas	1-95&99	1896
SMALLWOOD, Elisha	Ran	B1-9	1830
SMARR, William H.	War	A-295	1861
SMEDES, William C.	War	A-322	1862
SMITH, A. H.	Lau	1-341	1895
A. H.	Lee	1-171	1896
A. W.	DeS	2-472	1898
Alexander	Nes	A-55	1859
Alexander	Tis	1-110	1900
Allen	Laf	1-210	1871
Allen	Ran	1-200	1885
Amy	Ada	5-50	1894
Anaka	Low	1-570	1889
Anna Warrier	Wil	1-287	1845
Anthony	Ada	2-408	1852
B. O.	Cla	B-210	1850
Bartlett	Ada	1-342	1823
Benjamin	Cla	B-195	1846
Benjamin B.	Pon	1-12	1900
Bethunia	Mas	P.4-396	1843
Calvin	Ada	2-219	1840
Catharine	Ada	1-10	1803
Catherine	Mon	I.5-221	1887
Celiab	Cla	A-142	1825
Charles	Hol	1-184	1858
Charles	Jac	1-72	1890
Charles Percy	Tun	1-188	1857
Charlotte	Wil	2-51	1850
Colonel B.	Sun	1-30	1899
Daniel	Ada	1-291	1823
Daniel B.	Cop	AAA-120	1830
David	Hin	1-59	1835
David D.	Mad	A-324	1860
Dyce	Pan(1)	A-349	1859
Mrs. E. E.	Nes	A-119	1886
Edmund	Lef	A-22	1855

Edward M.	Cop	A-123	1897
Edwin	Car(1)	A-60	1846
Elijah	Ada	1-403	1828
Elizabeth	Ada	2-185	1839
Elizabeth	Clk	1-37	1877
Elizabeth	Cop	AAA-128	1845
Elizabeth	Mad	A-656	1889
Elizabeth B.	Car(1)	A-434	1862
Elizabeth Jane	Mad	A-451	1866
F. M.	Kem	A-52	1889
Fannie B.	Grn	A-88	1890
Fanny M. E.	Yaz	B-166	1884
Frank D.	Hol	3-85	1899
Frank H.	Cla	B-350	1875
G. M.	Cla	A-275	1833
George	Ada	1-378	1826
George W.	Yaz	B-301	1894
Gordon	War	A-331	1865
H. W.	Att	C-289	1892
Hannah	Yal(1)	A-277	1855
Hetty	Ada	1-359	1825
Howell J.	Ran	1-132	1874
Irene	Was	1-398	1873
Isaac	Jef	B-164	1884
Israel P.	Ada	2-430	1853
James	Cop	AAA-114	1857
James	DeS	2-106	1875
James	Hol	1-44	1844
James H.	Att	D-68	1898
James L.	Yaz	B-377	1898
James M.	Mad	A-28	1835
James P.	Hin	B-106	1865
James S.	Tat	1-10	1874
Jane Pryor	Was	1-454	1886
Jesse	Low	1-23	1859
John	Ben	1-9	1872
John	Yaz	B-164	1883
John C.	Tip	1-14	1866
John G.	Pan(1)	A-64	1849
John J.	Cla	3-173	1897
John Jr.	War	A-207	1853
John L.	Yaz	B-112	1879
John M.	Sco	A-310	1869
John P.	Ada	2-208	1840
John S.	Wil	2-270	1872
John W.	Mas	P.19-444	1870
John Wilson	Laf	2-50	1900
Jonah Dayton F.	Win	1-134	1892
Joseph	Grn	A-119	1896
Joseph B.	Mad	A-400	1864
Joshua	Cla	A-74	1818

Lemuel	Laf	1-1	1843
Lemuel O.	Mad	A-357	1861
Leonidas F.	Att	D-177	1900
Lewis	Hin	1-231	1849
Margaret	Ada	3-54	1856
Margaret Dulany	Hol	3-69	1899
Martha	Ada	4-483	1889
Martha	Mad	A-521	1871
Martha	Ran	1-128	1874
Martin L.	Jef	B-96	1867
Mary	Jac	1-107	1892
Mary	Jas	1-5	1851
Mary	Mad	A-218	1854
Mary E. G.	Was	1-454	1886
Mary Elizabeth	Coa(2)	1-45	1898
Mary O.	Hol	1-458	1882
Matilda	Cop	A-107	1896
Mike	Lea	1-174	1896
Mitchell	Ran	1-243	1892
Moses	Nox	B-337	1889
Nancy	Pon	1-7	1891
Nancy C.	Ben	1-79	1898
Nancy H.	Pan(2)	A-134	1898
Nathan	Jas	1-4	1857
Nicholas	Att	B-432	1884
Peter	Wil	1-177	1837
Peter	Wil	2-256	1869
Philander	Ada	1-330	1824
Plummer W.	Car(1)	A-102	1852
Priscilla	Ada	2-322	1846
R. C.	Mad	A-676	1891
R. W.	Att	B-332	1881
Reddick	Att	C-208	1890
Richard	Tip	1-21	1867
Richard L.	Ada	2-258	1842
Robert	Att	C-77	1889
Robert	Hin	1-394	1857
Robert D.	Ada	3-111	1858
Robert H.	Lau	1-145	1880
Robert Percy	Ada	2-339	1847
Russel	War	A-61	1836
S. H.	Clk	1-69	1884
Sallie C.	Laf	1-242	1874
Samuel	Hin	1-46	1835
Sarah	Pan(1)	B-30	1866
Sarah E.	Tat	1-35	1877
Sherwood	Mas	P.2-57	1840
Sid	Tal	A-214	1859
Susan D.	Mad	A-86	1844
Susan E.	Chi(2)	1-75	1898
Susan G.	Mad	A-628	1883

Thomas	Jef	A-1	1800
Thomas	Mas	P.12-438	1857
Thomas	Pre	1-74	1889
Thomas A.	Mad	A-193	1853
Thomas M.	Was	1-265	1859
W. C.	Isa	C-125	1870
W. H.	War	B-376	1899
Whiting W.	Hol	1-497	1888
William	Cla	B-170	1841
William	Hin	1-434	1858
William	Lea	1-52	1867
William	Pan(1)	A-27	1847
William	Win	1-37	1865
William B.	Ben	1-21	1875
William B.	Jef	P.E-355	1853
William B.	Yaz	B-42	1875
William Green	Mon	I.7-47	1897
William H.	Pan(1)	A-272	1858
William I.	Low	1-31	1859
William M.	Car(1)	A-461	1864
William U.	Pan(1)	B-208	1877
William W.	Pan(1)	A-352	1859
Zachariah	Wil	1-17	1831
SMITHERS, W. H.	Laf	1-269	1876
SMYTHE, George W.	Ada	2-25	1832
James S.	Lea	1-121	1885
Sallie J.	Was	2-118	1900
SNALES, Henry	Lea	1-62	1866
SNELL, Rebecca C.	Mas	1-53	1895
William M.	Low	2-43	1891
SNIDER, Nicholas C.	Grn	A-56	1884
SNODGRASS, John W.	Cla	B-298	1861
William	Ada	1-253	1822
SNOWDEN, Dora Blanche	Low	1-367	1874
Thomas J.	Ran	1-23	1860
SNYDER, George	Ada	2-238	1841
SOJOURNER, Hardy	Ada	2-300	1845
Readick	Cop	AAA-104	1883
Sylvester D.	Cop	A-138	1899
SOLAR, Needham	Hol	1-32	1841
SOLDINE, Joseph Louis	Ada	1-258	1822
SOLOMAN, William H.	Per	1-20	1888
SOLOMON, Augustus			
Marian	DeS	2-440	1896
Henry S	Ada	3-142	1860
Jacob S.	Lau	1-354	1896
SOMERVILLE, Percy R.	Car(1)	B-64	1899
SOMMOR, Christopher	Jef	B-75	1864
SORRELS, Martha D.	Hol	1-333	1869
Samuel P.	Cla	B-342	1873
SORIMER, John	War(1823-1827)-85		1824

SORSBY, Samuel K.	Mad	A-43	1838
SOUTHERLAND, Levy	Cho	A-3	1881
Louisa E.	Mad	A-207	1853
Samuel M.	Nox	A-36	1841
SPAIN, Nancy	Yaz	A-245	1860
William G.	Ada	2-429	1853
SPANN, Charles	Nox	A-209	1854
Charles G.	Car(1)	A-47	1840
Charles G.	Nox	A-28	1840
James	Nox	A-25	1840
SPARKE, Richard	Cla	A-61	1815
SPARKMAN, Jesse R.	Nox	B-164	1875
SPARKS, Lewis	Tis	1-95	1897
SPEARMAN, Lorenzo	Yal(1)	B-193	1882
Robert	Yal(1)	A-200	1851
Rutherford	Yal(1)	B-218	1891
Thomas	Yal(2)	1-70	1892
SPEARS, Allen	Mad	A-54	1840
Charlotte	War	B-188	1887
Charlotte	War	B-208	1888
James M.	War	A-193	1852
James M.	Wil	2-349	1879
Mason	Ami	1-254	1815
SPEED, Sarah Ann	Cop	AAA-107	1859
SPEER, Jacob	Ada	2-104	1835
SPEIGHTS, Green	Hin	1-109	1838
SPENCE, G. F.	War	A-256	1859
O. H.	Cop	A-121	1897
SPENCER, Eliza E.	Ben	1-41	1888
John	Ada	1-185	1819
John	Uni	1-51	1898
Lewis	Jas	1-99	1894
Marshal	Grn	A-15	1877
Robert	Laf	1-145	1862
Shepherd Jr.	Nox	A-58	1844
William	Web	A-11	1875
William M.	Chi(1)	1-88	1888
SPIARS, John W.	Yaz	A-242	1860
SPICER, Winfred	Car(1)	A-21	1841
SPIGHT, J. C.	Tip	1-214	1900
SPIVEY, Ruffin H.	Hol	1-67	1845
W. D.	Lef	A-90	1886
SPOFFORD, Ophelia M.	Mas	1-57	1894
SPOTORNO, A. J.	Han	A-204	1892
John B.	Han	A-123	1881
Louis	Han	A-67	1872
SPRAGINS, W. F.	Mon	I.7-45	1897
W. W.	Mon	I.7-144	1900
SPRAIN, Thomas	Jef	A-97	1827
SPRINGER, Benjamin	War	B-87	1878
J. S.	Uni	1-15	1888

SPROLES, Carter N.	Hol	1–462	1883
Richard	Hol	1–54	1845
SPROTT, Josephine	Cla	3–112	1889
SPROWL, John M.	Nox	B–267	1882
SPRUEL, Susan	Ada	3–383	1870
STACKHOUSE, William H.	Cop	AAA–110	1842
ST. CLAIR, Jasper	Jef	A–103	1829
ST. JOHN, Ellen	Cla	3–67	1881
Newton	Car(1)	B–73	1900
Richard R.	Ada	4–340	1885
STAFFORD, Charles	Lau	1–414	1899
Elizabeth	Lee	1–48	1880
Jane A.	Car(2)	1–26	1880
STALLINGS, J. T.	Okt	1–9	1882
Josiah	Low	1–466	1884
STAMPLEY, George	Jef	A–129	1802
Jacob	Cla	A–162	1826
Jacob	Cla	A–316	1835
Jacob	Jef	A–90	1826
John I.	Jef	P.D–1	1846
Richard	Yaz	A–208	1856
STAMPS, Jane	Cla	3–92	1885
Lucinda	Wil	2–281	1874
Volney	Cla	3–60	1879
STANCEL, Jesse	Mad	A–179	1852
STANCILL, Caswell	Lef	A–27	1856
Nathan	Lef	A–4	1849
STANDARD, Cynthia A.	Hin	1–436	1858
J. M.	Was	1–417	1880
William M.	Hin	1–320	1853
STANDEFER, Mary Ann	Mon	1–247	1848
STANFORD, William D. C.	Laf	1–185	1845
William L.	Yaz	A–344	1867
STANSBURY, Eugene A.	Hol	1–496	1888
STANTER, John	Hin	1–152	1828
STANTON, Abirl	Mon	1–153	1840
Anna E.	Ada	3–260	1865
Benjamin	Pan(1)	A–11	1846
Frederick	Ada	3–125	1859
Henry T.	Nox	A–103	1844
Huldah May	Ada	5–173	1898
John C.	Nox	B–70	1866
William	Ada	2–417	1852
STANWOOD, Isaac H.	Wil	3–14	1883
STAPLES, Frederick	Jac	1–164	1897
Mary	War	B–255	1891
Mary C.	Mot	1–106	1891
STARK, Caroline C.	Mas	P.15–335	1861
Margaretha	War	B–234	1890

189

STARKE, Douglass	Yal(1)	A-108	1825
Henry	Ada	1-253	1822
John C.	Tal	A-269	1861
Theodore	Ada	2-265	1843
STARNES, John H.	Cop	A-96	1894
Moses D.	Cop	AAA-94	1845
STARR, John	War	A-306	1861
STATEN, Mary Ann	DeS	1-45	1853
STATER, Warren	Law	1-12	1900
STATHAM, A. D.	Yal(1)	B-74	1862
Anna Elliot	Yal(1)	B-135	1868
STATHEM, Lafayett S.	Yal(1)	B-28	1859
STATON, Bithee	Tal	B-75	1884
Eli	Tal	B-49	1876
Harvey	Tal	A-202	1859
STEDMAN, Jesse B.	Car(1)	A-109	1855
STEED, Laura M.	Ran	B.1-664	1852
STEEL, James C.	Hin	1-150	1827
STEELE, James			
Montgomery	Ada	2-136	1836
John	Ada	1-176	1818
Robert Smith	Jef	P.D-227	1847
STEEN, John V.	Mot	1-107	1892
Thomas C.	Mad	A-606	1881
STEGAR, John	Mas	P.16-92	1864
STEGER, A. C.	Mad	A-257	1857
STEIKE, Rachael	War	B-104	1879
STEIN, Marks	Lef	A-111	1893
Rosalie	Lef	A-122	1897
STEINRIEDE, Bernhard	Yaz	B-174	1884
STEINRUDO, Ferdinand	Yaz	B-290	1893
STENNS, Calip Henry	Mas	1-101	1896
STEPHENS, Abednego	Ada	2-294	1845
Charles	Lau	1-74	1866
Daniel H.	Jef	B-23	1858
Eli E.	Chi(1863-1872)-27		1864
H. A.	Tip	1-10	1866
John R.	Pon	2-300	1844
Rebecca	Ada	2-286	1844
STEPHENSON, Eleanor	Wil	2-58	1851
Elizabeth R.	Low	1-500	1884
J. M.	Mas	P.16-1	1863
John	Tat	1-28	1877
Robert	Low	1-80	1861
W. D.	Low	2-239	1899
William	Mas	P.8-45	1851
. William R.	Mas	P.16-258	1865
STERLING, I. Bowman	Was	1-414	1878
STERLINGS, Allen	Law	P.B-68	1838
STERN, Samuel	Han	A-165	1886
STERNE, Peyton	Ada	1-175	1818

[handwritten, left margin, vertical: "Payton Steger / m. Francis R. Jefferson"]

[handwritten, next to STEGAR, John: "John Jefferson Steger"]

[handwritten, right margin: "d. 1861"]

STEVENS, Annie E.	Nox	C-107	1899
Edwin	Sha	A-12	1884
Franklin M.	Car(1)	A-118	1854
Harriett	Cla	B-291	1860
John R.	Hol	1-115	1852
Mary S.	War	A-242	1857
Rebecca	Yaz	A-221	1859
S. M.	Tat	1-150	1891
Thomas M.	Web	A-93	1892
William Hardy	Cly	1-136	1899
William Henry	War	A-356	1866
STEVENSON, John	Ada	4-492	1889
Miriam	Low	2-38	1891
STEWART, A. S.	Mas	1-31	1894
C. L.	Ben	1-3	1871
Charles	Wil	1-76	1833
Charles	Wil	1-126	1835
Duncan	Wil	1-75	1833
Isham	Mad	A-127	1848
J. C.	DeS	2-478	1898
J. G.	Pan(2)	A-27	1883
J. M.	Mas	1-42	1895
James	Win	1-150	1895
James	Yaz	B-54	1876
James A.	Nox	B-149	1873
Jency	Nox	C-119	1899
John	Hin	1-430	1858
John	Nox	A-40	1840
John	Wil	1-138	1835
Juliana	Wil	3-166	1898
Lorenzo R.	Grn	A-24	1878
Lucretia	Wil	1-53	1832
Mary	Han	A-137	1881
Mary	Wil	1-217	1839
Miller	Ada	1-492	1831
Philetas	Ada	1-494	1807
R. S.	Lee	1-121	1871
Robert	Ada	3-281	1866
Robert	Tat	1-45	1881
Robert G.	Mon	1-259	1850
Sarah	Mas	P.18-20	1867
Solomon	Lea	1-1	1852
Temple F.	Coa(1)	1-98	1866
Theresa E.	Wil	3-73	1891
W. E.	DeS	2-425	1895
Walter	Ada	3-220	1865
William	Jef	B-14	1859
William J.	Nes	A-73	1863
William M.	Mad	A-547	1873
STIER, John Henry	Ada	4-37	1874
STIERLIN, Julin	Wil	2-268	1872

STIGLER, George W.	Hol	1-340	1869
L. T.	Cho	A-18	1887
Martha E.	Hol	1-371	1873
Simeon	Hol	1-318	1866
William W.	Hol	1-376&380	1873
STINE, William E.	Pan(1)	B-7	1864
STINSON, James Turner	Mas	P.7-643	1851
STIRLING, Thomas S.	Clk	P.B-12	1839
STITH, Caroline	Ada	3-65	1856
STOCKARD, John P.	Laf	1-135	1860
STOCKDALE, James	Ada	1-268	1822
Thomas R.	Pik	1-119	1899
STOCKER, Sarah S.	Wil	2-112	1856
Susanna	Ada	1-376	1826
STOCKETT, Mary E.	Wil	3-34	1884
STOCKLEN, William H.	Hol	1-66	1845
STOCKTON, Ann	Ada	5-220	1898
Richard C.	Han	A-180	1889
STOCKWELL, Silas	Ada	3-156	1860
STOKELY, John	Lef	A-9	1852
STOKES, Arrabella P.	Lea	1-89	1877
Jacob	Han	P.(1853-1860)-306	1855
John C.	Grn	A-67	1885
Mrs. M. J.	Car(2)	1-28	1883
Mary A.	DeS	2-430	1896
Mary J.	Car(1)	A-508	1868
Reuben T.	Mad	A-648	1887
Young C.	DeS	1-35	1853
STONE, Dudley	Car(2)	1-31	1884
Jacob	DeS	2-496	1899
James	Mon	I.13-83	1857
James M.	Nox	B-395	1893
John	Mas	1-180	1900
John W.	Tun	2-102	1888
Lucinda B.	Mad	A-69	1842
Mahala	Mas	P.161-110	1864
Nannie E.	Pan(2)	A-82	1891
Susannah F.	Car(1)	B-49	1895
Thaddeus C.	Mas	P.15-447	1862
Thomas	Cla	B-214	1851
STONEBURNER, William	Lef	A-37	1859
STORM, John	Lin	1-31	1896
STOSTLY, Sarah	Mad	A-484	1868
STOUGHTON, John	War	B-356	1898
STOUT, Rosie Gannon	War	B-368	1899
STOVALL, Henry	Mas	P.5-421	1848
John	Car(1)	A-131	1855
Joseph	DeS	1-120	1850
Josiah	Hin	1-31	1834
Louisa Q.	Ada	4-326	1884
Margaret	Car(1)	A-446	1862

Nick	Yaz	B-237	1889
Ralph	Hin	1-132	1840
STOWELL, Benjamin	Ada	2-59	1834
STOWERS, Caleb	Ada	3-149	1860
James	Jef	B-27	1859
John	Ada	1-378	1826
Mandie	Laf	1-424	1896
Samuel	War	A-238	1856
STRAHAN, John	Mar	A1-126	1845
STRATTON, Joseph B. Jr.	Ada	4-466	1888
William S.	Hin	1-123	1839
STRAWER, Mrs. ?. C.	Uni	1-58	1899
STREET, Parke	Ada	2-289	1844
STRIBLING, W. B.	Lea	1-38	1863
STRICKLAND, Jacob L.	Pan(1)	B-192	1876
Matthew	Pan(1)	A-316	1858
P. H.	DeS	2-501	1900
P. H.	Mas	1-163	1899
T. K.	Lee	1-119	1889
STRICKLIN, Sarah A.	Tip	1-210	1899
W. L.	Coa(1)	1-115	1869
STRINGER, J. S.	Smi	1-5	1900
Josiah	Law	P.B-37	1837
Noah	Law	P.B-15	1836
STRONG, Benjamin	Mon	I.1-77	1882
C. W.	War	B-123	1880
Charles	Pan(1)	B-84	1871
Elisha H. Jr.	Cly	1-79	1887
Henry	War	A-225	1855
John	Cop	AAA-89	1838
John Hunt	Yaz	B-6	1871
Nelson	Laf	1-265	1875
William M.	Laf	1-327	1883
STROTHER, John	Hol	1-21	1840
Sarah	Wil	2-35	1848
STROUD, Elizabeth J.	Hol	1-245	1860
W. P.	Hol	1-384	1874
STUART, B. L.	DeS	2-386	1894
James F.	War	A-117	1841
Leonly	Jef	P.C-761	1845
James	Jef	P.B-209	1834
James	Jef	P.E-42	1851
Mary Emily	Lin	1-53	1899
Thomas	Mad	A-656	1888
Thomas H.	Jef	P.D-6	1847
W. B.	Jef	B-165	1872
STUBBINS, Nehemiah	Ada	1-299	1823
STUBBS, Francis	Cop	AAA-85	1859
STURDIVANT, Benjamin W.	Tal	B-108	1896

Charles	Low	1–365	1874
Eliza R.	Tal	B–125	1899
Jerry	Low	2–143	1896
STURGES, Alice			
Cornelia	Lau	1–403	1899
Frank	Cop	AAA–82	1870
SUBAT, Frank	Cop	A–10	1887
John Sr.	Cop	A–115	1897
SUCHETT, Martha A. A.	Lea	1–85	1876
Samuel	War	A–196	1853
SUDDUTH, John C.	Okt	1–35	1885
Sarah W.	Okt	1–35	1885
Spencer	Mad	A–145	1849
SUGGS, Rolen	Att	C–551	1870
Tabitha	Tip	1–121	1886
SULCER, Henry	Ada	2–217	1840
SULLEN, Catharine	Mad	2–78	1897
Laura	Was	1–410	1878
SULLIVAN, E. B.	Mas	1–2	1892
Elijah	Car(1)	A–119	1854
Ellen	Ada	3–322	1867
Hardy	Yaz	B–65	1877
Richard	Ada	4–147	1879
Timothy W.	Car(1)	A–438	1861
SULTAN, B. F.	Ran	1–197	1885
SULUEON, W. R.	Mas	1–90	1896
SUMMERALL, James T.	Chi(1)	1–35	1881
SUMMERHILL, J. W.	Att	B–476	1885
SUMMERS, George W.	Hin	B–80	1864
SUMRALL, David	Jac	1–62	1890
David	Jac	1–114	1892
W. A.	Wil	3–47	1887
SURGET, Eliza	Ada	3–256	1866
Eustis	Ada	4–238	1882
Francis	Ada	3–74	1856
Francis	Ada	3–294	1866
Mary Atwell	Ada	4–529	1890
SUTHERLAND, Daniel	Mad	A–190	1853
SUTHERLIN, Frances J.	Pre	1–39	1877
SUTPHEIR, Martha M.	Jef	B–149	1874
SUTPHIN, Abn. W.	Jef	B–186	1892
SUTTAN, John H.	Att	B–437	1885
SUTTLES, G. S.	Kem	A–68	1897
SUTTON, B. F.	Ran	1–197	1885
Elizabeth	Ran	1–58	1863
James M.	Was	1–436	1883
John	Nes	A–11	1846
Louisa C.	Ran	1–196	1885
Solomon	Cop	AAA–78	1851
Stephen	Mad	A–39	1836
William	Was	1–393	1872

SWAN, John C.	Was	1–232	1850
SWANN, Nicholas	Nox	A–289	1860
Porter	Nox	B–226	1879
W. M.	Hol	1–84	1848
SWANSON, Edward	War	A–25	1833
SWANZEY, J. A.	Kem	A–72	1898
SWASEY, Henry R.	Han	A–92	1875
SWAYZE, Caleb C.	Wil	3–20	1883
Elijah	Ada	1–114	1814
Gabriel	Ada	1–113	1814
Gabriel	Yaz	A–224	1859
Mary	Ada	3–1	1854
Nathan Sen.	Ada	1–182	1819
Richard	Yaz	B–292	1893
Sidney	Wil	2–221	1864
Solomon	Ada	2–42	1833
SWEARINGEN, Alfred	Tun	1–553	1871
Frederick	Nox	A–51	1842
John	Yal(1)	A–195	1851
William W.	Yal(1)	B–15	1859
SWEATMAN, Mary A.	Mot	1–49	1881
SWEET, Frank	Cly	1–135	1899
Sarah H.	War	B–124	1880
SWEETON, Ibby W.	Tip	1–20	1867
SWIGART, George H.	Wil	1–202	1839
SWILLEY, Selliff	Ran	1–9	1859
SWINEY, E. J.	Tip	1–187	1894
John K.	Hol	1–279	1862
William P.	War	A–199	1853
SWOFFORD, J. T.	Hin	1–229	1848
SWOOPE, Jacob K.	DeS	2–36	1871
SWORDS, Archibald	Cla	A–344	1836
James M.	War	B–27	1873
William	Hin	1–106	1838
SYKES, Adaline D.	Low	2–251	1900
Augustus J.	Mon	I.4–344	1882
Benjamin Sr.	Car(1)	A–53	1845
Georgia Augusta	Mon	I.7–68	1899
Joseph A.	Mon	I.17–183	1863
Louisa W.	Low	1–523	1887
Lucien M.	Mon	I.3–426	1879
Martha A.	Low	1–204	1866
Nelson	Low	2–185	1897
Sallie B.	Mon	I.3–290	1878
Sarah A.	Mas	1–155	1899
Simon B.	Mon	I.20–17	1866
Thomas B.	Mon	I.6–332	1894
Willian A.	Mon	I.2–609	1873
SYNNOTT, Sarah M.	Web	A–88	1891
TABB, John H.	Chi(1)	1–128	1895

TABOR, Aquila	Yal(2)	1-17	1881
TACKER, Victoria	Tis	1-15	1888
TACKETT, Phillip	Hol	3-47	1897
Pleasant C.	Mad	A-121	1848
TAIT, James M.	DeS	1-19	1852
TALABOT, I. C.	Ada	3-291	1866
TALBERT, James B.	Yal(1)	B-243	1899
Joseph H.	Yal(1)	A-114	1848
Michael D.	Yal(1)	A-227	1853
Nancy	Yal(1)	A-15	1835
TALBOT, James	Hin	1-93	1837
Rebecca	Mad	A-25	1826
TALIAFERRO, Ann	Cly	1-77	1886
Peachy R.	Cop	AAA-73	1852
Rhoda	Nox	B-231	1880
Roderick	Cly	1-3	1872
William	Cop	AAA-67	1840
William	Yal(2)	1-52	1887
TALLY, William	Nes	A-82	1865
TAM, Jane	Jac	1-97	1892
TANKERSLY, Reuben	Laf	1-3	1844
TAPP, M. E.	Tip	1-160	1891
TARPLEY, Colin S.	Hin	B-196	1866
Ephraim	Hin	1-344	1854
TARTT, Elnathan	Lau	1-121	1876
TARVER, Elizabeth	Pik	1-161	1900
Sarah J.	Lau	1-157	1881
TATE, John	Mad	A-148	1850
John M.	Nox	A-174	1851
John M.	Nox	A-276	1859
M. J.	Lea	1-180	1898
Mary Ann	Yaz	B-366	1898
Robert	Ada	2-361	1849
Thomas S.	Tat	1-48	1881
Waddy	Yaz	A-304	1865
Zack	Uni	1-4	1883
TATUM, Christopher	Jas	1-58	1871
Daniel	Mon	I.6-174	1892
Joel Haywood	Mon	I.5-203	1886
Robert	Yaz	B-14	1871
TAYLOR, A. M.	Yaz	B-380	1898
Abel John	Nox	A-91	1846
Benjamin F.	Cly	1-56	1883
Burrel	Mon	I.18-385	1865
Charlotte	Att	C-481	1871
Daniel	Ran	1-30	1861
Elias	Hol	1-251	1861
Elizabeth	Low	1-559	1888
Esther	Cop	AAA-63	1865
G. F.	Mas	1-124	1897
George W.	Ada	2-215	1840

Granville	Tun	2-151	1897
H. G. W.	Grn	A-106	1874
James I.	War	A-217	1854
James W.	Han	P.(1853-1860)-281	1854
Jefferson	Mon	I.3-67	1878
Jesse	Lau	1-151	1880
John P.	Car(1)	A-34	1843
John P.	Cla	3-144	1893
Joseph	Mon	1-208	1843
Kinchen	Jef	B-80	1865
Lee	Car(1)	A-164	1858
Levi	Ada	1-303	1823
Marcus Elvis	Pre	1-101	1896
Penelope	Win	1-105	1887
Rebecca	Lau	1-60	1865
Robert	Ada	1-192	1819
Robert L.	Laf	2-5	1897
Samuel	Lee	1-8	1869
Samuel H.	Lee	1-81	1883
Shepherd	Jef	A-88	1826
Swepson T.	Clk	1-153	1894
Thomas	Mas	P.9-7	1852
Thomas J.	Pan(1)	B-381	1883
Uriah	Laf	1-224	1872
TEAGUE, Daniel	Att	B-572	1887
John P.	Att	2-424	1864
Samuel Davis	Att	C-574	1896
TEASDALE, Thomas C.	Low	2-58	1891
TEAT, William H.	Lau	1-308	1893
TEMPLE, Eleanor E.	DeS	2-233	1885
J. W. F.	Lau	1-129	1880
William F.	Coa(1)	1-11	1846
TEMPLETON, Anthony	Ada	5-163	1897
John	War	A-86	1838
TENPELL, William	Nes	A-17	1848
TERRELL, Hilton	Hin	B-350	1884
James	Hin	1-7	1833
James F.	Nox	B-25	1862
John C.	Coa(1)	1-173	1884
Jonathan	Hin	1-56	1835
Micajah	Ada	1-18	1805
Sallie D.	Hin	B-224	1867
Vernon L.	Cop	A-98	1894
TERRILL, Charles N.	Hol	1-180	1857
TERRY, Asbury	Tip	1-23	1867
Curtis	Yal(1)	B-18	1859
George H.	DeS	2-454	1897
Isaac	Hin	B-402	1889
Joseph	Ran	1-68	1864
Mary	Cop	AAA-59	1858
Sarah	Cop	AAA-56	1834

Stephen	Hin	B-280	1871
W. D. Sr.	DeS	2-265	1886
William D.	Cop	AAA-52	1882
THACHER, Joseph S. B.	Ada	3-332	1867
THACKER, Ransom	Yal(1)	A-106	1846
Richard B.	Laf	1-246	1874
THAMES, David	Lin	1-4	1894
THARP, George W.	Cla	B-169	1841
W. L.	Tat	1-66	1883
THEOBALD, George P.	War	B-341	1898
Harriet B.	Was	1-468	1888
THERY, John B.	Ada	1-41	1808
THIGPEN, Isabella	Lau	1-181	1882
J. G.	Mad	A-617	1881
THOMAS, A. V. B.	Grn	A-90	1891
Alfred	Lau	1-296	1892
Andrew H.	Web	A-79	1891
Benjamin F.	Yaz	A-215	1858
Caroline	Cla	B-297	1861
Charles S.	Mas	P.13-268	1858
David	Lin	1-4	1894
Elijah	Nes	A-24	1849
Ezekiel	Lau	1-251	1889
Henry	Tal	B-45	1875
Hiram J.	Yaz	B-83	1878
J. H.	Lee	1-220	1900
James	Jas	1-20	1862
James P.	Mad	A-406	1865
John H.	Yaz	A-252	1865
Joseph F.	Ada	2-234	1841
Malcolm	Tal	A-231	1859
Mathew	Ada	1-163	1817
Nellie	Was	1-428	1882
Pleasant R.	Tip	1-69	1875
Richard	Hin	B-401	1890
Sarah M.	Ada	4-489	1890
Susannie	Coa(1)	1-227	1891
Thomas	War	B-289	1893
Wade R.	Lau	1-188	1882
William	Att	B-379	1882
William	Cla	A-37	1812
THOMPSON, Benjamin	Jas	1-77	1881
Benjamin	Mad	2-99	1897
C. Malon	Laf	1-232	1873
Carrie N.	Pre	1-112	1897
Catherine A.	Coa(1)	1-236&246	1891
Catherine A.	Laf	2-31	1899
Dougald B.	Wil	1-20	1831
E. C.	Yaz	B-246	1890
Elizabeth M.	Tal	B-40	1875
Eusebia	Tis	1-4	1887

Frances	Cop	AAA-48	1837
H. M.	Tat	1-26	1876
J. T.	Chi(1)	1-116	1893
Jacob	Coa(1)	1-241	1891
Jacob	Laf	2-23	1899
Jane	Mon	I.2-366	1876
Jane	Pan(2)	A-64	1886
Jennett	Hin	1-49	1835
Jesse	Cop	AAA-43	1855
John	Cla	1-290	1833
John M.	Tis	1-4	1887
John W.	Cop	AAA-38	1861
Joseph A.	Lau	1-51	1865
Joseph W.	Tal	A-247	1860
Lewis W.	Was	1-474	1888
Little Berry	Wil	1-205	1839
Margaret Ann	Mad	A-152	1850
Mary	Low	1-12	1858
Mary	Yaz	A-241	1860
Mary Eliza	Mad	A-292	1858
Peter G.	Low	1-57	1860
R. N.	Yaz	A-267	1863
Rebecca	Chi(1863-1872)-189		1870
Richard	Mas	P.15-579	1862
Robert H.	Yal(1)	B-207	1883
S. C.	DeS	1-330	1865
Thomas H.	New	1-127	1893
Thomas J.	Wil	2-122	1857
William	Car(1)	A-62	1846
William	Hol	1-386	1875
William	Tal	A-5	1835
William G.	Mad	A-516	1870
William J.	Mon	I.22-512	1871
THOMSON, James M.	Mas	P.5-292	1848
THORN, John Sr.	Smi	1-3	1894
Joshua	Ada	4-107	1876
Mary E.	Ada	5-303	1900
Patience S.	Han	A-222	1893
William	Tip	1-80	1876
THORNE, John	Ada	2-125	1836
THORNBURG, James N.	Ada	4-90	1875
THORNSBURG, John	Ada	3-177	1861
THORNTON, Benjamin F.	Ada	4-357	1885
Ella M.	Yal(2)	1-98	1895
J. W.	Jas	1-83	1886
John	Chi(1)	1-138	1899
K. H.	Nox	A-100	1847
Phillip H.	Tal	A-298	1864
Philip N.	Hol	1-403	1877
William B.	Mas	P.16-345	1865
THORTON, Richard M.	Hin	1-187	1846

THRAWER, Mary A.	Low	2-238	1899
THRELKELD, F. M.	Lee	1-178	1897
Stephen	Laf	1-324&362	1879
THURMAN, Hugh	Sim	A-1	1873
THURMOND, P. B.	Hol	1-267	1862
THWEATT, William K.	DeS	1-107	1855
TIBBS, James A.	Sco	A-452	1880
TICE, Annie	Hin	B-467	1899
TIDWELL, Falbia	Mad	A-12	1833
TIERMAN, Peter	Ada	1-187	1819
TIGNER, Clark H.	Wil	2-208	1863
Lydia	Wil	2-198	1863
William	Wil	2-92	1854
TIGRET, David P.	Tip	1-202	1898
TILGHMAN, John C.	DeS	2-138	1878
John P.	Mas	P.4-652	1847
Sherod	Mas	1-44	1895
William	Mas	P.16-123	1864
TILLERY, Joshua	Yaz	A-6	1834
TILLMAN, Alfred	Cop	AAA-35	1843
Mrs. Nickie	Ada	5-273	1900
Paschall	Yal(1)	B-54	1861
Salena C.	Cop	A-163	1900
William	War	A-351	1866
William B.	Cop	AAA-31	1855
TILSON, Nehemiah	Ada	1-118	1814
TINDALL, Bryant M.	Lef	A-45	1871
John L.	Mon	I.18-186	1865
TINER, Elizabeth	Laf	1-184	1865
TINNIN, David	Laf	1-59	1851
David	Pan(1)	A-110	1852
Mary	Yal(1)	A-103	1847
Robert	Pon E.(1844-1848)-164		1847
TINSLEY, Parmelia	War	B-232	1889
TINSON, Daniel B.	Wil	2-150	1859
TISDALE, Ran.	Car(1)	A-520	1869
William C.	Mad	A-362	1862
TITO, Fanny Francis	Han	A-118	1880
TITUS, James	DeS	1-154	1856
TODD, Jacob T.	Pon	1-22	1896
Joseph S.	War	A-179	1850
TOLAND, Mary	Hol	1-219	1859
TOLIAFERRO, Rhoda	Nox	B-231	1880
TOLLES, Reilly	Yaz	A-61	1842
TOLLIVER, Rainey	Pan(2)	A-67	1887
TOLS, Michael	Nox	B-8	1861
TOLSON, J. D.	New	1-117	1897
James D.	New	1-139	1895
TOMASICH, Joseph	Han	A-41	1868
TOMLINSON, Elizabeth	Ada	1-151	1816
J. G.	Lau	1-411	1899

John	Mas	P.10-33	1854
Nathaniel	Ada	1-105	1814
William E.	Ben	1-28	1879
TOMPKINS, Erelina F.	War	A-286	1860
Francis B.	War	A-288	1860
T. W.	War	A-253	1858
TONELLA, Theodore	War	B-299	1894
TONEY, Frank	War	B-331	1897
TOOLEY, Adam	Ada	1-108	1814
James	Ada	2-293	1845
TOPP, Jennings	Grn	A-114	1896
Mattie	Chi(2)	1-71	1894
TORIAN, Jacob	DeS	2-216	1883
TORNEY, James	Hol	1-201	1859
TORONES, Martha A.	Yal(1)	B-21	1859
TORPH, Ellen R.	Ada	3-132	1859
TORRY, George	Jef	A-39	1820
John L.	Cla	B-206	1849
TOUGH, David	Ada	4-33	1873
TOULINE, John B.	Han	A-1	1860
TOUNES, J. M.	Yal(1)	B-128	1867
TOWERS, Joel	Lau	1-183	1883
TOWLES, John S.	Pan(1)	B-134	1873
TOWNES, Allen	Yal(1)	A-100	1846
Allen	Yal(1)	A-284	1846
Armistead T.	Yal(1)	A-258	1855
James M.	Yal(1)	B-132	1867
Judith R.	Yal(1)	A-286	1856
Richard A.	Car(1)	A-111	1851
TOWNS, Isaac R.	Mot	1-34	1879
Joseph H.	Hol	1-24	1841
TOWNSEND, Abraham			
Thompson	Cho	A-25	1891
Alexander F.	Mot	1-109	1892
Clement	Wil	1-70	1832
Emily C.	Mot	1-151	1899
Mary P. B.	War	B-2	1869
Thomas	Low	1-73	1860
TOWNSLEY, Robert	Cla	A-362	1837
TOWSON, Daniel I.	Lef	A-41	1864
TRABUCCO, Gaetona			
Michelle	War	A-284	1860
TRACY, John Martin	Jac	1-126	1893
TRADER, H. G.	Tat	1-135	1890
TRAHERN, James	Hin	1-154	1831
TRAINER, Elizabeth	Hol	3-26	1895
TRASK, James S.	Wil	2-107	1855
TRAVIS, Joseph	Car(1)	A-167	1858
Seth	Jas	1-96	1893
TRAWICK, Cornelius	Cop	AAA-26	1863
TRAXLER, David D.	Ran	1-155	1872

Simeon	Smi	1-1	1893
TREADWELL, Elizabeth E.	Ben	1-44	1889
TREHERN, Mary	Jac	1-43	1886
TREMBLE, Walter	Cla	A-232	1832
TREVILLIAN, Temple States Sr.	Jef	P.C-768	1846
TREWALLA, Henry L.	Tal	B-102	1895
TREZVANT, Mary B.	DeS	1-26	1852
TRICE, Robert L.	Lee	1-159	1895
TRIGG, William	Ada	1-115	1813
William	Jef	A-37	1818
William A.	Laf	1-140	1861
TRIMBLE, John	Hin	1-292	1852
TRIMM, William H.	Cop	AAA-22	1859
TRIPLETT, E. J.	Win	1-98	1883
Susan	Lea	1-176	1897
W. D. C.	Nox	B-389	1893
TROTMAN, Thomas	Nox	A-296	1861
TROTT, J. C.	Pan(2)	A-153	1899
TROTTER, Elizabeth S.	Mas	P.4-280	1846
Silas F.	Tun	1-108	1853
TROUTMAN, John C.	Mad	A-565	1874
TROWBRIDGE, Sarah E.	War	A-303	1861
TRUEX, John William	Pik	1-27	1887
TRUITT, Elizabeth	Yal(1)	A-126	1848
TRULY, Martha	Jef	P.F-413	1855
TRUSS, Warren	Tis	1-35	1886
TRUSSELL, Henry	Grn	A-82	1888
TUBB, John	Mon	1-137	1839
William Lancaster	Mon	1-210	1843
TUCKER, Asa E.	Pan(1)	B-485	1896
Catharine C.	Pan(1)	A-379	1858
Heslip R.	Pre	1-114	1898
John E.	Chi(2)	1-29	1885
John S.	Mad	A-390	1863
Joseph	Jef	A-77	1823
P. W.	Cly	1-41	1879
Pleasant	Nox	A-194	1854
Rosannah	Yaz	A-197	1855
Sterling H.	Mon	I.8-207	1852
Thomas	Ada	1-277	1823
Thomas M.	Low	1-529	1887
William H.	Mad	A-350	1861
William W.	DeS	1-3	1851
TUDURY, Antoine	Han	A-100	1877
TUGGLE, John T.	Mas	P.17-569	1867
TULLIS, William	Yal(1)	A-102	1846
TUNLE, Elenora S.	Yaz	B-255	1891
TUNNELL, Steven M.	Chi(2)	1-23	1884
TUNSTALL, Elvia C.	Jef	A-31	1819

Joseph	Mad	2-129	1899
TUPPER, Tullius C.	Mad	A-443	1866
TURBEVILLE, J. W.	Cly	1-135	1899
TURK, Emma L.	Mad	A-687	1892
TURNAGE, Amos	Laf	1-154	1864
Amos	Laf	1-180	1865
Carney	Yaz	B-89	1878
TURNBULL, Elijah E.	Laf	1-187	1866
John	Was	1-6	1840
Judith	Yal(1)	A-64	1843
Robert J.	Isa	B-111	1854
Robert J.	Isa	C-134	1882
William	War	A-105	1840
TURNER, Alford	Yal(1)	B-130	1867
Celley	Was	1-480	1889
David R.	Car(1)	A-442	1862
Edward	Ada	3-146	1860
Elizabeth	Sim	A-83	1897
Hamp	Win	1-142	1894
Henry	Ada	1-232	1813
Henry	War	A-281	1860
Henry	War	A-364	1867
James	Clk	1-13	1873
James	Lee	1-128	1889
James W.	Car(1)	B-15	1886
John	Wil	1-109	1834
John T.	Car(1)	B-30	1888
Larken	Yal(1)	B-232	1897
Larkin T.	Cho	A-14	1885
Martha C.	Att	B-448	1885
Mathew	Mon	1-200	1842
Ransom	Yal(1)	B-101	1863
Robert	Car(1)	A-119	1854
Robert	Jef	A-92	1826
Sarah	Car(1)	A-494	1866
Simon T.	Car(1)	B-41	1891
Thomas W.	Kem	A-32	1887
William	Jef	P.B-344	1837
William	Laf	1-139	1858
William A.	Grn	A-84	1889
William George	Jac	1-121	1893
William H.	Yal(1)	B-148	1872
Wylie	Tip	1-40	1869
TURPIN, White	Ada	2-250&260	1842
TURRENTINE, Allen	Car(1)	A-159	1857
TURRY, David	Jef	A-93	1826
TUTT, Pierce B.	Yaz	A-11	1835
William G.	Was	1-423	1880
TUTTLE, Ichabod	Laf	1-121	1857
TWEED, Robert	Jef	B-203	1898
TWOMEY, John C.	Ada	3-279	1866

TYCER, Richard			
William	Ami	1–25	1811
TYER, James	Laf	1–91	1854
TYLER, A. G.	Ada	4–444	1888
Abden	Cop	AAA–19	1859
Alex	Nox	B–264	1881
John Jr.	Lef	A–95	1887
John L.	Nox	A–284	1860
Laura D.	Mon	I.22–516	1871
Sarah	Ada	2–458	1853
Thomas	Car(1)	A–17	1841
Thomas J.	Car(1)	B–37	1890
TYRE, James Sr.	Laf	1–79	1852
TYRONE, Sallie A.	DeS	2–384	1894
TYSON, Aaron L.	Car(1)	A–429	1861
Calvin M.	Mas	1–162	1900
Horatio	Mas	P.15–530	1862
Littleton	Cop	AAA–15	1833
Noah	Lef	A–19	1852
UHL, Joseph	Was	2–109	1899
ULLMAN, Simon	Ada	5–241	1899
ULMAN, Emma W.	Han	A–281	1895
James Augustus	Han	A–228	1893
ULMER, Sophia	Pik	1–132	1899
UMBORGEN, Charles	Ben	1–61	1891
UNDERWOOD, Henry	Mon	I.18–218	1865
John	Ada	1–317	1824
Thomas R.	Lau	1–20	1860
UNGER, James David	Att	C–343&362	1893
Solomon	Cla	3–80	1882
UNGLE, Harmond	Ada	2–190	1839
UPSHAW, Samuel W.	Hol	1–289	1864
URIE, Thomas	War	A–145	1844
USHER, William A.	Hol	1–223	1859
William W.	Hol	1–125	1853
VADEN, Peter T.	DeS	2–218	1883
VAIDEN, Cowles Mead	Car(2)	1–17	1880
VAIL, Stephen	Ada	3–391	1870
VALENTINE, Adaline W.	Okt	1–34	1895
Sarah J.	Cla	3–180	1898
VALLEY, Lewis	Lau	1–412	1899
VANARSDELL, Lucas	Mad	A–519	1867
VANCE, Elisha Q.	Pan(1)	A–186	1854
Eliza Ann Tate	DeS	2–114	1876
James J.	New	1–1	1875
Jno. W.	DeS	2–17	1870
William L.	Was	1–481	1888
VANDEVELDE, James			
Oliver	Ada	3–39	1855

James Oliver	Han	A-110	1855
VANDEVUNDER,			
Christopher	Kem	A-19	1885
VANDORN, Peter A.	Cla	A-346	1837
VAN EATON, Anna L.	Wil	3-135	1894
H. S.	Wil	3-169	1898
Sarah E.	Coa(2)	1-38	1895
VANHOOZER, Ina L.	Tat	1-239	1899
VANHORN, Benjamin	Yal(1)	B-204	1883
VANHOUTEN, Cornelius	Hol	1-100	1851
Susannah	Hol	1-299	1864
VAN NORMAN, Mary W.	Was	2-12	1894
VARDAMAN, Elijah	Cop	AAA-12	1857
VARNER, Samuel	Isa	A-170	1852
VASSAR, George W.	Car(1)	B-66	1899
VASSER, Mary H.	Mon	I.3-293	1878
VAUGHAN, Evans	Ada	2-129	1836
Thomas C.	Jef	P.B-479	1835
VAUGHN, Henry	Yaz	B-7	1870
Henry Sr.	Yaz	B-184	1884
Drury	Cho	A-19	1887
George W.	Low	2-94	1894
Hundley	Yal(2)	1-2	1878
Jessy Amanda	Jef	P.C-192	1840
Mary A.	Ben	1-53	1888
Murphy	Win	1-17	1862
Nancy	Cly	1-60	1883
Osmond J.	War	A-315	1862
Pleasant	DeS	2-467	1897
Sterling F.	Pan(1)	A-226	1855
Thomas	Pan(1)	A-296	1858
VAUSE, Thomas	Cla	A-13	1805
VEASEY, Mary E. A.	Tat	1-24	1876
Calvin	Tat	1-127	1889
Jonathan W.	DeS	1-232	1859
William J.	Tat	1-261	1900
VECIA, Catherine	Ada	4-368	1886
VENABLE, Elizabeth	War	A-231	1856
VENTRESS, Charlotte			
D.	Wil	2-330	1877
VERDERBER, Mattias	Han	A-154	1884
VERNER, Caleb	Mon	I.18-103	1865
VERUER, William E.	Low	2-89	1893
VESTAL, William S.	Mon	I.5-295	1887
VICK, Arington	Mas	P.7-555	1851
Charles W.	War	B-117	1879
Gray J.	Yaz	A-121	1849
Henry G.	Was	1-288	1860
John	War	A-65	1836
John E. W.	Jas	1-107	1897
John Wesley	War	B-197	1888

Kate B.	War	B-372	1899
Martha	War	A-181	1850
Mattie A.	Pan(2)	A-126	1896
Ransom	Mas	P.18-280	1868
Willis B.	War	A-4	1830
VICKERS, James	Nox	A-138	1850
Richard H.	Nox	B-90	1867
VISER, Lewis D.	Laf	1-297	1879
VIVERETT, Martha	Nes	A-104	1877
VOCAVICH. Peter	Jac	1-27	1883
VOGELSANGER,			
Catherine	Han	A-299	1896
VOGH, Valentine	War	A-168	1849
VOLKING, F. W.	Clk	1-119	1891
VONAN, Ignas	Han	A-44	1868
VOUSDAM, William	Ada	1-2	1802
WADDELL, Eliza			
Catherine	Hin	1-321	1853
WADDILL, Mary C.	War	B-201	1887
WADE, Elisha	Att	2-318	1863
James	Ada	1-56	1805
Mary	Mad	A-653	1888
Pleasant P.	Ada	2-154	1837
Sarah	Hol	1-253	1861
Seaborn L.	Att	D-173	1899
Walter	Jef	B-65	1862
William H.	Hol	1-87	1849
WADLINGTON, D. M.	Hol	1-419	1878
Mercer	Mad	A-9	1832
WADSWORTH, John A. C.	Mar	A2-18	1896
John B.	War	B-76	1877
WAGGONER, Sylvester			
G.	Lea	1-190	1899
WAGONER, Viney	Ada	4-222	1882
WAGSTER, Unicy	Clk	1-80	1885
WAHL, John M.	War	B-335	1898
John Matthews	War	B-63	1876
WAHRENDORFF, Henry	Jon	1-3	1897
WAILES, Benj. Leonard			
Covington	Ada	3-199	1862
WAINWRIGHT, Wash	Coa(1)	1-177	1885
WAITES, Emma	Lef	A-108	1893
WAKE, John M.	Grn	A-132	1898
WALCOTT, Robertz H.	Was	1-432	1883
Sarah A.	War	A-148	1845
WALDRESS, T. B.	Laf	1-377	1889
WALDRIP, Mitchell	Laf	1-167	1858
T. B.	Laf	1-377	1889
Thomas W.	Pan(1)	B-179	1875
WALDROP, Green B.	DeS	1-88	1854

McD.	DeS	1-192	1858
WALDRUP, Willis	Pan(1)	A-431	1863
WALES, Ann	Mad	2-26	1894
WALKER, A. W.	Hin	1-393	1856
Ajax	Mas	P.8-100	1852
Andrew	Ada	1-33	1808
Archibald	Tal	A-56	1844
Armstead	Yaz	B-56	1876
Caroline	Chi(2)	1-33	1886
Charles G.	Was	2-62	1897
Elisha W.	Jef	A-102	1827
Ezekiel	Tip	1-64	1873
Frederick S.	Hin	1-384	1856
George	DeS	2-398	1894
George H.	Tat	1-121	1878
George Washington	Sim	A-26	1885
Green B.	Mad	A-50	1838
Henry	New	1-181	1900
Henry	War	B-245	1890
Henry L.	Car(2)	1-56	1890
Hezekiah	Hin	1-242	1849
J. J. M.	Lee	1-11	1870
J. R.	Han	B-1	1898
J. V.	Tat	1-72	1884
James	Att	2-259	1865
James M.	Tat	1-203	1895
Jeremiah	Yaz	A-64	1842
John	Ita	E.5-123	1860
Joseph	Nox	A-200	1854
Josephus	Okt	1-47	1890
L. P.	Tis	1-115	1900
Mary L.	Clk	1-53	1883
Reuben	Chi(2)	1-74	1896
Robert	Ada	3-224	1865
Robert	Hin	1-223	1848
Robert B.	DeS	1-10	1852
Samuel	Mad	A-67	1842
Samuel	Yaz	A-209	1857
Samuel B.	Cla	B-316	1865
Thomas B.	Mas	P.10-12	1854
Thompson	Yaz	A-284	1861
W. A.	Tis	1-123	1900
W. Logan	Mas	1-108	1897
Washington T.	Yaz	B-418	1900
William	Hol	1-45	1844
William H.	Lau	1-352	1896
Zenn A.	DeS	1-75	1854
WALL, Durrett R.	Pan(1)	B-215	1877
Elizabeth	Mon	1-206	1842
George W.	Mon	1-126	1836
John	New	1-57	1878

Lucy	Mas	P.16–201	1864
Sarah	Wil	1–98	1833
W. G.	War	A–319	1862
William	Mon	1–195	1842
WALLACE, Andrew	War	A–71	1837
David	Cla	A–73	1818
Eliza	Tal	B–66	1881
Elizabeth E.	Hin	1–237	1847
J. M.	Laf	2–75	1900
J. R.	Hin	B–445	1896
James Monroe	Pan(1)	B–504	1900
James Monroe	Tat	1–254	1900
James Monroe	Tun	2–201	1900
James N. A.	Jas	1–74	1880
June	Cho	A–12	1885
Lewis	Sun	1–10	1890
William	Tip	1–8	1866
William L.	Lea	1–15	1857
WALLES, Joseph	Att	2–12	1861
WALLIS, Philip	Yaz	A–87	1846
WALLON, Ann C.	Mas	4–419	1846
WALMSLEY, Georgia	Tis	1–1	1887
WALSCER, Ferdinand B.	Jac	2–23	1900
WALSH, John	War	A–359	1867
Richard	Ada	1–432	1829
Thomas W.	Nes	A–18	1848
WALSTON, B. C.	Lau	1–416	1899
WALTER, Martha			
Fredonia	Mas	1–143	1898
WALTERS, Annis	Jon	1–1	1897
Asa	Nes	A–87	1866
George C.	Yal(1)	B–88	1863
Priscilla	Yal(1)	B–124	1867
WALTHALL, Edward C.	Grn	A–138	1898
Mary L.	Grn	A–143	1898
WALTON, Benbury	Pan(1)	B–247	1878
Boston	Hol	3–83	1899
Charles W.	Mon	I.19–674	1866
Charles	War(1827–1832)–165		1829
Harris	Yal(1)	B–79	1863
Horrace H.	Laf	1–380	1891
James	Hol	1–262	1861
James F.	Nox	A–79	1844
Jesse	Mon	1–128	1839
Jesse B.	Hol	1–209	1859
Jesse Pointer	Tat	1–210	1893
John	Nes	A–132	1895
John A.	Hin	1–445	1859
John J.	Ada	1–410	1828
Mary A.	Lef	A–106	1890
Thomas	Lef	A–60	1878

Susan E.	Jas	1–56	1868
William A.	DeS	1–346	1865
WALWORTH, John P.	Ada	4–280	1883
Sarah	Ada	5–187	1898
WALTERS, John H.	War	B–128	1881
WARD, A. G.	DeS	1–335	1865
A. S.	Chi(1)	1–132	1897
Benjamin N.	Yaz	B–318	1896
Daniel	Ada	1–445	1830
George	Mad	A–396	1864
Harriet I.	Low	2–220	1898
Hugh	Mad	A–302	1859
Jasper K.	Laf	1–144	1862
John W.	Was	1–139	1850
Mamie L.	Att	C–454	1894
Mamie L.	Mad	2–137	1894
Mary Lee	Tat	1–260	1900
Rachel K.	Mad	A–261	1857
Sarah	Lea	1–66	1872
T. W.	Tat	1–25	1876
Tabitha Elizabeth	Mas	P.15–40	1860
W. R.	Cly	1–50	1880
William	Pan(1)	A–45	1848
WARDE, Creighton	Hol	1–11	1832
James S.	Wil	1–14	1831
WARDLAW, Zachariah	Hin	1–347	1854
WARDLOW, J. P.	Tis	1–51	1892
WARE, James D.	Hin	1–334	1854
Margaret S.	Hin	1–454	1859
WARF, John	Mad	A–627	1878
WARFIRLD, Henry N.	Hol	3–10	1894
WARMACK, John	Hol	1–451	1882
WARNER, Nancy	Jas	1–18	1862
WARREN, A.	Clk	1–20	1874
Bushrod B.	Coa(1)	1–3	1843
Elizabeth	Hin	B–66	1861
George B.	Coa(1)	1–98	1866
Jeru	Lin	1–7	1894
Josiah	Jef	B–209	1890
Mary	Lea	1–8	1856
Reuben	Yaz	B–239	1889
Seth W.	Ada	3–115	1858
Thomas D.	Ada	5–107	1896
Thomas M.	Win	1–34	1864
WARTCKE, Mina	Was	1–488	1890
WARTON, Edmond D.	Hol	1–123	1852
WASHBURN, A. W.	Yaz	B–137	1881
WASHINGTON, Dilsie	Qui	1–7	1896
George	Sun	1–22	1898
Minnie	Was	1–488	1890
Shepherd S.	Hin	B–152	1862

209

WASSON, John A.	Att	B-332&355	1881
WATERER, Needham	Yaz	B-32	1873
WATERS, Arnold E.	Cla	A-274	1833
W. Brice	Hol	1-214	1859
WATFORD, James A.	Ran	1-124	1871
WATHEN, B. J.	War	B-25	1872
WATKINS, A. S.	DeS	2-408	1894
Asa	Jef	P.C-15	1840
Calvin C.	Jef	B-147	1877
Hudson A.	Pan(1)	B-18	1865
Isham L.	Tal	A-38	1843
Israel	Lea	1-98	1880
J. M.	Nox	C-24	1897
Maryatt H.	New	1-7	1882
Mattie E.	Mon	I.6-462	1895
Minor Walton	Tal	A-132	1851
Oliver P.	Jef	P.E-532	1854
Robert L.	Ada	3-38	1855
S. G.	Mon	I.5-533	1889
Tolbert Kyle	Chi(1)	1-135	1899
W. P.	Pan(2)	A-137	1898
William A.	Mas	P.16-273	1865
William H.	Ada	4-224	1882
A. C.	Jef	B-218	1900
WATSON, Amasa B.	For(2)	1-10	1888
Amasa B.	Gre	1-30	1900
Ede T.	Low	1-563	1888
Elisha M.	Pan(1)	A-138	1852
Gideon	Web	A-26	1878
Hugh A.	Mon	I.5-57	1885
J. M.	Lee	1-101	1887
James	Uni	1-54	1899
James M.	Ran	1-184	1883
Jesse	Pan(1)	A-437	1863
John F. Jr.	Hin	B-203	1866
John R.	Mot	1-24	1877
Mary Ann	Pan(1)	B-122	1872
Mikel M.	Laf	1-22	1848
R. H.	Tis	1-73	1894
Robert	Yal(2)	1-106	1896
Rufus W.	Mon	I.19-117	1865
WATT, George	War	B-192	1887
Margaret	Cla	3-87	1884
William T.	Nox	B-47	1863
WATTHALL, Sarah S.	Mas	P.18-30	1867
WATTLES, Mary Ann	Ada	3-307	1867
WATTLEWORTH, Charles	Jac	1-12	1881
WATTS, James Wilson	Laf	1-429	1896
Jarrell	New	1-76	1888
John	DeS	2-30	1871
Mary L.	New	1-106	1893

Nancy	Cla	A-226	1831
Samuel	DeS	1-256	1860
WAVER, James M.	Mad	A-351	1861
WAYMOUTH, John	Ada	2-411	1852
WEAR, Julia A.	Car(1)	B-51	1896
WEAST, Sarah	Ada	2-437	1853
WEATHERALL, James L.	Mas	P.9-391	1854
Sallie	Hol	3-48	1897
WEATHERBY, George M.	Hol	1-240	1860
N.	Hol	1-284	1863
Sallic	Hol	1-465	1884
Septimus	Att	A-642	1861
WEATHERLY, Rhoda A.	Grn	A-94	1892
Tabitha	Laf	1-145	1858
Scott Watson	Cla	3-156	1894
William M.	Yal(1)	A-13	1836
WEATHERSBEE, Fort	Hin	B-244	1868
WEATHERSBY, Forten	Sim	A-78	1897
Julia C.	Ran	1-220	1887
T. H.	Mad	A-629	1884
William	Ran	1-201	1885
WEATHERSLY, Jonathan	Sim	A-54	1889
WEATHERSPOON, Esther	Yaz	A-34	1838
WEAVER, Ellen	Low	2-147	1896
WEBB, David H.	Coa(1)	1-108	1863
Elizabeth	Grn	A-8	1874
G. W.	DeS	1-301	1862 —
George E.	Ran	1-300	1895
Noah S.	Wil	1-238	1841
Robert D.	Yaz	B-323	1897
Stephen W.	Ran	B.1-8	1829
Thomas D.	Coa(1)	1-100	1866
Thompson B.	Ran	1-236	1890
William	Laf	1-165	1866
WEBER, Benedict	Hin	B-220	1866
Elizabeth	Tip	1-38	1869
WEBSTER, Elizabeth	Clk	1-201	1898
George W.	Cla	A-210	1830
Henrietta	Lau	1-337	1894
Sarah	Laf	1-243	1874
Shadrach	Mas	P.5-32	1847
WEDEKIND, F.	Nox	B-220	1879
WEED, Ann	Wil	2-266	1871
Nathaniel	Mas	P.15-554	1862
WEEKLEY, Mary	Wil	1-255	1842
WEEKS, J. F.	Cla	3-158	1895
Jabez	Att	B-226	1876
WEEPS, M.	Cho	A-53	1897
WEIBEN, R. E.	Fra	A-13	1892
WEIR, Calvin S.	Yal(1)	A-153	1849
Margaret R.	Nox	B-240	1880

Penelope W.	Laf	1-151&183	1857
Thomas	Win	1-30	1864
WEISS, Morris	Was	1-451	1886
WELBOURN, John	Yal(1)	B-201	1883
WELCH, Edward O. K.	Ada	1-40	1808
James	Cop	AAA-8	1838
John D.	DeS	1-448	1869
WELE, Isabella	Grn	A-71	1887
WELL, Margaret	Ada	3-4	1854
WELLDON, Thomas	Ada	4-13	1872
WELLE, Samuel G.	Low	1-443	1880
WELLONS, James	Car(1)	A-512	1868
W. B.	Tat	1-105	1888
WELLS, Albert G.	Low	1-261	1869
Banister	Mad	A-208	1851
Clarissa	Mas	1-149	1898
Ebenezer M.	Att	B-189	1875
Edward	Mad	A-129	1848
Emily A.	Low	2-109	1895
George	Hin	1-74	1836
Jerry	Mot	1-40	1879
John	Jef	P.C-294	1840
Lallie	Hin	B-387	1887
Margaret V.	Hin	B-414	1891
Mary	Mad	A-496	1869
Mary M.	Uni	1-24	1891
Miles	Hin	1-226	1848
Mills	Hin	B-36	1859
Minerva G.	Hin	B-381	1879
Nancy	Hin	B-341	1882
Noel	Cla	B-326	1868
Polly	Hin	1-359	1855
Stephen	Hin	1-52	1835
Thomas	Hin	B-351	1884
William M.	Hin	B-270	1871
WENTE, Mary E.	War	B-345	1897
WENZEL, H. H.	Nox	B-302	1885
WESSON, John L.	DeS	2-524	1900
Joseph M.	Tip	1-62	1873
Rebecca	DeS	2-462	1897
WEST, Absolom M.	Mas	1-39	1894
Aley S.	Hol	1-322	1866
Charles	Jef	B-60	1861
Charlotte Frances	Ada	4-516	1890
George R.	Laf	1-249	1874
John A. A.	Hin	B-415	1890
John M.	Hol	1-288	1863
John M.	Laf	1-407	1892
Levi	Ran	1-131	1874
Margaret	Ada	5-279	1900
O. F.	Tat	1-38	1879

R. D.	Hol	3-58	1898
Richard	Ran	1-208	1885
Thomas	Jef	A-23	1818
William A.	Laf	1-410	1894
William N.	Tal	A-75	1846
WESTBROOK, Lemuel	Low	1-89	1862
Samuel	Mon	I.14-578	1860
WESTEMIER, A.	War	B-214	1889
WESTER, Daniel	Lee	1-94	1886
Jonathan	Lee	1-200	1898
WESTMORELAND, Mary			
Ann	Low	2-172	1897
WETHERBEE, Andrew M.	Cly	1-98	1890
WETHERED, Polly	Nox	A-196	1854
WEYMOUTH, Sarah R.	Ada	3-216	1865
WHATLEY, Daniel	Lea	1-152	1892
Jessey	Cla	B-214	1851
Oliver	New	1-166	1896
WHEAT, J. J.	Grn	A-104	1893
WHEELER, J. A.	Jas	1-81	1883
James W.	Wil	3-111	1893
John H.	Wil	1-264	1843
Leodicia	Ran	1-79	1865
Levin	DeS	2-238	1885
WHEELISS, Samuel G.	Yal(1)	B-198	1882
WHEFFIN, Julin W.	Chi(1)	1-2	1876
WHIELDON, William	Ada	3-144	1860
WHISTLER, Jackson	Yal(1)	B-19	1859
WHISTON, Philander	Hin	1-228	1848
WHITAKER, Abraham	Hin	1-96	1837
Agnes C.	War	B-55	1875
Austin	Mas	1-147	1898
Daniel	War	A-335	1865
James	Jef	A-42	1820
M. H.	Lau	1-287	1892
Robert	Mas	P.4-359	1846
WHITE, Aaron Kennedy	Mad	A-636	1885
Alfred H.	Lau	1-264	1890
Ann	Nox	B-293	1885
Anne M.	Hin	B-425	1893
Archibald	DeS	2-175	1881
Archibald	Wil	3-163	1897
Benjamin	Wil	2-79	1853
Benjamin A.	Tip	1-50	1871
C.	Web	A-128	1898
Christopher	Nox	A-122	1847
Creecy	Yaz	B-300	1894
David S.	Pan(1)	A-357	1859
David S.	Pan(1)	A-438	1864
Dempsey	War (1823-1827)-6		1823
Eliza	Mas	P.7-600	1851

F. B.	DeS	2-282	1887
George	Wil	2-44	1849
Gideon B.	Low	2-50	1892
H. R.	Law	1-11	1896
Henry	Att	D-250	1900
Henry	Mas	1-38	1894
Henry M.	Hin	B-214	1866
Isaac	Tip	1-101	1882
J. W.	DeS	2-311	1889
James	Mon	I.2-43	1873
James Thomas	DeS	2-12	1870
John	Kem	A-13	1884
John	Lea	1-63	1866
John	Nox	A-39	1842
John C.	Wil	2-8	1846
John W.	Lef	A-88	1885
Joseph	Cla	A-204	1828
Joseph B.	Hol	1-23	1841
Larkin	Cla	A-97	1820
Mrs. M. B.	DeS	2-508	1900
Maria	Low	1-319	1872
Mary	Ada	4-324	1884
Miles	DeS	2-156	1880
Miles	Sim	A-57	1876
Miles	Ran	1-228	1889
Nathan	Yaz	A-16	1835
R. P.	Tat	1-157	1892
Reuben	Cla	A-227	1831
Reuben	Law	P.B-126	1840
Rhody	Ada	2-41	1833
Richard	Hin	1-390	1856
Robert	Wil	1-34	1832
Samuel	Nox	A-20	1839
Stephen	Ada	5-39	1893
T. W.	DeS	2-303	1889
Thomas	Cla	A-41	1813
Thomas I.	Car(1)	A-2	1834
Thomas Sr.	Cla	A-8	1804
William	DeS	1-376	1866
William J.	War	A-302	1861
William M.	Mad	A-682	1891
William W.	Tun	2-35	1876
Wilson	Nes	A-21	1848
Wylie	Lea	1-28	1859
Zena	Laf	1-120	1857
WHITEHEAD, E. D.	Mot	1-78	1885
Edmond G.	Car(1)	B-21	1884
Edwin D.	Coa(1)	1-84	1861
James	War(1823-1827)-157		1825
Joseph B.	Hin	1-254	1850
Urban J.	Yaz	A-30	1836

W. W.	Car(1)	B-13	1870
Wilson W.	Hol	1-58	1845
William	Ada	1-66	1811
WHITEHORN, Sarah	Tip	1-149	1889
WHITEHURST, Elizabeth	Ada	4-342	1885
William N.	Ada	4-527	1891
WHITESIDE, Hugh S.	Pre	1-18	1873
John F.	Pre	1-19	1873
WHITESIDES, James	Ita	E.5-372	1860
WHITFIELD, Mills W.	War	A-180	1850
Nancy	War	A-220	1855
Needham H.	Mon	I.7-19	1897
Needham Sr.	Mon	I.1-548	1873
WHITLEY, John	War	A-349	1866
WHITLOCK, Sarah Sage			
Huntington	Lea	1-127	1886
WHITMORE, Charles	Ada	3-232	1865
WHITSEL, William	Tat	1-3	1874
WHITTEN, D. M.	Pan(2)	A-35	1883
Silas R.	Tip	1-145	1888
WHITTFIELD, James B.	Yaz	A-10&17	1835
WHITTIER, Jesse	Tun	1-111	1853
WHITTINGTON, Amelia	War	A-56	1836
G. E.	Lea	1-161	1894
Isaiah	Hol	1-454	1882
Levi	War	(1823-1827)-42	1824
WHITTLE, Elizabeth	Ada	1-398	1826
James E.	Kem	A-84	1900
WHITWELL, Robert	Laf	1-141	1858
WIER, Caroline M.	Nox	B-50	1864
H. H.	Car(1)	A-172	1859
Robert N.	Nox	A-272	1859
WIGGIN, Thomas D.	Low	1-17	1858
WIGGINS, David M.	Mad	A-384	1862
Edley	Web	A-103	1893
George W.	Car(1)	A-133	1855
WIGGINTON, James			
Benjamin	Jac	1-143	1896
WIGHTMAN, Isaac A.	Ada	3-320	1867
WILBORNE, James	Low	2-273	1899
WILBOURN, Chloe M.	Pan(1)	B-182	1875
E. J.	Yal(1)	B-244	1899
Elijah	Pan(1)	B-256	1878
Elijah	Pan(1)	B-369	1879
M. Wallace	Pan(1)	B-40	1867
Quince Anna	Pan(1)	B-349	1881
William R.	Pan(1)	B-53	1868
WILCOX, Agnes	Ada	4-518	1890
P. B.	Cla	A-221	1830
WILCZINSKE, J.	Was	1-397	1873
WILCZINSKI, Joseph	Was	2-43	1897

WILD, Joanna C.	Wil	2-399	1881
WILDER, Lou E.	Mad	2-104	1898
William	Nox	C-125	1900
WILDS, Mary E.	Car(1)	A-103	1852
WILEMAN, Benjamin	Pre	1-45	1880
WILDY, William J.	Mad	A-3	1830
WILES, A. B.	Mad	A-467	1868
WILEY, Alexander D.	Yal(1)	A-39&50	1841
John	Wil	1-164	1837
Leroy M.	Yaz	B-276	1891
M. W.	Tip	1-189	1894
Yancy	Laf	1-359	1886
WILGUS, John B.	Han	A-268	1895
WILKENS, Elen	Mas	P.10-213	1854
WILKERSON, John	Tat	1-53	1882
Nancy	New	1-148	1896
WILKINGS, Eliza Jane	Yal(1)	A-240	1853
WILKINS, Catherine			
Lintot	Ada	2-362	1849
D. G.	Uni	1-33	1895
Dimmond H.	Mot	1-143	1897
James	Mas	P.4-4	1844
James H.	DeS	1-318	1862
Thomas	Ada	1-75	1812
Thomas	Wil	1-211	1839
WILKINSON, Alice T.	Tat	1-218	1897
Benjamin R.	Yaz	A-205	1856
Cornelia	Yaz	B-17	1871
Daniel W.	Ran	1-98	1867
Edward C.	Yaz	A-204	1855
Eliza C.	Yaz	B-119	1880
George B.	Yaz	B-2	1870
Henry	Yaz	A-159	1852
John	Nes	A-12	1847
Margaret A.	Mas	P.5-363	1848
Micajah	Ada	1-377	1826
Peter	Jef	B-37	1860
Sarah	Lau	1-274	1889
Thomas V.	Ran	B.1-322	1847
William Alex.	Yaz	A-51	1840
William B.	Yaz	A-127	1846
William J.	New	1-120	1895
WILKS, William B.	Mon	I.4-155	1882
WILLBORN, Thomas	Pon	2-90	1826
William B.	Nox	B-129	1873
WILLCOX, Joseph D.	Laf	1-279&312	1877
WILLETT, William T.	Pon	2-20	1841
WILLIAM, Randell	Coa(1)	1-200	1888
WILLIAMS, Basil	Yaz	A-101	1848
Benjamin W.	Mas	P.4-654	1847
Billy	Low	1-498	1885

Bryan T.	Nox	B-35	1863
Mrs. C. N.	Mot	1-146	1898
C. S.	Hin	1-197	1847
Caroline M.	Ada	3-244	1865
Daniel	Low	1-136	1863
Daniel	Wil	1-72	1833
David	Ada	1-243	1821
David E.	Laf	2-20	1899
Eliza	Cla	B-212	1850
Eliza	Mad	2-48	1895
Elzey	Low	1-315	1872
Emma	Cla	3-126	1890
Enoch	Att	A-194	1859
Eugene F.	Cly	1-138	1900
Fred	Yal(1)	B-186	1881
George W.	Pan(1)	B-25	1866
George W.	Yal(1)	B-68	1862
Guilford	Ada	3-69	1856
Henry	DeS	1-194	1858
Isaac	Ada	1-139	1816
Jacob	Isa	C-130	1874
James C.	Ada	1-484	1830
James P.	Lau	1-37	1863
James S.	Cly	1-117	1895
James Turley	Yal(1)	A-90	1845
John	Ada	1-17	1804
John	Hol	1-269	1863
John	Mon	1-252	1848
John	Nox	A-5	1836
John	Nox	A-75	1839
John	Yal(1)	A-66	1843
John	Yal(1)	A-210	1851
John D.	DeS	2-278	1886
John F.	Yaz	B-271	1892
John Lee	Nox	B-216	1878
John Sr.	Yal(1)	A-203	1852
John W.	Pan(1)	A-261	1857
Joseph D.	Hol	1-97	1851
Josiah B.	Chi(1863-1872)-108		1865
Kershaw	Yal(1)	B-82	1863
Lewis	Cla	B-270	1857
Lydia Carter	Ada	1-327	1824
M. M.	Nox	C-144	1900
M. Corneleu	DeS	1-308	1862
Martha	Low	1-10	1858
Mary	Yal(1)	A-60	1842
Mary A.	Grn	A-51	1884
Nancy G.	DeS	1-87	1854
Nathaniel T.	War	A-175	1849
Nehemiah	Pik	1-102	1898
Philander	Ran	1-67	1864

Priscilla A.	DeS	2–266	1886
Rebecca H.	Mon	I.8–212	1852
Samuel	Chi(1863–1872)–131		1858
Samuel	Ran	1–316	1900
Sanford C.	DeS	2–240	1885
Sarah	Yal(2)	1–17	1881
Sarah C.	Pan(1)	B–491	1898
Seaborn J.	Yaz	B–310	1896
Susan B.	Ran	1–181	1883
T. J.	DeS	1–354	1866
Tedo	Isa	C–135	1882
Thomas	Coa(1)	1–125	1878
Thomas	Tat	1–100	1887
Thomas E.	Lau	1–163	1881
Thomas W.	DeS	1–4	1851
Wiley H.	Low	1–420	1879
William	Coa(1)	1–2	1842
William	DeS	1–430	1868
William	Hin	1–73	1836
William	Ran	1–211	1885
William B.	DeS	1–285	1861
William W.	Mad	A–1	1829
WILLIAMSON, Charles			
Carter	War	A–89	1838
Elizabeth	War(1823–1827)–213		1826
George W.	Grn	A–62	1886
H.	Lef	A–72	1883
H. T.	Kem	A–70	1897
John	Ada	3–179	1861
Lea	Pan(1)	B–501	1900
Mildred P.	DeS	1–167	1858
Russell	Mad	*	1845

* Available only at the Canton Public
Library, Canton, MS.

S. M.	Sim	A–75	1896
W. W.	War	A–256	1859
WILLIFORD, William L.	DeS	1–111	1856
WILLINGHAM, Mary A.	DeS	2–68	1872
WILLIS, Adaline	Hin	B–65	1859
Asenath	Ada	1–64	1806
Augustin Jr.	Mon	1–202	1842
Augustin Sr.	Mon	1–171	1842
Augustine	Mon	I.3–220	1878
David G.	Mas	P.19–74	1869
Eliza	Sha	A–23	1896
Elizabeth F.	Cla	3–119	1889
Esther A.	Cla	A–364	1837
George	Lea	1–155	1892
James	Mas	P.19–524	1870
Joel	War	B–7	1869
John W.	Yal(1)	1–3	1837

Julia B.	Hin	B-291	1874
Margaret	Cop	AAA-6	1857
Robert	Ran	1-100	1867
Robert	Win	1-8	1861
Thomas C.	Hin	1-292	1852
William	Cla	A-104	1821
William T.	Yal(1)	A-280	1856
WILLISON, John	Yaz	A-31	1837
WILLISTON, Ebenezer B.	Ada	2-295	1838
WILLOUGHBY, Wyatt	Car(2)	1-60	1892
WILLS, William	Cla	A-98	1820
WILROY, William W.	DeS	2-126	1877
WILSON, Alexander J.	Mas	P.8-366	1852
Alexander L.	Ada	3-174	1861
Arva	Cla	A-264	1833
Asaph	Mas	P.9-386	1854
Charles W.	Cla	B-224	1852
David	Ran	1-223	1887
E. W.	Ada	4-451	1888
Eleanora	Ada	5-71	1895
Eliza P.	Yaz	B-152	1883
Ephraim	Laf	1-435	1894
Franklin P.	Mad	A-32	1837
H. Van	Tat	1-71	1884
Hardin D.	Cop	AAA-4	1863
Jane E.	Ada	2-259	1842
Jane M.	Car(2)	1-39	1887
James M.	Hol	1-480	1885
Joe Davis	Car(2)	1-79	1899
Joel F.	Att	D-66	1898
John	Was	1-434	1883
John J.	Yaz	A-168	1853
John P.	Cla	3-182	1899
John R.	Yaz	A-189	1854
Joseph	War	A-83	1837
Joseph	War	A-280	1860
Legrand W.	Mas	P.15-449	1862
M.	Laf	1-436	1898
M. A.	Mad	A-662	1889
Margaret	Laf	1-89	1854
Margaret	Mas	P.13-488	1858
Martha E.	Mad	A-526	1871
Mary F.	Yaz	B-28	1873
Mary Jane	Hol	1-327	1868
Middleton Ford	Pan(1)	B-495	1899
Miller	Hin	1-239	1849
Newton	DeS	2-150	1879
Robert	Laf	1-63	1851
Robert	Yaz	B-160	1883
Ruth C.	Mas	P.4-140	1845

Sally L. S.	Yaz	B-15	1871
Samuel	Mad	A-16	1833
Samuel J.	Nes	A-39	1855
Shemuel	Mas	P.11-93	1855
Simpson A.	Yaz	B-297	1894
Thomas F.	Pan(1)	B-211	1877
William Sidney	Cla	B-308	1862
Winifred C.	Mas	P.5-333	1848
WIMBERLY, F. D.	Cop	A-88	1893
Louis	Laf	1-372	1888
WINANS, William	Wil	2-127	1857
WINBISH, William R.	Tis	1-16	1888
WINBORN, Mary	Mas	P.18-308	1868
WINCHELL, W. H.	Laf	1-411	1894
WINCHESTER, Josiah	Ada	4-446	1887
Francis K.	Ada	5-45	1893
WINDHAM, Ann Ogden	Wil	2-389	1881
WINDLEY, Samuel H.	Hin	1-412	1857
WINFREY, William	Nox	B-52	1865
WING, Frederick D.	Jac	1-145	1895
WINGARD, Samantha	Att	C-75	1889
WINN, A. O.	Car(1)	A-162	1858
George	Ada	2-4	1832
Miner F.	War(1823-1827)-198		1826
Saphrona	Was	1-433	1883
Selia	Hol	1-70	1847
WINSETT, Elizabeth	Mas	P.15-289	1861
WINSTEAD, John	Wil	2-75	1852
WINSTED, Joseph J.	Ran	1-120	1872
WINSTON, Fountain	Ada	2-81	1834
John Anthony	Nox	B-206	1872
Lucretia	Lef	A-121	1896
Mary	Cop	A-104	1895
Mary Elizabeth	Ada	5-1	1892
Mary Newell	Ada	2-240	1841
Rebecca	Low	1-196	1866
William H.	Cly	1-111	1889
WINTER, Elvira A.	Grn	A-128	1897
Richard	Mad	A-498	1870
Rosa	Hin	B-234	1867
Thomas J.	Hin	1-311	1853
William Hovi	Grn	A-43	1880
WINTERS, Willis G.	Att	C-69	1888
WISE, Eugenia	Yaz	B-236	1889
John	Hin	1-126	1840
Louis	Yaz	B-390	1899
Lydia	Cly	1-89	1888
Sarah	Hin	1-176	1844
Solomon	Was	1-396	1873
William H.	DeS	1-113	1856
WISEMAN, Devenport	Cla	A-101	1820

Hugh	Tip	1–2	1866
WITHERS, David Dunham	Wil	3–75	1892
Sterling	Mas	P.15–548	1862
WITHERSPOON, Elias			
Bourdenot	Low	1–294	1870
Mary C.	Ada	5–207	1897
WITT, Elias	Ada	1–173	1818
WITTY, William H.	Mot	1–75	1885
WOATEN, S. D.	Tat	1–126	1889
WOFFORD, Absolom L.	Web	A–13	1875
Isaac	Web	A–8	1875
WOHNER, Lizzie	Mad	2–73	1876
WOLFE, Charles W.	Was	1–400	1875
Emma A.	Pan(2)	A–39	1884
WOLLARD, S. W.	Chi(1863–1872)–193		1870
WOMACK, Mark S.	Web	A–90	1871
WOMBLE, Harrison	Tal	A–176	1857
WOMMACK, Keziah	Cop	AAA–1	1864
WOOD, Charles Thomas	Grn	A–146	1900
David	Ada	1–438	1829
Eliza C.	Ada	2–390	1851
Elizabeth	Mas	P.16–5	1863
George	Jac	1–25	1883
Hannah	Car(1)	A–14	1833
Irene	Car(1)	B–42	1890
J. H.	Yal(2)	1–53	1888
James G.	Jef	P.C–621	1845
James N. H.	Ada	2–252	1842
James W.	Mot	1–59	1882
Joseph A.	Cop	A–30	1889
Leonard Whitaker	Han	B–46	1900
Margaret B.	Ada	4–403	1887
Mary A.	Jef	B–177	1890
Spencer	Ada	4–70	1875
Thomas H.	DeS	1–280	1861
William B.	Lef	A–56	1877
William H.	Cla	B–213	1851
William S.	Tis	1–49	1891
WOODALL, Elvira T.	Coa(2)	1–15	1893
Thomas Rhodes	Att	D–184	1900
WOODBURN, Isaac			
Leonard	Was	1–302	1861
John	Was	1–247	1853
WOODFIN, G. W.	Att	C–473	1895
WOODHAM, A. B.	New	1–172	1899
WOODHOUSE, John	Cla	B–283	1859
Nancy	Cla	B–198	1848
WOODHULL, John	Ada	1–477	1824
WOODNEFF, F. M.	Wil	2–117	1857
WOODRUFF, Baker	Yaz	A–346	1865
James H.	Wil	2–233	1865

WOODS, Ephraim	Jef	B–161	1884
Hezekiah W.	Att	B–426	1884
Lena S.	Lau	1–366	1898
Robert	Was	1–257&271	1843
William F.	Mas	P.11–211	1856
WOODSIDES, William	Wil	1–64	1833
WOODSWORTH, James W.	Clk	1–188	1894
WOODWARD, B. J.	Lea	1–26	1858
David	Ada	1–236	1821
J. O.	Win	1–109	1888
William	Cho	A–28	1893
William	Yaz	A–107	1848
WOOLDRIDGE, Cecile	Yaz	B–309	1896
David	Yaz	1–363	1870
Edmond	Ada	1–25	1807
Josiah J.	Yaz	A–123	1849
William H.	Cla	A–53	1814
WOOLEY, John	Cla	3–97	1886
WOOLFOLK, William R.	Ran	B.1–15	1839
WOOLLARD, G. B.	Tat	1–42	1880
WOOLS, Washington	War	A–115	1841
WOOLSEY, James	DeS	2–41	1871
WOOTEN, Hardy	Car(1)	A–44	1840
Narcissa	Mas	P.13–489	1858
R. K. Sr.	Nox	C–57	1898
Shadrach	Mas	P.5–549	1849
Spencer D.	Tat	1–118	1889
WOOTTEN, Jane M.	Nox	B–261	1881
John L.	Pan(2)	A–69	1887
Richard	Jef	P.B–557	1840
WOOTTON, Lewis B.	Jef	P.B–263	1838
WORD, Benjamin N.	Lea	1–162	1895
James	Tis	1–26	1890
John T.	DeS	1–77	1854
Nathaniel R.	Car(1)	A–99	1851
WORRELL, William	Mad	A–231	1855
WORTHINGTON, Ann	Was	1–427	1879
Josephine M.	Was	1–439	1880
William W.	Was	1–493	1892
WORTMAN, William	Yaz	B–144	1882
WRAY, John F.	Pon E.(1844–1848)–382		1847
WREN, Elizabeth	Ada	3–440	1870
Francis	Ami	1–139	1816
Mary	Ada	3–108	1858
WRENN, Belfield	War(1827–1832)–227		1830
Cecilia	War	A–144	1844
Henry M.	War	A–201	1853
Jones	War	A–28	1833
WRIGHT, Catherine W.	Han	A–202	1892
Della	Mad	A–650	1887
Mrs. E. D.	War	B–259	1891

G. W.	Tip	1-207	1899
George W.	Yal(1)	B-209	1892
J. L.	Tip	1-209	1899
J. W.	DeS	2-27	1870
Jesse C.	Pan(1)	A-127	1852
John	Tip	1-55	1871
John M.	Cla	B-181	1844
John W.	Mas	P.7-298	1850
Joseph N.	Pan(1)	B-63	1869
Mallie V.	Yal(1)	B-238	1899
Mary	War	B-305	1895
Mary Allen	Lee	1-12	1871
Mary M.	Ada	4-465	1888
Michael Sr.	Pan(1)	A-168	1854
Nancy J.	War	B-25	1873
Nathaniel H.	Tip	1-1	1864
Newton Barton	Pan(1)	B-266	1878
Peter	Ada	2-57	1834
R. L.	Was	2-47	1897
Mrs. S. S.	Was	2-47	1897
Sarah G.	Pan(1)	A-223	1855
Sophenia	Tat	1-73	1884
Thomas	Hol	1-152	1856
W. C.	Tip	1-195	1896
William	Coa(1)	1-103	1867
William H.	Nox	A-224	1855
WRIGLEY, John Lees	Was	1-442	1884
WYATT, Elizabeth D.	Was	1-426	1876
Willis H.	Yal(1)	B-44	1860
WYCHE, George	Hin	1-108	1838
William H.	Cla	A-303	1834
WYLEY, Hannah	Mad	2-19	1893
R. C.	Mad	A-609	1881
WYNETH, Augusta F.	Grn	A-134	1898
WYNN, Elizabeth A.	Hol	1-476	1885
L. T.	Laf	1-182	1864
Lewis T.	Laf	1-148	1859
Selia	Hol	1-70	1847
W. C.	Att	C-338	1893
William T.	Yal(1)	A-290	1856
WYSE, Joseph	Att	B-287	1879
YAGER, Andras	Was	1-472	1888
YALE, Cyrus	Cop	A-41	1890
YANCY, William F.	Mad	A-372	1862
YARBROUGH, John	DeS	1-9	1852
Thomas	Yaz	A-67	1843
YATES, George C.	DeS	2-205	1883
Samuel	Cov	1-4	1892
Sarah G.	Wil	2-155	1861
Susan	Web	A-74	1889

YEAGER, Elijah R.	Grn	A-73	1887
YEISER, Eleanor A.	Hin	1-36	1834
YELLOWLY, James B.	Mad	A-219	1854
YERGER, George S.	Hin	B-48	1860
Mary H.	Was	1-496	1892
William G.	Was	2-115	1899
YERK, Zebulon	Ada	5-299	1900
YONGUE, E. V.	Mot	1-94	1889
YORK, Alonza	Laf	1-194	1870
YOUNG, A. S.	Cly	1-109	1891
Benjamin Farrar	Ada	3-139	1860
Clarissa	Cla	3-31	1877
Dorrel M.	Mas	P.8-432	1852
Elijah	Mad	A-363	1862
Eliza A.	Ada	3-486	1871
Emily M.	Ada	5-263	1900
Garth Ann	Hol	1-370	1873
James William	War	A-308	1862
John	Ada	2-99	1835
John	Hin	B-78	1866
John	Yal(2)	1-107	1892
John C.	Yaz	B-264	1891
John J.	War	A-191	1852
John W.	Ada	4-91	1875
Lucy	Wil	1-189	1838
Manervia	Mon	I.6-74	1890
Nancy	Mas	P.8-8	1851
Sam	Att	B-185	1875
Thomas	Nes	A-37	1854
Thomas D. M.	Lea	1-102	1880
William	Cla	B-314	1863
William A.	Pan(i)	A-405	1860
William C.	Laf	1-47	1848
William H.	War	A-118	1841
William J.	Att	C-420	1869
YOWELL, Joel	Jef	A-68	1818
ZINN, Jacob	Pon E.(1844-1848)-281		1847
ZOLLACOFFER, George	Laf	1-1	1843